CONCISE DICTIONARY OF CHEMISTRY

A Perfect Reference for Aspirants of IAS, IIT-JEE, AIEEE, CBSE-PMT, and Students of All Age Groups

I0129610

Editorial Board

V&S PUBLISHERS

Published by:

V&S PUBLISHERS

F-2/16, Ansari road, Daryaganj, New Delhi-110002
☎ 23240026, 23240027 •Fax: 011-23240028
Email: info@vspublishers.com

Branch : Hyderabad
5-1-707/1, Brij Bhawan (Beside Central Bank of India Lane)
Bank Street, Koti, Hyderabad - 500 095
☎ 040-24737290
E-mail: vspublishershyd@gmail.com

Follow us on: t f in

All books available at **www.vspublishers.com**

© **Copyright:**
ISBN 978-93-815886-2-8
Edition: 2012

Printed at: Param Offsetters, Okhla, New Delhi

Contents

Publisher's Note

Innumerable books are available in the market on science and its allied branches, like, physics, chemistry, and biology et al, both as textbook and reference manual. Written for different age-groups and class, quite a number of these books come replete with jargon-filled terms; and just fail to connect with readers' inclination and curiosity level. On top of that, new words keep finding their way into the books every other day. Every new addition contributes to difficulty in comprehending the matter.

An average reader is interested only in knowing what a specific word means without getting lost with heavy sounding inputs.

Following an open-ended discussion with a cross-section of students and other stakeholders we realised that many books on science (physics, chemistry and biology) take readers' understanding of scientific terms for granted and make short passing references while alluding to the term in the text. Presentations of this nature in no way assist readers in understanding the subject properly.

You need to suffer no longer.

V&S Publishers has come out with four dictionaries of terms; in science, physics, chemistry and biology. These have been compiled to help readers grasp the meaning of popular scientific terms. For easy reference terms have been arranged alphabetically. Terms that have come into the reckoning even in the early 2012 have been incorporated and suitably explained in such a way that an average secondary and senior secondary student can grasp them easily. High resolution images, illustrations and examples, where appropriate, have been added for reader's convenience. For all readers, who have not made a special study of any science subject, explanations of terms will be found to be easily comprehensible.

An attempt has been made to include important scientific charts, tables, constants, conversion tables as appendices to make this dictionary more useful. A glossary of Nobel Prize winners and their contributions is an added attraction.

We would be happy to have your views and comments about the book.

Introduction

What is Chemistry?

Chemistry is the branch of science that deals with the identification of the substances of which matter is composed; the investigation of their properties and the ways in which they interact, combine, and change; and the use of these processes to form new substances.

Why is the study of Chemistry Important?

Chemistry has a reputation for being a complicated and boring science, but for the most part, that reputation is undeserved. Fireworks and explosions are based on chemistry, so it's definitely not a boring science. If we take classes in chemistry, we'll apply math and logic, which can make studying chemistry a challenge if we are weak in those areas. However, anyone can understand the basics of how things work, and that's the study of chemistry. In a nutshell, the importance of chemistry is that it explains the world around us.

Everyone can and should understand basic chemistry, but it may be important to take a course in chemistry or even make a career out of it. It's important to understand chemistry if we are studying any of the sciences because all of the sciences involve matter and the interactions between types of matter. Students wishing to become doctors, nurses, physicists, nutritionists, geologists, pharmacists, and (of course) chemists all study chemistry. We might want to make a career of chemistry because chemistry-related jobs are plentiful and high-paying. The importance of chemistry won't be diminished over time, so it will remain a promising career path.

How is Chemistry Classified?

Chemistry deals with the structure and composition of matter and the chemical reactions that are responsible for changing the state and properties of matter. Chemistry is the science of atoms, molecules, crystals and other aggregates of matter and the chemical processes that change their energy and entropy levels as also their structure and composition. Chemistry has been sub-divided into distinct disciplines that deal with specific branches of chemistry. The different branches deal with different aspects of the study of matter. Take a look at them:

Organic Chemistry: This branch of chemistry deals with the study of the organic matter. The substances that primarily consist of carbon (C) and hydrogen (H) are termed as organic. The discipline that deals with the study of the structure, composition and the chemical properties of organic compounds is known as organic chemistry. This branch also deals with the chemical reactions that are used in the preparation of organic chemical compounds.

Inorganic Chemistry: It is the branch of chemistry that relates to the structure, composition and behaviour of inorganic compounds. All the substances other than the carbon-hydrogen compounds are classified under the group of inorganic substances. Oxides, sulphides and carbonates form the important classes of inorganic compounds. Industrial inorganic chemistry deals with the branch of applied science such as the manufacture of fertilizers, while the descriptive inorganic chemistry deals with the classification of compounds based on their properties.

Analytical Chemistry: This is a very important branch of chemistry that deals with the analysis of the chemical properties of natural and man-made materials. The study does not restrict itself to any particular type of chemical compounds. Instrumental analysis is a prominent part of modern analytical chemistry. Analytical chemistry primarily deals with the study of the chemicals present in a substance, in what quantity they are, and how they define the chemical properties of the substance.

Physical Chemistry: This branch of chemistry applies the theories of physics to atoms and subatomic particles. When physical chemistry is applied to the chemical interaction between atoms and subatomic particles, the study is known by the name, quantum mechanics. It is a relatively vast field that deals with intermolecular forces, rates of chemical reactions as well the conductivity of different materials.

Biochemistry: This discipline of chemistry represents a peep of biology into chemistry. It deals with the structure and behaviour of the components of cells and the chemical processes in living beings. The complex and large bio-molecules are usually composed of similar units that repeat. The complex molecules are known as polymers and the basic units they are composed of are known as monomers. Biochemistry deals with the study of cellular constituents like proteins, carbohydrates, lipids, and nucleic acids as also the chemical processes that occur in cells.

Nuclear Chemistry: It is a popular and one of the very important branches of chemistry that studies radioactivity. It revolves around the study of the nuclear properties of and the chemical processes in radioactive substances. This branch also covers the study of the equipment used for the performance of nuclear processes. The effects of the absorption of radiation, the production and use of radioactive materials and radiotherapy come under this branch of chemistry. Nuclear chemistry also deals with the non-radioactive areas of life.

Chemistry is a very vast subject as it delves into the enormity of the universe. While dealing with the study of the structure and behaviour of matter, it makes an attempt to encompass the study of the fundamental units that make up the universe.

Chemistry in Everyday Life

Chemistry is important in our day-to-day life. See how:

Cooking - Chemistry explains how food changes as we cook it, how to preserve food, how it rots, how our body uses the food we eat, and how ingredients interact to make food.

Cleaning - A very significant Part of the importance of chemistry is it explains how cleaning works. We use chemistry to help decide what cleaner is best for dishes, laundry, ourselves, and our home. We use chemistry when we use bleaches and disinfectants and even ordinary soap and water. How do they work? That's chemistry!

Medicine - We need to understand basic chemistry so that we understand how vitamins, supplements, and drugs can help or harm us. A substantial part of the importance of chemistry lies in developing and testing new medical treatments and medicines.

Environment - Chemistry is at the heart of environmental issues. What makes one chemical a nutrient and another chemical a pollutant? How can we clean up the environment? What processes can produce things we need without harming the environment?

We're all self-proclaimed chemists. We use chemicals every day and perform chemical reactions without thinking much about them. Chemistry is important because everything we do is chemistry! Even our body is made of chemicals. Chemical reactions occur when we breathe, eat, or just sit there reading. All matter is made of chemicals, so the importance of chemistry is that it's the study of everything.

Great Chemists of All-time

1. Dmitri Mendeleyev (Russian) - Mendeleyev devised the Periodic table of elements. He predicted that several more elements would be discovered.

2. Antoine Lavoisier (French) - Lavoisier showed that air is a mixture of oxygen (O) and nitrogen (H). He disproved the old Theory of phlogiston and determined the nature of combustion. Lavoisier wrote the first modern book on chemistry and explained the law of conservation of matter.

3. Henry Cavendish (British) - Cavendish showed that water could be produced from two gases and discovered hydrogen.

4. Amedeo Avogadro (Italian) - Avogadro is the first to distinguish molecules from atoms. He developed Avogadro's Constant (The number of particles of a substance in a mole). He also studied the effect of combining volumes.

5. Jons Jakob Berzelius (Swedish) - Berzelius developed symbols for many of the chemicals. He calculated the atomic weights accurately of many of them and discovered Selenium, Silicon and Thorium.

6. John Dalton (British) - Dalton developed an atomic theory of matter and explained the laws of partial pressure.

7. Robert Boyle (Irish) - Boyle studied gases and showed how pressure and

volume at constant mass were indirectly proportional to one another.

8. Joseph-Louis Gay-Lussac and Jacques Charles (Both French) - Studied gases and showed that gas volume at constant pressure increases with temperature.

9. Friederich Wöhler (German) - Friederich Wöhler is considered as the father of Organic Chemistry. He was the first chemist to synthesise an organic compound, Urea.

10. Carl Scheele (Swedish) - Carl Scheele was co-discover of oxygen (O) with Joseph Priestley. He also discovered chlorine, manganese and molybdenum.

11. Marie Curie (Polish) - He isolated radioactive elements radium and polonium.

12. Josiah Gibbs (American) - Founder of Chemical Thermodynamics.

13. Jacobus van't Hoff (Dutch) - He was one of the earlier chemists to speak about the 3-D nature of molecules.

14. Frederick Sanger (British) - Sanger revealed the Amino sequence for insulin. He worked out methods for determining the molecular structure of nucleic acids. He was two time Nobel Prize winner.

15. Humphry Davy (British) - He showed the connection between electrochemistry and the elements. He discovered the elements Potassium, Sodium, Barium, Calcium and Magnesium amongst others.

16. Joseph Priestley (English) - Oxygen co-discoverer.

17. Henri Le Chatelier (French) - Chatelier developed the principle that every change in a stable chemical equilibrium will result in a shift in the direction of the equilibrium to reduce the effects of the change.

18. Frederick Soddy (British) - Introduced the isotope theory of elements.

19. Svante Arrhenius (Sweden) - Established modern electrochemistry.

20. Germain Hess (Swiss/Russian) - Introduced Hess's Law for determining the heat of reactions.

21. Wilhelm Ostwald (Latvian) - Discovered Dilution law. He also invented process to make nitric acid by oxidising ammonia. He also developed a theory of colour.

22. Daniel Rutherford (Scottish) - Discoverer of Nitrogen.

23. Friederich Kekulé (German) - Kekulé was an organic chemist. He described the ring structure of benzene.

24. Stanislao Cannizzaro (Italian) - Cannizzaro established the use of Atomic weights in Chemical formulas and calculations.

25. Linus Pauling (American) - Pauling applied Quantum Theory to determine Chemical Structure (especially of proteins). He also showed how electrons effect the formation of molecules.

26. Johannes Brønsted Danish and Thomas Lowry (British) - Independently introduced the Brønsted-Lowry definition of an acid as something that

donates a proton and a base as something that accepts a proton.

27. Leo Baekland (Belgian/American) - Father of the Plastics Industry.

28. William Ramsay (Scottish) - Co-discovered Argon with Lord Rayleigh. Ramsay was the first to identify Helium, Neon, Krypton and Xenon.

29. Henri Moissan (French) - Moissan isolated fluorine. He invented the electric furnace and also discovered Carborundum and produced artificial diamonds in a laboratory.

30. Theodore Richards (American) - Richards performed extensive work on atomic weights to reveal the existence of isotopes.

31. Dorothy Hodgkin (British) - Crystallographer. He used x-ray crystallography to reveal the structure of such molecules as penicillin and insulin.

32. Thomas Graham (Scottish) - He developed Graham's Law of Diffusion. He was the founder of Colloidal Chemistry.

33. Fritz Haber (German) - He invented the process to make ammonia from nitrogen in the air known as the Haber process. His invention allowed Germany to continue making explosives after the World War I ban in spite of the blockade on the importation of nitrates.

34. Irving Langmuir (American) - Langmuir was a High Temperature chemist. His works led to the development of the tungsten lamp. He also studied gases. Research in this field would have practical implications with respect to the use of atomic hydrogen in welding torches.

35. Peter Debye (Dutch) - Worked on molecular structure. He pioneered x-ray powder photography.

36. Harold Urey (American) - Harold isolated Heavy water and discovered deuterium.

37. Paul Flory (American) - Paul Flory was a leading figure in the field of Polymerisation. He also studied properties of plastics, rubbers and fibres.

38. William Perkin (British) - Perkin was noted for his work on dyes. He also invented mauve.

39. George Washington Carver (American) - Agricultural chemist. His research involved the synthesis of products from peanuts, sweet potatoes and soybeans.

40. François Raoult (French) - Raoult developed the law which relates vapour pressure of a solution to the number of molecules of solute dissolved in it.

Future of Chemistry

As chemists, biologists and other scientists continue to unveil nature's secrets, a flood of facts accumulates with stunning momentum. Each answer is a new beginning - material for new experiments. After much effort was spent in the last century finding individual puzzle pieces, scientists can now revel in the process of fitting the pieces together.

Not that everything has been figured out - not by a long shot. Perhaps ironically, as science grows larger in scope and broader in focus, some of the most promising tools to synthesise the hows, whats, and wheres of human biology are exceedingly tiny.

Unravelling - and making sense of - different components of chemistry that aid the genetic instructions that spell life for organisms as diverse as flies, plants, worms, and people have sparked the most exciting revolution. Every minute of every day, scientists all over the world work feverishly, weaving a compelling tale of the chemistry that underlies our health.

It's all very exciting, but the progress mandates still more work. Much more work!

Among the questions still awaiting answers are these:

- How to synthesise foods that feed the growing number of people?
- How to manufacture clothes that clean themselves automatically?
- How to prevent ageing?
- How to produce medicines that prevent sickness?
- How to keep our brain alert for all-time?
- How to convert bacteria to our benefit?
- How do the 6-foot long stretches of DNA in every cell in our bodies know how to keep our biochemical factories running smoothly?
- When will someone figure out how to fight disease by manipulating the intricate sugar coatings on our cells?
- Who will invent the tools that will revolutionise chemistry labs of the future?
- What unexpected places hold treasure troves for new medicines?

A

Abatement

Action taken to reduce air pollution which involves the use of control equipment or some new process. This refers to a reduction or lessening as opposed to elimination of a type of discharge or pollutant.

Ablation

The weathering of a glacier by surface melting, or rock weathering by hydraulic erosion.

Abrasion

1. The susceptibility of the surface of a paper sample to being abraded during a standard test.
2. The tendency of papermaking materials to abrade slitter knives, dies, etc.

Absolute density

The absolute density is a measure of the mass of one millilitre of gas at standard temperature and pressure.

Absolute zero

Absolute zero is the theoretical temperature of -273.16ºC or -459.67ºF or 0 k at which entropy reaches its minimum value. The laws of thermodynamics state that absolute zero cannot be reached using only thermodynamic means. A system at absolute zero still possesses quantum mechanical zero-point energy, the energy of its ground state. The kinetic energy of the ground state

cannot be removed. However, in the classical interpretation it is zero and the thermal energy of matter vanishes. The zero point of any thermodynamic temperature scale, such as Kelvin or Rankine, is set at absolute zero.

Absolute Zero
Thermometers compare Fahrenheit Celsius and Kelvin scales

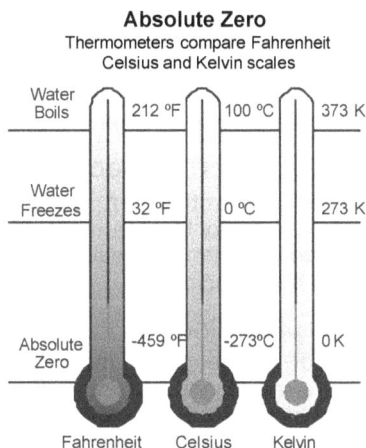

	Fahrenheit	Celsius	Kelvin
Water Boils	212 ºF	100 ºC	373 K
Water Freezes	32 ºF	0 ºC	273 K
Absolute Zero	-459 ºF	-273ºC	0 K

Absorbance

The logarithm (must be specified as to base 10, lg, or base e, ln) of the reciprocal of transmittance [ln (I_o/I_t) or lg (I_o/I_t)], where I_o and I_t are the monochromatic radiances (intensities) of light incident on and transmitted through, respectively, a sample which is usually contained in a sample cell.

Absorber

A device used commonly for sampling by absorption in which a gaseous or liquid material is removed from another gas or liquid by selective absorption; these include: scrubber, impinger, packed column, spray chamber, etc. A substance used to absorb energy form any type of radiation.

Absorption
The process of one material (absorbent) being retained by another (absorbate); this may be the physical solution of a gas, liquid, or solid in a liquid, attachment of molecules of a gas, vapour, liquid, or dissolved substance to a solid surface by physical forces, etc. In spectrophotometry, absorption of light at characteristic wavelengths or bands of wavelengths is used to identify the chemical nature of molecules, atoms or ions and to measure the concentrations of these species. The transfer of a component from one phase to another.

Absorption cross section
A measurement of an atom or molecule's ability to absorb light at a specified wavelength, measured in square cm/particle.

Absorption line
A narrow range of wavelengths in which a substance absorbs light; a series of discrete absorption lines can be used as an unambiguous identification for many relatively simple chemical species.

Abstraction reaction
A reaction that takes any atom away from another chemical species. Classical examples in atmospheric chemistry are the gas phase removal of hydrogen from methane by hydroxyl radical or the following solution phase reaction:
$$HSO_3 + H_2O_2 \quad HSO_4^- + H_2O$$

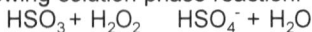

Acceleration
Measure of how fast velocity is changing, so we can think of it as the change in velocity over change in time. The most common use of acceleration is acceleration due to gravity, which can also appear as the gravitational constant (9.8 m/s^2).

Accommodation coefficient
Also sticking coefficient. A measure of the efficiency of capture of molecules or atoms which collide with aerosol particles, cloud droplets, etc. The accommodation coefficient is the fraction of the collisions which result in the capture of the molecules (atoms,radicals, etc.) by the particle, cloud droplet, etc., fraction of colliding molecules which are not reflected but which enter the surface of an aqueous aerosol.

Accretion
The process by which aerosols grow in size by external addition of various chemical species; a form of agglomeration.

Accumulation mode particles
(Also known as secondary particles) These are particles that are formed in the atmosphere due to both the chemical and physical processes that take place with the interactions of primary gaseous emissions. The primary gaseous emissions are injected into the atmosphere by combustion processes such as from a car or from a coal burning plant.

Accuracy
An indication of how close a measurement is to its accepted value.

Acetal
Acetal is an organic compound, pleasant smelling, formed by addition of ethyl alcohol to ethanal (acetaldehyde). It is used as a solvent and in synthetic organic chemistry. Acetals are used as protecting groups for carbonyl groups in organic synthesis as they are stable with respect to hydrolysis by

bases and with respect to many oxidizing and reducing agents.

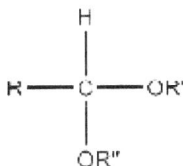

Acetaldehyde

CH_3CHO, a fairly simple aldehyde (second in the analogous series after formaldehyde) that is found in the atmosphere as a result of emissions from the manufacture of acetic acid, plastics, raw materials, and as a product in some polluted air oxidation reactions, for instance, acetaldehyde is found in urban air all over the world. Also called Ethanal.

Acetic acid

CH_3COOH, a carbonyl compound that is emitted into the troposphere by both natural and anthropogenic processes. In the troposphere, acetic acid is present in the gas phase and is highly water soluble. Since acetic acid is highly water soluble, it is found in high concentration as acidic precipitation, such as in fog water and cloud droplets in urban areas. Also known as Ethanoic Acid.

Acetone

CH_3COCH_3, a carbonyl compound that is found in the atmosphere as a reactive gas. Acetone is considered to be a volatile organic compound (VOC), which is emitted into the atmosphere by industrial processes. Acetone has been linked to the formation of ozone in the troposphere due to the fact that it is a source of free radicals. Also known as Propanone.

Acetyl

A functional group with chemical formula -COCH3.

Achiral

A group containing atleast two identical substituents.

Acicular

Another word for "needle-shaped," as in the case of aragonite calcium carbonate particles.

Acicular habit

An acicular habit describes the shape of a large crystal that looks like spikes coming out from one point. Think about those koosh balls for this example.

Acid

A species which reacts in liquid water to generate hydrogen ions (conventionally represented as cations H^+ or hydronium, H_3O^+); anions (e.g., sulphate, SO_4^{2-}; nitrate, NO_3^-) which were associated with the H^+ in the acid are also released. Important acids in the atmosphere include sulphuric acid (H_2SO_4), nitric acid (HNO_3), and organic acids (e.g., formic acid, HCO_2H; acetic acid, CH_3CO_2H, etc.).

1. **Brønsted acid**—A molecular entity capable of donating a proton to a base, (i.e. a "proton donor") or the corresponding chemical species. For example: H_2O, H_3O^+, $CH_3CO_2H, H_2SO_4, HSO_4^-$.
2. **Lewis acid**—A molecular entity (and the corresponding chemical species) that is an electron-pair acceptor and therefore able to react with a Lewis base to form a Lewis adduct, by sharing the electron pair furnished by the Lewis base.

Acid alum

A mixture of aluminium sulphate (papermaker's alum) and sulphuric acid.

Acid anhydride

Hydrocarbon containing two carbonyl groups.Acyl group attached with carboxylate group.eg- RCOOCOR'

Acid deposition

A broad term that includes any forms of acids that accumulate in the atmosphere, for instance, acid rain, fog, haze. The term can be used to explain the long term effects of these events on the environment as well as the main causes of acid rain, fog or haze. The term functions as a category that any aspect of anthropogenic acid in the environment can be placed.

Acid halide

Acyl group with any halogen attached with carbon of carbonyl group.eg.-RCO-X(X=F,Cl,Br,I).

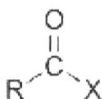

Acid rain

Acidified particulate matter in the atmosphere that is deposited by precipitation onto a surface, often eroding the surface away. This precipitation generally has a pH less than 5 and sometimes much lower depending on the concentration of acidic components.

Acid-base indicator

A dye that changes colours under different conditions of pH Values.

Acid-base titration

The procedure used to determine the concentration of an acid or base involving the gradual addition of either an acid or base.

Acidic

Describes a solution with a high concentration of H^+ ions.

Acidic paper making

Forming paper from stock that has a pH value usually in the range of 3.5 to 6.5, and usually in the presence of aluminium species, e.g. alum.

Acidification

In the gas phase this process happens when compounds like nitrogen oxides and sulphur oxides are converted in a chemical reaction in the gas phase or in clouds into acidic substances. These acids are rained-out or dry deposited. Significant amounts of the compounds containing nitrogen and sulphur are a direct result of anthropogenic activity. An example reaction that takes place in soil occurs from the oxidation of reduced sulphur (for instance, pyrite) exposed during, for instance, strip mining of lignite. This can be represented as:

$$2FeS_2 + 6H_2O + 7O_2 =$$
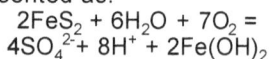

Acidity

Ability of an aqueous sample to contribute hydrogen ions during a titration with base.

Acid-pulse (dry deposition)

Deposit of powder-like substance over the ground surface; especially effecting plant leaves; that when contacted by water has a very low pH.

Acrolein (CH_2CHCHO)

The simplest double-bonded aldehyde, produced in urban smog, contributing greatly to eye and lung irritation. It is a constituent of internal combustion engine exhaust, cigarette smoke, and biomass burning, and from the incomplete combustion of plastics and fuels. Also called Propenal.

Acrylic acid

Acrylic acid (propenoic acid) is a colourless liquid, smelling like acetic acid. It can be formed by acrolein oxidation. It readily polymerizes and is used in the manufacture of acrylic resins, transparent plastic materials (organic glass).

Actinide series
The actinide series is one of two series of inner transition elements. Elements 89 through 103 are a part of this series. The elements include uranium, berkelium, and nobelium.

Actinium
Symbol: Ac Atomic Number: 89 Atomic Mass: 227.03amu. It is one of the elements in the actinide series of inner transition elements. It may also be classified as a rare earth element. Actinium is the first element of the actinide series. It is used as a source of neutrons in experiments that involve radioactivity. You will not find the element in regular use anywhere in the natural world.

Activated charcoal
Activated charcoal or activated carbon is charcoal that has been activated for adsorption by steaming or by heating in a vacuum. Charcoal is obtained by burning wood, nutshells, coconut husks or other materials. Charcoal becomes activated by heating it with steam to approximately 1000 °C in the absence of oxygen. The chemical nature of amorphous carbon, combined with a high surface area makes it an ideal medium for the adsorption of organic chemicals. A single gram of such material can have $400 \ m^2$ to $1\ 200\ m^2$ square meters of surface area. Activated charcoal is widely used to decolourize liquids, recover solvents, and remove toxins from water and air.

Activated complex
An unstable, short-lived particle formed as the result of a collision of particles in a chemical reaction. The activated complex is located at the top of a potential energy diagram. Bonds are in the process of both being formed and being broken.

Activating group
Any group which activate any molecule by increasing positive or negative charge on carbon atom.Mainly towards neucleophilic or electrophilic substitution reactions.

Activation energy
When reactions proceed, a certain amount of energy is needed for the whole process to begin. The energy needed to get the reaction started (get it over the hump) is called the activation energy. The energy required to start a chemical reaction. If a reaction is not spontaneous, it requires a specific amount of energy to proceed. That required energy is the activation energy. Enzymes and catalysts can decrease the activation energy of a reaction.

Active chlorine
Active chlorine can be a single chlorine atom that is a radical ("Cl dot") and therefore highly reactive. It can also be a molecule containing chlorine that is reactive (ClO). Active chlorine's most notable role in atmospheric chemistry is in catalytic destruction of ozone in the stratosphere and the accumulation of active chlorine at the earth's polar stratosphere during the polar night that leads to major ozone hole formation during the spring.

Active transport
Active transport is the carriage of a solute across a biological membrane from low to high concentration that requires the expenditure of (metabolic) energy.

Activity series
a list of metals and hydrogen arranged in order of their chemical reactivity, such that any element in the series will displace ions of the elements below it from aqueous solutions of their salts.

Activity series of metals
A list of metals arranged in decreasing order of chemical reactivity. Very active metals react with water. Active metals react with acids. Least reactive metals do not react with acids.

Acyl group
A group having alkyl or aryl group with a carbonyl group RCO-

Adam's catalyst
A catalyst for hydrogenation and hydrogenolysis in organic synthesis. Also known as platinum dioxide

Addition reaction
A reaction where a product is created from the coming together of 2 reactants.

Additivity principle
The hypothesis that each of several structural features of a molecular entity makes a separate and additive contribution to a property of the substance concerned. More specifically, it is the hypothesis that each of the several substituent groups in a parent molecule makes a separate and additive contribution to the standard Gibbs energy change (or Gibbs energy of activation) corresponding to a particular equilibrium (or rate of reaction).

Address-message concept
Address-message concept refers to compounds in which part of the molecule is required for binding (address) and part for the biological action (message).

Adduct
A new chemical species AB, each molecular entity of which is formed by direct combination of two separate molecular entities A and B in such a way that there is change in connectivity, but no loss, of atoms within the moieties A and B. Stoichiometries other than 1:1 are also possible, e.g. a bis-adduct (2:1). An "intramolecular adduct" can be formed when A and B are groups contained within the same molecular entity. This is a general term which, whenever appropriate, should be used in preference to the less explicit term complex. It is also used specifically for products of an addition reaction.

Adhesion
Adhesion is one type of attraction force between the molecules of a substance and the container or another object. You stay wet when you get out of the bathtub because of adhesive forces. Some of the water molecules want to stick to you.

Adiabatic lapse rate
The rate of decrease of temperature with increasing altitude in the atmosphere. If heat is neither gained nor lost from the air parcel under consideration, then the lapse rate is said to be adiabatic and the energy to expand the volume of the parcel or rising air comes from the kinetic energy of the gas molecules in that parcel. The expansion of the parcel causes these molecules net kinetic velocity to decrease and this is equivalent to cooling the air. In dry air the dry adiabatic lapse rate is about 9.8 C/km (the sign is traditionally positive although the temperature is decreasing with altitude).

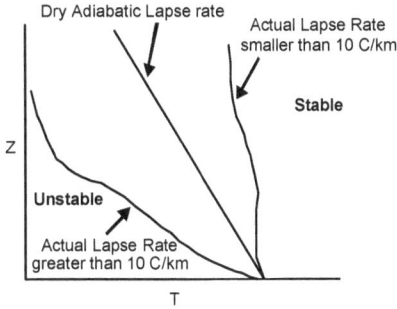

Adsorbed

Solid material used to capture either a gas or liquid; often activated carbon is employed as the solid because of its high surface area per unit mass.

Adsorbent

An adsorbent is the solid material to which another species is adsorbed in a surface layer. A condensed phase at the surface of which adsorption may occur.

Adsorption

The process by which molecules of gas, dissolved substances, or liquids adhere to the surface of solids through either weak physical forces (physical adsorption) or stronger chemical forces (chemical adsorption). The enrichment (positive adsorption, or briefly, adsorption) of one or more components in an interfacial layer.

Advection

The transport of air, its properties (such as heat), trace materials, fog, cold air, etc., solely by mass motion of the atmosphere, generally in a horizontal direction.

Aeration

The process by which a volume filled with a liquid becomes permeated with air or another gas; aeration is often accomplished by spraying the liquid into the air, bubbling air through a liquid, or agitating the liquid to promote surface absorption of air.

Aerobic

Oxygen-dependent or requiring oxygen.

Aerobic respiration

Organisms utilize oxygen to break down components, derive energy, and generate needed biomolecules. Carbohydrates are cycled into water and carbon dioxide.

Aerometer

Instrument used to measure the density of gases.

Aerometric measurements

Measurements of the temperature, pressure, air motion (velocity vectors), or other physical measurements to characterize an air mass.

Aerosol particles

One of the components of an atmospheric air parcel, comprised of minute solids particles part of which is almost certainly water.

Aerosol scavengers

Cloud droplets which attract an aerosol into snow, rain or some other water precipitate by coagulation and accretion.

Affinity

Affinity is the tendency of a molecule to associate with another. The affinity of a drug is its ability to bind to its biological target (receptor, enzyme, transport system, etc.) For pharmacological receptors it can be thought of as the frequency with which the drug, when brought into the proximity of a receptor by diffusion, will reside at a position of minimum free energy within the force field of that receptor.

Afforestation

The process or act of changing land into forest by planting trees, seeding, etc. on land formerly used for something other than forestry. This can obviously be contrasted with deforestation.

Agglomerate

The most general term indicating that small particles come together and stick.

Agglomeration

A process by which atmospheric particles collide and stick to each other forming a new particle. Many of the particles emitted from automobile tailpipes are agglomerations of smaller particles formed in the combustion process.

Agonist

An agonist is an endogenous substance or a drug that can interact with a receptor and initiate a physiological or a pharmacological response characteristic of that receptor (contraction, relaxation, secretion, enzyme activation, etc.).

Agostic

The term designates structures in which a hydrogen atom is bonded to both a carbon atom and a metal atom. The term is also used to characterize the interaction between a CH bond and an unsaturated metal centre, and to describe similar bonding of a transition metal with Si-H compounds. The expression " -hydrido-bridged" is also used to describe the bridging hydrogen.

Air mass

A qualitative term to describe a widespread body of air with approximately uniform characteristics which had been identified at a given time over a particular region of the earth's surface. Sometimes an air mass is marked by inert tracers such as SF_6 which may be added to it. The composition of a given air mass undergoes alteration as it migrates, chemical changes occur, compounds are removed by dry and wet deposition, and new impurities are added to the mass.

Air parcel

A volume of air, the component makeup and concentrations of which remain relatively static, that tends to travel around the earth changing geographic location and position above earth as an intact unit. Air parcels can be tracked.

Air pollutant

A substance, gaseous material or aerosol which has been introduced into the air (either by human activity or by natural processes) in sufficient concentration to produce a measurable effect on humans, animals, vegetation, or materials (monuments, etc.): SO_2, NO_2, H_2S, CO, hydrocarbons, etc.

Air pollution

Usually the presence of substances in the atmosphere, resulting either from human activity or natural processes, present in sufficient concentration, for a sufficient time and under circumstances such as to interfere with comfort, health or welfare of persons or the e nvironment.

Air pollution control

Measures taken to control the purity of the air to some degree specified by law.

Air pollution control district

A geographical region designated by law in which the emissions of some specified air pollutants are controlled to a degree specified by law.

Air pollution index or air quality index

A mathematical combination of the concentrations of air pollutants (weighted in some fashion to reflect the estimated health impact of the specific pollutant) which gives an approximate numerical measure of the quality of the air at a given time. These indices have little scientific basis but have been used to inform the public (in a qualitative fashion) of the degree of pollution present at a given time.

Air pollution survey

A study of the concentrations and geographical distribution of specified air pollutants in a given area and an assessment of the damage, if any, which the pollutants have caused.

Air quality act of 1967

The first national act in the United States to regulate emissions into the atmosphere; the act was closely related to a previous act created in 1963. The bill was created in response to growing urban areas that were having obvious pollution problems.

Air quality assessment

A prescribed level of atmospheric pollution allowed for a certain compound during a specific time in a specific geographical area. Standards are set by some regulating body, office or agency.

Air quality characteristic

One of the quantifiable properties relating to an air sample: concentration of a constituent, wind speed, temperature, etc. The quantity of air quality characteristic is the true value of the characteristic being investigated; it is recognized that in practice, this value can only be approximated by existing methods.

Air quality index (aqi)

An accounting or measurement of specified toxic levels of pollutants in the air. Based on the EPA air quality act, it gives the indicator (number) of different gas phase concentration levels to determine if it is hazardous to be outside or not, that is to breathe the air is a specific region.

Air resource management

The detailed planning and the implementation of air pollution control programmes designed to preserve the health and welfare of the people in the region, the plant and animal life, physical property, good visibility, and other factors which determine the air quality and the maintenance of an aesthetically acceptable environment.

Air sampling network

A number of air sampling stations which are established in a given geographical region at which measurements of both pollutant concentrations and meteorological quantities (wind speed, direction, rain fall, humidity, etc.) are made to determine the extent and the nature of the air pollution and to establish trends in the concentrations of the air pollutants with time.

Air stripping

Air stripping is a process for the removal of volatile organic contaminants from groundwater. The groundwater flows downward inside a tower filled with materials (the packing) over a large surface area. Air is introduced at the bottom of the tower and is forced upward past the falling water. The volatiles evaporate from the water and are collected in air filters or released to the atmosphere.

Air, composition of pure

The composition of air is variable with respect to several of its components (e.g., CH_4, CO_2, H_2O) so "pure" air has no precise meaning; it is commonly considered to be air which is free of dust, aerosols, and reactive gaseous contaminants of anthropogenic origin. The composition of the major components in dry air is relatively constant (percent by volume given): nitrogen, 78.084; oxygen, 20.946; argon, 0.934; carbon dioxide, 0.033; neon, 0.0018; helium, 0.000524; methane, 0.00016, krypton 0.000114; hydrogen 0.00005; nitrous oxide, 0.00003; xenon, 0.0000087. The concentration of carbon dioxide, methane, nitrous oxide, the chlorofluorocarbons and some other species of anthropogenic origin are increasing measurably with time. Relative clean air which is free of most reactive anthropogenic pollution (NO, NO_2, SO_2, non-methane hydrocarbons, etc.), often used as a reference sample in the calibration and operation of instruments, is purchased under the designation of zero air.

Air-float clay

A type of kaolin clay products that are prepared for use by an air-sorting process to obtain particles a good size range for the application.

Aitken particles

Aerosol particles below 0.1m in diameter. These generally are the most numerous among all particles in the air. Their concentrations can be determined with the Aitken counter which measures total particle number density. Owing to their small size, Aitken particles contribute little to the total mass concentration of all aerosol particles; this is determined primarily by particles of diameter > 0.1m.

Akd

Alkylketene dimer, a synthetic sizing agent in the form of an aqueous dispersion of waxy particles, useful for wet-end addition.

Albedo

The fraction of the energy of electromagnetic radiation reflected from a body (or surface) relative to the energy incident upon it. The reflection of light from a surface is, of course, dependent on the wavelength of the light, the nature of the surface, and its angle of incidence with the surface. The term albedo usually connotes a broad wavelength band (visible, ultraviolet, or infrared), whereas the terms reflectivity and spectral albedo are used to describe the reflection of monochromatic (single wavelength or small band of wavelengths) radiation.

Alchemy

Alchemy is an ancient, non-scientific form of chemistry. In the middle ages, alchemists were people who tried to turn one element into another (usually lead (Pb) into gold (Au)).

Alcohols

When the elements making up an organic compound are Carbon, Hydrogen and Oxygen and the Hydrogen and Oxygen combine in such a way as to form a -C-OH group, the Organic Compounds formed are referred to as Alcohols and the Functional Group (-OH) is referred to as the "O H" Group. The most common Alcohol is Ethyl Alcohol or Ethanol (C_2H_5OH) which is present in all beers, wines and liquors.

Aldehyde

A class of organic compound of general formula: R(C=O)H, where R is an hydrogen atom or hydrocarbyl group (e.g., CH_3, C_2H_5, etc.). These are products of hydrocarbon oxidation. The simplest aldehydes are formaldehyde (methanal, HCHO), acetaldehyde (ethanal, CH_3CHO), and propionaldehyde (propanal, CH_3CH_2CHO). They also react rapidly with HO-radicals in the atmosphere to produce acyl (RCO) and acylperoxyl ($RCOO_2$) radicals. Formaldehyde is the most abundant aldehyde in the atmosphere (formed from the natural hydrocarbon, CH_4, as well as other hydrocarbons) where its mixing ratios are often > 0.2 ppbv even in relatively clean air. Acetaldehyde is a major precursor to peroxyacetyl nitrate (PAN) in the troposphere.

Aldol reaction
When two similar aldehydes are reacted with each other,a product having both aldehyde(>C=O) and alcohol(OH) group is formed.This reaction is called aldol reaction.

Alert levels
Also referred to as air quality index (AQI). This is a measure of different levels of concentration of air pollutants in the air. This index by another name was originally established in 1976. With each pollutant level, there is a warning depending on the concentration and its effects to the public. Alert levels can be found for any of five pollutants and the levels have colour and number indicators that warn the public. The pollutants upon which the air quality index is based are ground-level ozone, particulate matter, carbon monoxide, sulphur dioxide, and nitrogen dioxide.

Aliphatic
A non-cyclic, non-aromatic, hydrocarbon chain (e.g. alkanes, alkenes, and alkynes)

Aliphatic compounds
Hydrocarbons that contain only single covalent bonds, double covalent bonds separated by more than two carbon atoms, or a triple covalent bond are referred to as Aliphatic Compounds. The Aliphatic Compounds make up the majority of Hydrocarbons.

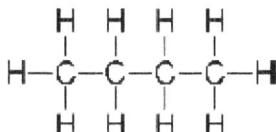

Aliquot
A representative portion of the whole.

Alkaline papermaking
Forming paper from stock that has a pH value in the range from about 7 to 9.5.

Alkalinity
Ability of an aqueous sample to contribute hydroxyl ions during a titration with acid.

Alkaloid
Alkaloids are basic nitrogen organic compounds (mostly heterocyclic) derived from plants and having diverse pharmacological properties. Alkaloids include morphine, cocaine, atropine, quinine, and caffeine, most of which are used in medicine as analgesics or anaesthetics. Some alkaloids are poisonous, e.g. strychnine and coniine, and colchicine inhibit cell division.

Alkanes
Alkanes are hydrocarbons containing only Single Covalent C-C Bonds are called Alkanes.

Alkenes
Alkenes are hydrocarbons containing at least one Double Covalent C=C Bond.

Alkoxide ion

The conjugate base of an alcohol without the terminal H atom. For any alcohol R-OH, the corresponding alkoxide form is R-O⁻.

Alkyl

A hydrocarbon having formula C_nH_{2n+1}

Alkyl group

Part of an organic chemical compound that is made up mainly of carbon and hydrogen atoms in the approximate ratio of two hydrogen atoms per carbon atom (-CH2-).

Alkylation

Addition of alkyl group in a compound.

Alkyne

An unsaturated hydrocarbon containog triple bond.and having general formula C_nH_{2n-2}

Allosteric binding sites

Allosteric binding sites are contained in many enzymes and receptors. As a consequence of the binding to Allosteric binding sites, the interaction with the normal ligand may be either enhanced or reduced.

Allosteric enzyme

An allosteric enzyme is an enzyme that contains a region to which small, regulatory molecules ("effectors") may bind in addition to and separate from the substrate binding site and thereby affect the catalytic activity.

Allosteric regulation

Allosteric regulation is the regulation of the activity of allosteric enzymes.

Alloy

A mixture of a metal with one or more other elements. eg. steel (iron & carbon), solder (lead & tin), bronze (copper & tin) and brass (copper & zinc).

Allyl

An alkene hydrocarbon group with the formula:

H2C=CH-CH2-.

Allylic substitution reaction

A substitution reaction occurring at position 1/ of an allylic system, the double bond being between positions 2/ and 3/. The incoming group may be attached to the same atom 1/ as the leaving group, or the incoming group becomes attached at the relative position 3/, with movement of the double bond from 2/3 to 1/2.

Alternant

A conjugated system of pi electrons is termed alternant if its atoms can be divided into two sets so that no atom of one set is directly linked to any other atom of the same set.

Example of alternate   system

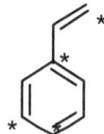

Example of non-alternate   system

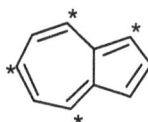

(two atoms of unstarred set are dircetly linked)

Alternative energy source

Any energy source that can be harnessed without the use of burning fossil fuels. Such alternative sources are almost always a renewable energy source such as hydroelectric power, wind power, and solar power.

Alum

Its formula $K_2SO_4.Al_2(SO_4)_3.24H_2O$. A white or Colourless Crystalline compound. It is used as mordant for dyeing and in tanning of leather goods.

24

Aluminium

Symbol: "Al" Atomic Number: "13" Atomic Mass: 26.98amu. Aluminium is a light element and classified as a basic metal. There is more aluminium than any other metal in the Earth's crust. You will also find aluminium in utensils, foil wrap, power lines, soda cans, and airplane structures.

Aluminium trihydrate

A very bright mineral having the same chemical composition as alum floc.

Ambient air

The outdoor air in the particular location.

Ambient air quality

A general term used to describe the quality of the outside air. Usually adjectives such as good, fair, bad, etc. are used by the media to describe this; often some form of air pollution or air quality index is employed to determine the specific descriptive term to be used. These are very qualitative terms of little or no scientific value.

Americium

Symbol: "Am" Atomic Number:"95" Atomic Mass: (243)amu. Americium is one of the elements in the actinide series of inner transition elements. It may also be classified as a rare earth element. This element is radioactive and can be safely used in small amounts. You might find it in nuclear reactors and some smoke detectors.

Ames/salmonella test

A screening test employed in predicting the mutagenic and the potential carcinogenic activities of chemicals in the environment. It employs Ames test strains of salmonella bacteria (his⁻) which lack the ability to produce histidine. The compound to be tested, the bacteria and a small amount of histidine (insufficient to permit colony growth but enough to allow sufficient growth for expression of mutations) are added to agar. The bacteria are allowed to incubate for about 63 hours at 37 °C. If a significant increase in colonies above background is observed in the sample containing the test compound, then it is concluded that the chemical tested is a direct mutagen for the particular Ames strain of bacteria.

Amide

Amide is an organic compound that contains a carbonyl group bound to nitrogen. The simplest amides are formamide ($HCONH_2$) and acetamide (CH_3CONH_2).

Amides

When Organic Acids have the Oxygen in the terminal -OH group of O=C-OH replaced by an Nitrogen, then the resulting compound has the terminal group O=C-NH_2 and is called an Amide.

Amines

When the Oxygen of the -OH functional group of Alcohols is replaced by Nitrogen the functional group becomes -NH_2 and the compounds are called Amines. The simplest Amine is Methyl Amine (CH_3NH_2).

Amino acids

A group of 20 different kinds of small molecules that link together in long chains to form proteins. Often referred to as the "building blocks" of proteins. The sequence of amino acids in a protein determines the structure and function of the protein.

Amino group

The amino group is a functional group with one nitrogen and two hydrogen atoms. You will find them on all of the amino acids. It can be synthesized from ammonia.

Ammonia

The molecular formula for ammonia is NH_3. Ammonia is one of the most important inorganic nitrogen compounds in atmospheric water droplets. It reacts with strong acids and is one of the only known basic, gas phase atmospheric components. Atmospheric ammonia can also enhance the nucleation rate and the production of new particles in the atmosphere. These new particles can be activated to become condensation nuclei and then, through various processes, grow to a particle size of 0.05 micrometer or larger which can then be effective as cloud condensation nuclei. This process can, therefore, affect the global radiation budget. The major sources of ammonia are decaying natural organic matter, livestock wastes, fertilizers, and industrial activity.

Amorphous

A solid that has no definite shape or form because the particles are arranged randomly. eg. glass, flour, soot.

Amorphous solid

An amorphous solid has no specific organization of molecules. The other end of the spectrum would be a crystal with a highly organized set of molecules. Plastic is an example of a vitreous solid. Because of their combination of atoms, amorphous solids do not have a specific melting point. They become a liquid over a wide temperature range.

Amphipathic

Amphipathic molecules have one hydrophobic end and one hydrophilic end. You can find these molecules in the cell membrane.

Amphiphilic

A compound containing a large organic cation or anion which possesses a long unbranched hydrocarbon chain, e.g. $H_3C(CH_2)_nCO_2^-M^+$ $H_3C(CH_2)_nSO_3^-M^+$ $H_3C(CH_2)_nN(CH_3)_3^+X^-$ ($n > 7$). The existence of distinct polar (hydrophilic) and non polar (hydrophobic) regions in the molecule promotes the formation of *micelles* in dilute aqueous solution.

Amphiprotic

a substance that can function as an acid in some reactions and a base in others.

Amphiprotic (solvent)

Self-ionizing solvent possessing both characteristics of Brønsted acids and bases, for example H_2O and CH_3OH, in contrast to aprotic solvent.

Amphoteric

A chemical species that behaves both as an acid and as a base is called amphoteric. This property depends upon the medium in which the species is investigated: H_2SO_4 is an acid when studied in water, but becomes amphoteric in superacids.

Amylopectin

The branched-chain form of natural starch molecules, making up almost 100% of starch from waxy maize, a hybrid corn.

Amylose

The linear-chain form of natural starch molecules present in the most widely used form of corn, and also in potato and tapioca starch.

Anaerobic respiration

Living or acting in the absence of oxygen. Cellular respiration in the absence of oxygen.

Analog

An analog is a drug whose structure is related to that of another drug but whose chemical and biological properties may be quite different.

Analyser selectivity of analyses with

Ability of a device to exhibit a low or zero sensitivity to analytes (see interferant) other than the one it is intended to measure. The selectivity is described by a coefficient of interaction; it is the ratio of the device response to the substance to be measured to that of the interferant, both being at the same concentration.

Analyser sequential indication of

Indication obtained following sequential sampling or received from a sequential cell or from data processing comprising a succession of predetermined repetitive operations (or a combination of the three).

Analyser, accuracy of an analysis with

The ability of a measuring instrument to give indications approaching the true value of the quantity measured.

Analyser, continuous

An analyser in which subassemblies operate continuously.

Analyser, continuous indication

An analysis with a permanent indication related to the sample concentration. To obtain a continuous indication, the sampling and measuring cell need to be continuous. A time lag may exist between sampling and indication of measured concentration.

Analyser, dead time of

Time which elapses between the moment at which a sudden change in concentration (or a new sample) is introduced and the moment at which the detector response indication reaches the measurement threshold of the analyser, a value conventionally fixed at 10% of the final change in indication.

Analyser, discontinuous

An analyser with at least one discontinuous subassembly.

Analyser, discontinuous indication of

Indication related to the concentration during intervals of time which are not continuous.

Analyser, fall time of

When following a change in concentrations from a definite value c to 0, the time which elapses between the moment when this change is produced and the moment when the indication reaches a value conventionally fixed at 10% of the final change or indication.

Analyser, measurement threshold of

The minimum concentration of a substance which produces a quantifiable signal with a given uncertainty.

Analyser, precision of measurements with

The quality which characterizes the ability of a device to give for the same value of the quantity measured, indications which agree among themselves, not taking into consideration the systematic errors associated with variations of the indications. Repeatability characterizes the ability of a device to give indications which are unaffected by random errors.

Analyser, range of measurement of
Range of concentration between the measurement threshold and the maximum usable indication.

Analyser, resolution of
A general term which defines the ability of a device to differentiate between adjacent signals.

Analyser, response time of
Time which elapses, when there is a stepwise change in the quantity to be measured, between the moment when this change is produced and the moment when the indication reaches a value conventionally fixed at 90% of the final change in indication.

Analyser, rise time of
The difference between the response time and the dead time.

Analyser, sensitivity of
The response of the measuring cell of a system in indicated output units per unit concentration of the component being measured. It is the slope, at the concentration being measured, of the tangent to the calibration curve.

Analyser, sequential
A discontinuous analyser in which at least one subassembly operates sequentially.

Analytical unit; analyser
An assembly of sub-units comprising: suitable apparatus permitting the introduction and removal of the gas, liquid or solid to be analysed and/or calibration materials; a measuring cell or other apparatus which, from the physical or chemical properties of the components of the material to be analysed, gives signals allowing their identification and/or measurement; signal processing devices (amplification, recording) or, if need be, data processing devices.

Anatase
A crystalline form of titanium dioxide having the second-highest refractive index of commonly used fillers. .

Aneroid barometer
An instrument for monitoring the atmospheric pressure in which no liquid is employed, but rather changes in pressure between the atmosphere and a closed vessel bend a diaphram which moves a pointer on a scale.

Anion
an ion carrying a negative charge. Anions result when atoms or groups of atoms (polyatomic ions) gain electrons.

Anionic
Having a negative charge (usually balanced by counter-ions in the adjacent solution).

Anionic trash

Informal term meaning negatively charged colloidal and dissolved polymeric materials in paper furnish, usually coming from the wood.

Anionotropic rearrangement (or anionotropy)

A rearrangement in which the migrating group moves with its electron pair from one atom to another.

Annelation

Alternative, but less desirable term for annulation. The term is widely used in German and French language.

Annulation

A transformation involving fusion of a new ring to a molecule via two new bonds. Some authors use the term "annelation" for the fusion of an additional ring to an already existing one, and "annulation" for the formation of a ring from one or several acyclic precursors, but this distinction is not made generally.

Annulene

Mancude (i.e. having formally the maximum number of noncumulative double bonds) monocyclic hydrocarbon without side chains of the general formula C_nH_n (n is an even number) or C_nH_{n+1} (n is an odd number). Note that in systematic nomenclature an annulene with seven or more carbon atoms may be named [n]annulene, where n is the number of carbon atoms, e.g. annulene for cyclonona-1,3,5,7-tetraene.

Anode

the site of oxidation (loss of electrons) in an electrochemical cell or electrolytic cell.

Anoxic

The lack of oxygen such as the inadequate oxygenation of the blood (anoxia). In aquatic environmental chemistry it refers to water that has become oxygen poor due to the bacterial decay of organic matter.

Antagonist

An antagonist is a drug or a compound that opposes the physiological effects of another. At the receptor level, it is a chemical entity that opposes the receptor-associated responses normally induced by another bioactive agent.

Antarafacial, suprafacial

When a part of a molecule ("molecular fragment") undergoes two changes in bonding (bond-making or bond-breaking), either to a common centre or to two related centres, external to itself, these bonding changes may be related in one of two spatially different ways. These are designated as "antarafacial" if opposite faces of the molecular fragment are involved, and "suprafacial" if both changes occur at the same face. The concept of "face" is clear from the diagrams in the cases of planar (or approximately planar) frameworks with isolated or interacting pi orbitals. The terms antarafacial and suprafacial are, however, also employed in cases in which the essential part of the molecular fragment undergoing changes in bonding comprises two atoms linked only by a sigma bond. In these cases it is customary to refer to the phases of the local sigma-bonding orbital: occurrence of the two bonding changes at sites of like orbital phase is regarded as suprafacial, whereas that at two sites of opposite phase is antarafacial. The possibilities are shown for C-C and C-H sigma bonds in Figs. c and d. There may be two distinct and alternative stereochemical outcomes of a suprafacial process involving a sigma bond between saturated carbon atoms, i.e. either retention or inversion at both centres. The antarafacial process results in inversion at one centre and retention at the second. For examples of the use of these terms see cycloaddition, sigmatropic rearrangement.

Antarctic ozone hole

Recent data suggest that due to the release into the atmosphere of CFCs by human activities, the ozone hole can be as large as North America during a given astral spring. The CFCs are broken apart by UV light to form free radicals of chlorine after they have diffused into the upper stratosphere from the troposphere. This long term movement from the troposphere to the stratosphere is possible for these chlorine containing chemicals because of there long atmospheric lifetimes; however, this type of movement is not important for more reactive species such as tropospheric ozone because of their reactivity and therefore short atmospheric lifetime. In the Antarctic stratosphere, the reaction that converts reservoir species of chlorine into an active form—which destroys ozone—takes place on the surface of particles in polar stratospheric clouds as the temperature drops below about 200K. This is possible because of the unique isolation of the south polar vortex during the austral winter. The surfaces of these (nitric acid/water) clouds act as catalysts for reactions that release molecular chlorine which quickly photolyzes to chlorine's (radical) active state. It is this radical which destroys ozone.

Antarctic vortex

The combination of a drastic temperature and corresponding pressure drop along with the rotation of the Earth on its axis produces a spinning/rotating volume of air. The rotational speed of the winds commonly reaches as high as 180 mph. The motion of these winds form an impenetrable barrier such that the trapped air inside is unmixed, as it is separated from the air outside, and remains quite cold (temperatures drop below 80 Celsius). Inside the whirling volume of freezing air, the cold temperatures facilitate the condensation of gases into particles that eventually form polar stratospheric clouds.

Anthropogenic

Refers to something originating from humans and the impact of human activities on nature.

Anthropogenic forcing

Influence exerted on a habitat or chemical environment by humans. This obliquely refers to the idea of managed environment as opposed to a wild or non-disturbed environment. The variability of assumptions about radiative forcing can cause significant changes in the results from computer models that require an estimate of those values.

Anti bonding molecular orbital

Molecular orbitals having higher energy than bonding molecular orbitals after combination of atomic orbitals.denoted by an astric over Sigma or pi notations.

Antichlors

Additives such as sodium sulfite or hydrosulfite that reduce chlorine or related oxidants so that they do not attack wet-strength agents.

Anticyclone

An anticyclone (that is, opposite to a cyclone) is a weather phenomenon defined by the United States' National Weather Service's glossary as "[a] large-scale circulation of winds around a central region of high atmospheric pressure, clockwise in the Northern Hemisphere, counterclockwise in the Southern Hemisphere".[1] Effects of surface-based anticyclones include clearing skies as well as cooler, drier air. Fog can also form overnight within a region of higher pressure. Mid-tropospheric systems, such as the subtropical ridge, deflect tropical cyclones around their periphery and cause a temperature inversion inhibiting free convection near their center, building up surface-based haze under their base. Anticyclones aloft can form within warm core lows, such as tropical cyclones, due to descending cool air from the backside of upper troughs, such as polar highs, or from large scale sinking, such as the subtropical ridge. Anticyclonic flow spirals in a clockwise direction in the Northern Hemisphere and anticlockwise in the Southern Hemisphere.

Anticyclonic flow

The air flow produced about a high pressure center by the combination of two forces: the pressure gradient accelerating the air away from the center and the Coriolis force acting inward. Anticyclonic flows are clockwise in the northern hemisphere and counterclockwise in the southern hemisphere.

Antifoam

A defoamer product that has been formulated with the aim of preventing the formation of visible foam, not killing existing visible foam.

Antimetabolite

An antimetabolite is a structural analog of an intermediate (substrate or coenzyme) in a physiologically occurring metabolic pathway that acts by replacing the natural substrate thus blocking or diverting the biosynthesis of physiologically important substances.

Antimony

Symbol: "Sb" Atomic Number:"51" Atomic Mass: 121.75amu. Antimony has been used for thousands of years. The pure metal is quite brittle. You will find the element used in batteries, alloys, and in the creation of paints and enamels.

Antisense molecule

An antisense molecule is an oligonucleotide or analog thereof that is complementary to a segment of RNA (ribonucleic acid) or DNA (deoxyribonucleic acid) and that binds to it and inhibits its normal function.

Apparent density

The mass of a sample of paper per unit area, divided by its thickness, as measured by smooth platens at a defined pressure, usually in a stack of sheets.

Appearance energy (appearance potential)

Refers to ionization of a molecule or atom by electron collision or photon absorption. In mass spectrometry it has often been reported as the voltage which corresponds to the minimum energy of the electrons in the ionizing beam necessary for the production of a given fragment ion. In photoionization it is the minimum energy of the quantum of light which produces ionization of the absorbing molecule. It is recommended that the term appearance energy replace the term appearance potential and that the energy should be stated in SI units.

Approach flow
The part of a paper machine, including the pressure screens and intake manifold, just before the thin stock reaches the headbox.

Aprotic (solvent)
Non-protogenic (in a given situation). (With extremely strong Brønsted acids or bases, solvents that are normally aprotic may accept or lose a proton. For example, acetonitrile is in most instances an aprotic solvent, but it is protophilic in the presence of concentrated sulphuric acid and protogenic in the presence of potassium tert-butoxide. Similar considerations apply to benzene, trichloromethane, etc.)

Aquation
The incorporation of one or more integral molecules of water into another species with or without displacement of one or more other atoms or groups. For example the incorporation of water into the inner ligand sphere of an inorganic complex is an aquation reaction.

Aqueous
Made of, with, or by water.

Aqueous solution
a homogeneous solution of particles dissolved in water.

Aragonite
A crystalline form of precipitated calcium carbonate that tends to adopt a needle-like shape, often used in coatings.

Area
Measures the size of a surface using length measurements in two dimensions.

Arene
Another name for an aromatic hydrocarbon.

Argogel
Trademark of Argonaut Technologies, San Carlos, California, USA. Beaded solid support with a crosslinked polystyrene core and grafted linear poly (ethylene glycol) (PEG) chains with terminal functional groups.

Argon
Ar, an element that is a member of the 8A group (Noble Gases) of the periodic table. Argon is represented by the atomic symbol Ar, has an atomic number of 18, and an atomic weight of 39.948. It is colourless, odorless, and a very inert gas. It comprises about 1% of the Earth's atmosphere.

Aromacity
A chemical property in which a conjugated ring of unsaturated bonds, lone pairs, or empty orbitals exhibit a stabilization stronger than would be expected by the stabilization of conjugation alone.

Aromatic compounds
There is a special class of Hydrocarbons where the carbon-carbon bonds are arranged such that a ring of carbon-carbon bonds is formed. These compounds are called Cyclic Alkanes. There is a very special class of compounds that are formed when Cyclic Alkanes become Cyclic Alkenes in which every other carbon-carbon bond is a double bond. This special class of very stable Hydrocarbons is referred b as Aromatic Compounds. The simplest

Aromatic Compound is Benzene (C_6H_6).

Aromatic hydrocarbons

Hydrocarbon compounds in which the carbon atoms are connected by a ring structure that is planar and joined by sigma and pie bonds between the carbon atoms. An example of an aromatic compound is benzene, C_6H_6.

Array

An ordered arrangement

Array synthesis

Form of parallel synthesis in which the reaction vessels are maintained in a specified spatial distribution, e.g. the wells of a 96-well plate or pins held in a rack.

Arrester

Equipment designed to remove particles from a gaseous medium.

Arrhenius equation

The equation, $k = Ae^{-Ea/RT}$, which describes the rate coefficient (k) for an elementary reaction in terms of a preexponential factor A, activation energy E_a, temperature T (K), and gas constant R.

Arrhenius theory

All acids produce hydrogen ions when they are dissolved in water, and all bases produce hydroxide ions; the hydrogen ions are responsible for the acidic properties of a solution and the hydroxide ions are responsible for the basic properties.

Arsenate mineral

A mineral that is made up of compounds with an arsenic atom or arsenic oxide group bonded to a metal. Erythrite is a good example of a arsenate mineral.

Arsenic

Symbol: "As" Atomic Number: "33" Atomic Mass: 74.92amu. Classified as a semi-metallic element, Arsenic is probably best known as a poison. While highly toxic, this grey, semi-metallic element is used in lasers, insecticides, and in some fireworks.

Artificial cure

Placement of paper, taken from a paper machine, into an oven to achieve an equivalent curing effect of the same paper being stored in a hot roll of paper for many hours.

Asa

Alkenylsuccinic anhydride, a synthetic sizing agent that usually is emulsified with cationic starch just before addition to a paper machine wet end.

Ash

The solid residue which remains after the combustion of a fuel such as coal. Ash consists largely of heat treated mineral matter, but it may contain some products of the incomplete combustion of the fuel as well.

Ash content

The amount of filler in paper, as determined by incineration (which can dehydrate the filler or convert it into a different chemical form).

Aspirator

Any apparatus that produces a movement of a fluid by suction (e.g., a squeeze bulb, pump, Venturi, etc.)

Assay

A biological test, measurement or analysis to determine whether compounds have the desired effect either in a living organism, outside an organism, or in an artificial environment.

Assay equivalent

An aliquot of a library which will allow the library to be screened in a single assay. Particularly applicable to libraries prepared by split/pool procedure, where it pertains to the number of particles required to sample a library. Generally consists of a specified number of library equivalents.

Assimilation cycle

A natural process by which a water body uses microbes, which convert nonliving substances into protoplasm or cells, to purify itself from pollutants.

Association

The assembling of separate molecular entities into any aggregate, especially of oppositely charged free ions into ion pairs or larger and not necessarily well-defined clusters of ions held together by electrostatic attraction. The term signifies the reverse of dissociation, but is not commonly used for the formation of definite adducts by colligation or coordination.

Associativity

A property in math which states that:
    (A+B)+C=A+(B+C) and
    (A*B)*C=A*(B*C).

Astatine

Symbol: "At" Atomic Number: "85" Atomic Mass: (210)amu. Astatine is a member of the halogen group. This element is often found during reactions with uranium in nuclear reactors. It is not found in nature and has no uses.

Asymmetric

Molecules that are not symmetrical.

Asymmetric induction

The traditional term describing the preferential formation in a chemical reaction of one enantiomer or diastereoisomer over the other as a result of the influence of a chiral feature in the substrate, reagent, catalyst or environment. The term also refers to the formation of a new chiral feature preferentially in one configuration under such influence.

Atmosphere

The sum total of all the gases surrounding the Earth, extending several hundred kilometres above the surface in a mechanical mixture of various gases in fluid-like motion. The permanent constituents are molecular nitrogen; 78.1%, molecular oxygen; 20.9%, argon; 0.934%, and approximately 0.037% carbon dioxide (but this is increasing...). Various other components exist in trace amounts. Not to be under emphasized, these trace components are where the interesting atmospheric chemistry occurs. The atmosphere can also be artificially divided into layers.

Atmosphere (of the earth)

The entire mass of air surrounding the earth which is composed largely of nitrogen, oxygen, water vapour, clouds (liquid or solid water), carbon dioxide, together with trace gases and aerosols; see air, composition of pure.

Atmosphere (unit of pressure measurement)

A unit of pressure measurement which has been employed in describing the pressure of gases in storage tanks. It is roughly related to the average pressure of the atmosphere at sea level. One atmosphere = 1.01325×10^5 N m^{-2} or 1.01325×10^5Pa or 760 Torr. The use of the atm unit of pressure measurement is no longer recommended by international scientific bodies; it has been recommended that standard pressure be redefined as 10^5 Pa.

Atmospheric chemistry

The scientific study of the relationships and interactions of the substances in the gases around the earth. Examples would be determination of the concentrations, sources, and sinks of ozone in the troposphere and stratosphere and the greenhouse gases that surround earth. This includes all reactions of and sources and sinks on the surface of the earth of particles released in the air.

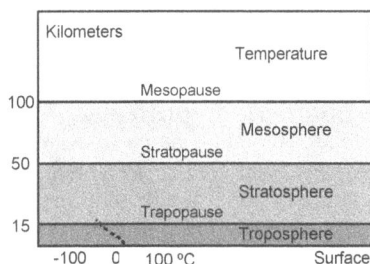

Atmospheric convection

Process in which heat energy is transported through a medium, usually a gas or liquid. An example, in the atmosphere occurs when warm air with a lower density experiences an upward force until it cools and its density matches the surrounding air, generally termed convection cells.

Atmospheric window

This is a gap in the atmosphere's spectral absorption. It is created because not enough molecules in the atmosphere are absorb in the wavelengths 8-12 micrometers. Absorption is caused by the molecules in the air, therefore adding more gases to the atmosphere the window can become reduced and cause more of these wavelengths to stay in earths atmosphere causing global warming.

Atom

The smallest particle of an element that can enter into chemical change. Atoms consist of a central nucleus, containing protons and usually neutrons, surrounded by electrons.

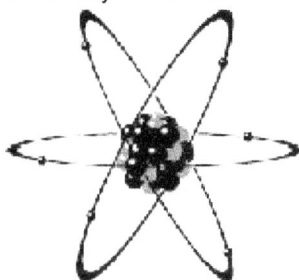

Atomic heat

This is a measure of the atomic weight of a substance multiplied by its specific heat.

Atomic mass

The atomic mass is the total mass of one atom of an element. It is the mass of the protons, electrons, and neutrons combined. The mass of all atoms is based on the mass of carbon. Carbon's mass is twelve AMU. Atomic mass is not measured in pounds or grams, scientists used something called Daltons. One Dalton is equal to one-twelfth the mass of a carbon atom.

Atomic number

The atomic number is the number of an element on the periodic table. It is also equal to the number of protons inside of an atom. A neutral atom has equal numbers of electrons and protons. The atomic number for oxygen is 8.

Atomize

To subdivide a liquid into very small particles; methods include: impact with a jet of gas, use of a spinning disk generator, vibrating orifice generator, etc.

Attraction forces

Attraction forces hold molecules next to each other. When something is in a liquid, the attraction forces hold the liquid together. If you raise the temperature of the liquid, the molecules are given more energy and break free of the attraction forces to become a gas.

Austral spring

Related to Antarctic ozone depletion, this denotes the season of spring in the southern hemisphere when the greatest amount of ozone is lost, generally beginning in September. Astral relates to the hemisphere that the observer is currently in and the season that relates to the observer, while austral refers to the south.

Autacoid

An autacoid is a biological substance secreted by various cells whose physiological activity is restricted to the vicinity of its release; it is often referred to as local hormone.

Autoreceptor

An autoreceptor, present at a nerve ending, is a receptor that regulates, via positive or negative feedback processes, the synthesis and/or release of its own physiological ligand.

Autoxidation

Autoxidation, autooxidation is a oxidation is caused by exposure to air. Rust is an example of autoxidation. Autoxidation makes ether taken from half-filled bottles very dangerous, because air oxidises ether to highly explosive organic peroxides.

Autumnal equinox

Point at which on the celestial sphere that the equator and the Ecliptic intersect. Generally the autumnal equinox occurs on or about September 23 in the northern hemisphere; this also signifies spring in the southern hemisphere.

Auxo-chromes

Chemical substituent groups on dye molecules that have the effect of changing the hue.

Average energy

This is a measure of the overall energy of a sample. Some areas might be hotter and some might be colder, but the average energy is how scientists measure the temperature of a system.

Avogadro's hypothesis

Amadeo Avogadro came up with this idea. He said that if you have two volumes of gas, they would have the same number of molecules inside if the pressure and temperatures inside were equal. One liter of oxygen and one liter of carbon dioxide (at the same temperature and pressure) would have an equal number of molecules.

Avogadro's Constant

This is one of the constants of Chemistry. Amadeo Avogadro determined that there were 6.02×10^{23} atoms in one mole of any substance. So if you have one gram of hydrogen, you have that many 6.02×10^{23} atoms. 60,220,000,000,000,000,000,000 atoms. Formally, it was called Avogadro's Number.

Axial bond

The bond parellel or anti parellel to axial coordinate passing center of gravity.

Azide synthesis

Dutt-Wormall reaction in which a diazonium salt reacts with a sulfonamide first to a diazoaminosulfinate and then on hydrolysis the azide and a sulfinic acid.

Azo compounds

Azo compounds are organic compounds containing the group -N=N- linking two other groups. They can be formed by reaction of a diazonium ion with a benzene ring.

B

Back scattering

Process by which up to 25% of radiant energy from the sun is reflected or scattered away from the surface by clouds. Serves the greatest importance in the atmospheric heat budget. Large errors in the assumed value of this variable may have important effects on computer models of the atmosphere.

Background concentration (level)

Synonymous with baseline concentration. The concentration of a given species in a pristine air mass in which anthropogenic impurities of a relatively short lifetime are not present. The background concentrations of relatively long-lived molecules, methane, carbon dioxide, halocarbons (CF_3Cl, CF_2Cl_2, etc.), and some other species continue to rise due to anthropogenic input, so the composition of background air is undergoing continual change.

Baffle chamber

A chamber used in incinerator design to promote the settling of fly ash and coarse particulate matter by changing the direction and/or reducing the velocity of the gases produced by the combustion of the refuse.

Bag filter

A large bag constructed of a suitable fabric which is often tubular in shape, into which a particle-containing air stream flows. Modern bags are constructed of a fabric which is capable of collecting all but very fine particles in the gas stream. The efficiency of the removal of particles of various size ranges changes with the amount of particles captured by the filter and the filtering time. The bag operates on the same principle as the one on a household vacuum cleaner.

Baghouse

An installation which contains many bag biters in parallel so that the resistance to air flow in a large installation is not seriously increased by the addition of these controls.

Balanced equation

A balanced chemical equation has equal numbers of atoms on each side of the equation. If one side of the equation has five oxygen atoms, the other side must also have five (to be balanced).

Baldwin's rules

A set of empirical rules for certain formations of 3- to 7-membered rings. The predicted pathways are those in which the length and nature of the linking chain enables the terminal atoms to achieve the proper geometries for reaction. The disfavoured cases are subject to severe distortions of bond angles and bond distances.

Barium

Symbol: "Ba" Atomic Number: "56"
Atomic Mass: 137.33amu. Barium is
a member of the alkaline metals
group. Barium is only found as a part
of compounds when found in nature.
The element is used in paints,
fireworks, medicine, and the process
of making glass.

Barometric pressure

The downward pressure, at any given
point in the atmosphere, of the gases
directly above that point. Average
pressure globally at sea level is
1,013,000 dynes per centimetre
squared or 760 Torr. This is defined
as one atmosphere.

Barrier chemistry

A very dilute spray of high-charge,
water-loving cationic polymer,
sometimes with a surfactant,
continuously applied to a forming
fabric or roll.

Base

A species which when dissolved in
water generates hydroxide (OH^-) ions
or is capable of reacting with an acid
to form a salt. A Brønsted base is a
molecular entity capable of accepting
a proton from an acid (i.e. a "proton
acceptor") or the corresponding
chemical species. For example:
   OH^-, H_2O, $CH_3CO_2^-$, HSO_4^-, SO_4^{2-}
A Lewis base is a molecular entity
(and the corresponding chemical
species) that is able to provide a pair
of electrons and thus capable of coordination to a Lewis acid, thereby
producing a Lewis adduct.

Base anhydride

Type of oxide that can form a base if
water is added.

Baseline in gas chromatography

Portion of a chromatogram
corresponding to the signal delivered
by the detector when, under normal
conditions of operation, only the carrier
gas passes through the detector. The
slow desorption of strongly adsorbed
substances previously passed
through the column may contribute to
this baseline position (column bleed).
The signal trace recorded as a
function of time in the absence of
analyte.

Basic

Having the characteristics of a base.

Basic dyes

Colourant molecules that have a
positive charge due to amine groups
and have a strong affinity for the
surfaces of high-yield fibers.

Basicity

A measure of the amount of base in a
solution.

Bathochromic shift (effect)

Shift of a spectral band to lower
frequencies (longer wavelengths)
owing to the influence of substitution
or a change in environment. It is
informally referred to as a red shift and
is opposite to hypsochromic shift (blue
shift).

Beer's Law (Beer-Lambert law)

For monochromatic radiation,
absorbance (A) is determined by the
relationship: A = abc, with a =
absorptivity, b = path length through
the medium, and c = concentration of
the absorbing species. The intensity
of a ray of light which has gone
through a medium is a function of the
path length through which the light
passes and the concentration of
absorbing matter in that medium.

Bentonite

An informal term for "montmorillonite",
a platey microparticle product often
used in sequential addition with

cationic PAM for retention and drainage and sometimes also for pitch control.

Benzene

C_6H_6, an aromatic hydrocarbon. It can be found in the air by several different ways of transmission. It can be produced for use with plastic or produced through the burning of fossil fuels. Benzene can also be found in the soil as well as some areas of groundwater pollution. In urban setting its presence correlates with the presence of NO_x and CO. Exposure to benzene has been linked to leukemia.

Benzyl group

The radical or ion formed from the removal of one of the methyl hydrogens of toluene (methylbenzene).

Berkelium

Symbol: "Bk" Atomic Number: "97" Atomic Mass: (247)amu. Berkelium is only one of the elements in the actinide series of inner transition elements. It may also be classified as a rare earth element. It is a radioactive metal with no known applications.

Beryllium

Symbol:"Be" Atomic Number:"4" Atomic Mass: 9.01amu. Beryllium is ember of the alkaline metals family. Beryllium is a silvery, very light metallic element. You might find the element in nuclear reactors, springs, satellites, and the space shuttle.

Bias error

Systematic deviation of the results of a measurement process from the true value of the air quality characteristic. This deviation cannot be detected by merely repeating the method several times under prescribed conditions. Characterizes the systematic error in a given analytical procedure and is the (positive or negative) deviation of the mean analytical result from the (known or assumed) true value.

Bimodal distribution

The occurrence of two maxima in a frequency distribution.

Bimolecular reaction

A second order reaction where the concentration of two compounds determine the reaction rate.

Binary acid

An acid whose molecules each consist of two elements; HCl for example.

Binary code

Relationship between a set of tags and their corresponding ligands where building block identity is denoted by the presence or absence of a given tag or set of tags (i.e. the two "bits" 1 and 0).

Binary compound

A binary compound is a compound that only has two atoms. Think about sodium chloride for binary compounds (NaCl).

Binding energy

Energy that holds nucleus' neutrons and protons together.

Bioassay

A bioassay is a procedure for determining the concentration, purity, and/or biological activity of a substance (e.g., vitamin, hormone, plant growth factor, antibiotic, enzyme) by measuring its effect on an organism, tissue, cell, enzyme or receptor preparation compared to a standard preparation.

Bioavailability

The percentage of drug that is detected in the systemic circulation after its administration. Losses can be attributed to an inherent lack of absorption/passage into the systemic circulation and/or to metabolic clearance. Detection of drug can be accomplished pharmacodynamically (quantification of a biological response to the drug) or pharmacokinetically (quantification of actual drug concentration). Oral bioavailability is associated with orally administered drugs.

Biochemicals

Compounds that are either naturally occurring or identical to naturally occurring substances. Examples include hormones, pheromones, and enzymes.

Biocides

Chemical additives designed to kill slime-forming bacteria or fungi.

Biogenic emissions

The chemical compounds that living organisms put into the atmosphere, usually related to respiration or fermentation. Monitoring the biogenic emissions helps determine the source and sink of chemicals as well as atmospheric cycles. Examples of atmospheric components from biogenesis are methane, nitrous oxide, or terpenes.

Biogeochemical carbon

The biological and geographic study of the properties of carbon's chemical properties in relation to gases in the atmosphere. Models that study this often incorporate atmospheric carbon dioxide, carbonates in the ocean, organic carbon, and dissolved inorganic carbon in an attempt to determine the temporal characteristics of the planet's carbon cycle.

Bioisostere

A bioisostere is a compound resulting from the exchange of an atom or of a group of atoms with another, broadly similar, atom or group of atoms. The objective of a bioisosteric replacement is to create a new compound with similar biological properties to the parent compound. The bioisosteric replacement may be physicochemically or topologically based.

Biological Amplification or Bioaccumulation

Increase in concentration of DDT, PCB, and other slowly degradable, fat-soluble chemicals in organisms at successively higher levels.

Biomass

The complete dry weight of organic material found in the biosphere or less strictly, the matter in the biosphere that is contained in living organisms.

Biomass burning

the process of oxidizing living material. This process produces atmospheric particulates as well as the production of greenhouse and reactive tropospheric gases. These gases include CO_2, CO, NO_x, CH_4, CH_3Cl along with the addition of black carbon. All of these chemical species can be lofted relatively high in the atmosphere due to the convective heating of a fire.

Bioprecursor prodrug

A bioprecursor prodrug is a prodrug that does not imply the linkage to a carrier group, but results from a molecular modification of the active principle itself. This modification generates a new compound, able to be transformed metabolically or chemically, the resulting compound being the active principle.

Biosphere
A volume including the lower part of the troposphere (as high as living organisms can fly or be lofted) and the surface of the earth including the oceans. This region, by definition, encompasses all the living matter of the earth. Some very important atmospheric chemicals are produced in this region and pass into the atmosphere. This region exchanges chemicals and particulate m atter with the atmosphere and soils and waters of the earth.

Biotechnology
The industrial application of living organisms and/or biological techniques developed through basic research. Biotechnology products include pharmaceutical compounds and research materials.

Biotransformation
Biotransformation is the chemical conversion of substances by living organisms or enzyme preparations.

Biradical
An even-electron molecular entity with two (possibly delocalized) radical centres which act nearly independently of each other, e.g.

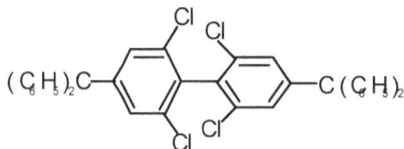

Species in which the two radical centres interact significantly are often referred to as "biradicaloids". If the two radical centres are located on the same atom, the species are more properly referred to by their generic

names: carbenes, nitrenes, etc. The lowest-energy triplet state of a biradical lies below or at most only a little above its lowest singlet state (usually judged relative to k_BT, the product of the Boltzmann constant k_B and the absolute temperature T). The states of those biradicals whose radical centres interact particularly weakly are most easily understood in terms of a pair of local doublets. Theoretical descriptions of low-energy states of biradicals display the presence of two unsaturated valences (biradicals contain one fewer bond than permitted by the rules of valence): the dominant valence bond structures have two dots, the low energy molecular orbital configurations have only two electrons in two approximately nonbonding molecular orbitals, two of the natural orbitals have occupancies close to one, etc.

Bismuth
Symbol: "Bi" Atomic Number: "83" Atomic Mass: 208.98amu. It is classified as a basic metal and is the most diamagnetic metal in the periodic table. Bismuth is a brittle metal often found with tin and lead. You will find it used in magnets, nuclear reactors, alloys, and even cosmetics.

Bivane
A wind vane used in turbulence studies to obtain horizontal and vertical components of the wind vector.

Black carbon
Emitted during the burning of coal, diesel fuel, natural gas and biomass and is part of the composition of soot. Black Carbon can absorb and reflect sunlight cooling the Earth's surface, but also increase solar energy absorbed in the atmosphere, warming it. These effects are thought to effect global climate and rainfall

cycles. Black carbon increases the effect of global warming, visibility problems, and health problems.

Blackbody radiation

Any physical body absorbs and emits electromagnetic radiation when its temperature is above absolute zero. Planck's law determines the radiant flux of a body at a specific wavelength. In atmospheric chemistry, the calculation involving the earth's blackbody radiation shows that the earth's surface temperature would be below the freezing point of water if it did not have an atmosphere which absorbed some of the outgoing radiation.

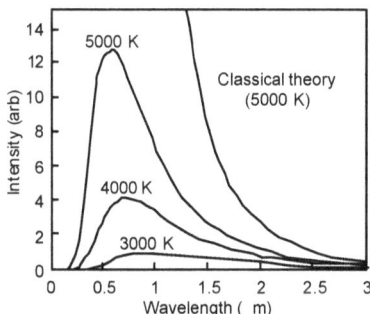

Bladed habit

This is a crystal shape that resembles a knife blade because is has very thin layers. You may also think of a messy deck of cards for this example.

Blank reading or blank value

Instrument reading for a zero sample. A reading originating from the matrix, reagents and any residual bias in the measurement instrument or process, but not from the analyte.

Bleedfast-ness

The ability of a dye to remain attached to fibers in paper even when exposed to fluids or to sweaty hands.

Blowdown

Hydrocarbons purged during refinery shutdowns and startups which should be piped to storage systems for safe venting, flaring, or recovery. This term also applies to the purging of water in boiler operation, and serves in the control of dissolved solids in the boiler water.

Boat cyclohexane

A less-stable conformation of cyclohexane that somewhat resembles a boat.

Bohr structure

Bohr atomic structure is considered the classic structure of an atom. Niels Bohr came up with the idea that there is a nucleus with protons and neutrons. Surrounding that nucleus are spherical shells where electrons can orbit the nucleus. While there are areas where you can expect to find electrons, we now know that they are not always in spherical shells.

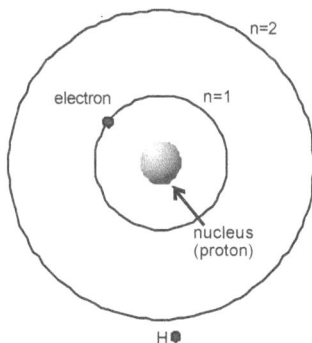

Bohrium

Symbol: "Bh" Atomic Number: "107" Atomic Mass: (264) amu. Bohrium is of the postactinide elements. Scientists have created these in labs and may have found only a few atoms of the element. You will not find it in use anywhere on Earth.

Bohr's atom

Bohr made significant contributions to the atom. He understood the line spectra-the reason why only certain wavelengths are emitted when atoms jump down levels.

Boiling point

The boiling point is the temperature when a liquid begins to boil and becomes a gas or vapour. It requires the addition of energy for the matter to move from one state to another.

Boiling Water

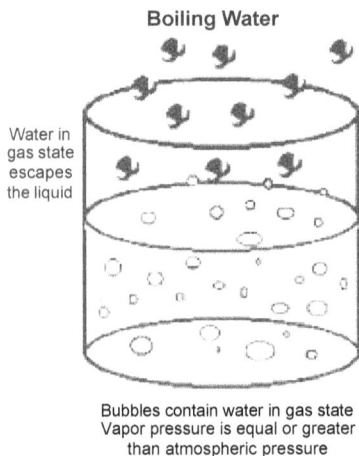

Water in gas state escapes the liquid

Bubbles contain water in gas state Vapor pressure is equal or greater than atmospheric pressure

Boil-out

The occasional cleaning of a paper machine system, during a shut-down, by filling the system with a hot solution the usually contains detergent and either NaOH, an acid, or an enzyme.

Bolide impacts

Asteroids or comets striking the earth; a possible cause of major climate changes and mass extinctions in the Earth's history.

Bond

The attractive forces that create a link between atoms. Bonds may be covalent or ionic.

Bond angle

The angle formed between three atoms across at least two bonds.

Bond energy (mean bond energy)

The average value of the gas-phase bond-dissociation energies (usually at a temperature of 298 K) for all bonds of the same type within the same chemical species. The mean bond energy for methane, for example, is one-fourth the enthalpy of reaction for $CH_4(g)$ C(g) + 4H(g) Tabulated bond energies are generally values of bond energies averaged over a number of selected typical chemical species containing that type of bond.

Bond enthalpy

The amount of energy stored in a single chemical bond between two atoms.

Bond length

The average distance between the centers of two atoms bonded together in any given molecule.

Bond number

The number of electron-pair bonds between two nuclei in any given Lewis formula. For example in ethene the bond number between the carbon atoms is two, and between the carbon and hydrogen atoms is one.

Bond order

A theoretical index of the degree of bonding between two atoms relative to that of a normal single bond, i.e. the bond provided by one localized electron pair. In the valence-bond theory it is a weighted average of the bond numbers between the respective atoms in the contributing structures. In molecular-orbital theory it is calculated from the weights of the atomic orbitals in each of the occupied molecular orbitals. For example, in valence-bond theory (neglecting other than Kekulé structures) the bond order between adjacent carbon atoms in benzene is 1.5; in Hückel molecular orbital theory it is 1.67. Other variants of molecular orbital theory provide other values for bond orders.

Bond strength
The degree to which each atom linked to a central atom contributes to the valency of this central atom.

Bond, chemical
A chemical bond is created when two atoms share or give electrons to each other. There are single, double, and triple bonds. Two major types of bonds are ionic and covalent.

Borderline mechanism
A mechanism intermediate between two extremes, for example a nucleophilic substitution intermediate between S_N1 and S_N2, or intermediate between electron transfer and S_N2.

Boron
Symbol: "B" Atomic Number: "5" Atomic Mass: 10.81amu. Boron is a non-metallic element never found alone but always with other elements. It is a trace element in your diet. You might find boron in clay pots, detergent, glass, flares, or fiberglass.

Boundary layer
That well-mixed region of the lower atmosphere in which the turbulence is maintained largely by convective buoyancy induced by the upward heat flux originating from the solar-heated surface of the earth. During the afternoon this often extends from 1 to 5 km in height. Surface boundary layer is that region of the lower atmosphere where the shearing stress is constant. It is separated by

the Ekman layer from the free atmosphere, where the behaviour of the atmosphere approaches that of an ideal fluid in approximate geostrophic equilibrium.

Boyle's law
A scientist named Robert Boyle came up with an understanding of the way pressure and volume are related (at constant temperatures). His formula shows that the volume of a gas is inversely proportional to the pressure. The idea was written down as $P = (1/V)k$ (where k is a constant).

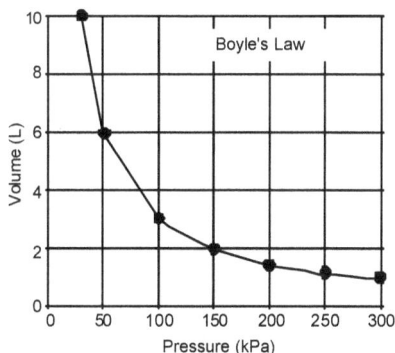

Bravais lattice
The Bravais lattice is the basic structure of a crystal. Each point of the lattice represents the compounds found in the mineral. The shape of an iron pyrite lattice would be cubic. The smallest combination of elements or atoms that forms the lattice is called the unit cell.

Breaking length
A measure of the tensile strength of paper; in theory, the maximum length of a strip of paper that can support itself without tensile failure.

Breaks of the web
Ripping of the paper as it is in the process of being made, resulting in lost production.

Bredt's rule

A double bond cannot be placed with one terminus at the bridgehead of a bridged ring system unless the rings are large enough to accommodate the double bond without excessive strain. For example, while bicyclo[2.2.1]hept-1-ene is only capable of existence as a transient, its higher homologues having a double bond at the bridgehead position have been isolated: e.g.

Bicyclo[3.3.1]non-l-ene   Bicyclo[4.2.1]non-l(8)-ene

Breeching

The passage or conduit through which the exhaust products of combustion are carried to the stack or chimney.

Breeze

A term sometimes used to describe very fine particles of coke. Also a meteorological term for a gentle wind. Bridge solution (in ph measurement) Solution of high concentration of inert salt, preferably comprising cations and anions of equal mobility, optionally interposed between the reference electrode filling and both the test and standard solution, when the test solution and filling solution are chemically incompatible. This procedure introduces into the operational cell a second.liquid junction formed usually in a similar way to the first.

Bridged carbocation

A carbocation (real or hypothetical) in which there are two (or more) carbon atoms that could in alternative Lewis formulae be designated as carbenium centres but which is instead represented by a structure in which a group (a hydrogen atom or a hydrocarbon residue, possibly with substituents in non-involved positions) bridges these potential carbenium centres. One may distinguish "electron-sufficient bridged carbocations" and "electron-deficient bridged carbocations". Examples of the former are phenyl-bridged ions (for which the trivial name "phenonium ion" has been used), such as (A). These ions are straightforwardly classified as carbenium ions. The latter type of ion necessarily involves three-centre bonding. Structures (C) and (D) contain five-coordinate carbon atoms. The "hydrogen-bridged carbocation" (B) contains a two-co-ordinate hydrogen atom. Hypercoordination, which includes two-coordination for hydrogen and five- but also higher coordination for carbon is generally observed in bridged carbocations.

   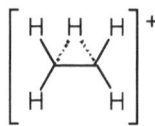

(A)   (B)

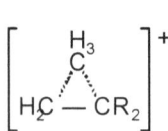   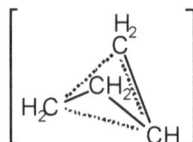

(C)   (D)

Bridging

A mechanism of action of very-high-mass retention aid polymers, in which the molecules attach simultaneously onto two surfaces.

Brightness

The diffuse reflectivity of paper at a mean wavelength of light of 457 nm.

Britt jar

The Dynamic Drainage/Retention Jar apparatus to evaluation effectiveness of retention aids by measuring the solids in filtrate passing through a screen in the absence of fiber mat formation.

Brittle

The breakage into fragments when a force is applied.

Broke

Paper trim or reject material from the paper machine or other paper mill operations that is repulped and used again to make paper.

Bromine

Symbol: "Br" Atomic Number: "35" Atomic Mass: 79.90amu. Bromine is a member of the halogen group. Bromine is the only non-metallic element that is a liquid at room temperature. While it is poisonous you will still find this reddish-brown element used in flame-retardants, water purification systems and dyes.

Bromochlorodifluoromethane

Chemical formula $CBrClF_2$ Synonyms: Halon 1211, Freon 12B1, chlorodifluorobromomethane. This chemical belongs to the freon family. Halon 1211 was introduced in the 1960s as an effective gaseous fire suppression agent for application in the protection of computer control rooms, museums, telecommunication switches and other areas containing highly valuable materials.

Bromomethane

CH_3Br, a volatile compound with a high mixing rate in the atmosphere. Methyl bromide escapes easily into the atmosphere where it can contribute to the depletion of ozone in the upper atmosphere. It works similarly to CFCs in its reaction with ozone molecules (O_3). In the stratosphere, with the sun's UV light as a catalyst, methyl bromide breaks down and exchanges a bromide ion for oxygen from ozone. By breaking down the ozone molecules in the stratosphere, methyl bromide thins the ozone layer and lets more UV light pass through.

Bromotrifluoromethane

Also known as Halon-1301, this chemical with formula $CBrF_3$ is one of the most ozone destructive substances known to man. It is listed as a Class I ozone depleting chemical in the United States Clean Air Act amendments of 1990. This chemical is commonly used in fire fighting equipment used around sensitive electronic equipment such as computer rooms, telecommunication centers, and aviation equipment. It is know to cause headache and unconsciousness in humans.

Brownian motion

The movement of particles in a colloidal system such as an aerosol caused by collision with the molecules in the fluid in which the particles are imbedded.

Brown-stock washers

Cylinder-type vat washers (usually) for removal of black liquor from unbleached kraft pulp.

Bubbler

An apparatus used to absorb certain water soluble components in a gas stream for later analysis. Usually it involves the use of a glass fritted tube which forces the air into small bubbles of high surface area during operation.

Buffer

A system of weak acid(s) or base(s) dissolved in water that tends to hold the pH near to a constant value when acid or base are added.

Buffer solutions

Solutions that resist changes in their pH, even when small amounts of acid or base are added.

Bulk

The reciprocal of apparent density.

Butanal

A highly flammable, corrosive compound that causes burns; the aldehyde of butane. Also a colourless liquid, with a pungent smell that condenses and oxidizes in higher temperature of the atmosphere and contributes to photochemical smog. Its chemical formulea is C_3H_7CHO

C

Cadmium

Symbol: "Cd" Atomic Number: "48" Atomic Mass: 112.41amu. Cadmium is one of the transition elements. This bluish metal is actually very soft and can be cut with a knife. You will find it used in nickel-cadmium batteries, nuclear reactors, and as a pigment. It is toxic.

Cage compound

A polycyclic compound having the shape of a cage. The term is also used for inclusion compounds.

Cahn-Ingold-Prelog priorities

A rule for assigning priorities to substituents off of carbon in a double-bond or in a chiral center.

Calcined clay

A product that results from heating of ordinary clay in a furnace, making it white and bulky.

Calcite

The most common crystalline form of calcium carbonate, including almost all ground calcium carbonate and most PCC products.

Calcium

Symbol: "Ca" Atomic Number: "20" Atomic Mass: 40.06amu. Member of the alkaline earth metals group. Calcium can be found in three percent of the Earth's crust, your bones and cells, and in the shells of ocean creatures.

Calcium carbonate

A white mineral filler, tending buffer the pH in the alkaline range, that is available as ground limestone (GCC) and in various shapes as precipitated calcium carbonate (PCC). It is a white solid: Formula $CaCO_3$

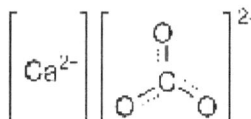

$$\left[Ca^{2-} \right] \left[O^{-}{-}C{\overset{O}{\underset{}{\parallel}}}{-}O \right]^{2-}$$

Calcium oxalate

A type of scale that forms when oxalate (a byproduct of bleaching) encounters hard water. Formula is $Ca(COO)_2$.

Calibration component

A component of a calibration mixture, present in the gaseous or vapour state, quantitatively and qualitatively defined, and used directly for testing and for calibration.

Calibration function

Instrument reading, X, as a function of measurable properties of the air quality characteristic under investigation represented by the reference material, with all interferants, C_i remaining constant.

Calibration gas mixture

A gas mixture of known composition, generally comprising one or more calibration components and a complimentary gas.

Calibration gas mixture, methods of preparation of

(a) Gravimetric method—A method in which each component of a mixture is successively added a gas cylinder which is weighed first empty and then after each addition. The concentration of each component is expressed as a mass ratio or mole ratio.

(b) Manometric method—A method in which each component of a mixture is added successively to a gas cylinder previously emptied and where the pressure is measured after each addition. The mole ratio can only be calculated from the pressure data if the deviation from ideality of the particular system is known.

(c) Static volumetric method—A method in which a mixture is prepared by combining two or more gases, contained in two or more separate calibrated volumes, all at known temperatures and pressures.

Calibration mixture

A gaseous or liquid mixture of known composition, generally comprising one or more calibration components and an inert diluent, used directly for testing and calibration of analytical instruments.

Californium

Symbol: "Cf" Atomic Number: "98" Atomic Mass: (251)amu. Californium is one of the elements in the actinide series of inner transition elements. It may also be classified as a rare earth element. It is a very radioactive element and you might find it used in medicine.

Caliper

Paper thickness, determined by measuring the distance between smooth, flat plates at a defined pressure.

Calorie

A calorie is a unit Scientific measure for heat and energy. You have probably heard of calories in your food. Scientists measure one calorie as the amount of energy needed to raise the temperature of water (one gram of water) one degree Celsius.

Calorimeter

An insulated device used to measure the amount of heat absorbed or released during a physical or chemical process.

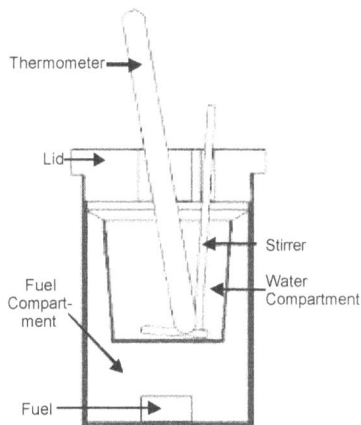

Calorimetry

Used to describe the study of the flow of heat.

Cap and Trade

For carbon regulation, a method of decreasing carbon emissions by setting (annual) regulatory limits on large, industrial CO_2 emitters and fining them if they surpass that limit. Emitters that can decrease their annual CO_2 emissions are allowed to sell the rights to emit the balance to other emitters which can't as easily decrease emissions. These traded emission right prices are set by the market and, in theory, allow those who need to purchase the emission rights a chance to save money over the fines. Gradually the regulatory emission limits are lowered and this pushes total emissions down over time.

Captodative effect

Effect on the stability of a carbon centred radical determined by the combined action of a captor (electron withdrawing) and a dative (electron releasing) substituent, both attached to the radical centre. The term is also used for certain unsaturated compounds.

Carbene

Generic name for the species H_2C: and substitution derivatives thereof, containing an electrically neutral bivalent carbon atom with two nonbonding electrons. The nonbonding electrons may have antiparallel spins (singlet state) or parallel spins (triplet state). Use of the alternative name "methylene" as a generic term is not recommended.

Carbenium centre

The three-coordinate carbon atom in a carbenium ion to which the excess positive charge of the ion (other than that located on heteroatoms) may be formally considered to be largely attributed, i.e., which has one vacant p-orbital. (N.B. It is not always possible to uniquely identify such an atom.) This formal attribution of charge often does not express the real charge distribution.

Carbenium ion

A generic name for *carbocations*, real or hypothetical, that have at least one important contributing structure containing a tervalent carbon atom with a vacant p-orbital. The term was

proposed (and rejected) as a replacement for the traditional usage of the name carbonium ion. To avoid ambiguity, the name should not be used as the root for the systematic nomenclature of carbocations. The corresponding difficulty confused carbonium ion nomenclature for many years. For example, the term "ethylcarbonium ion" has at times been used to refer either to $CH_3CH_2^+$ (ethyl cation) or (correctly) to $CH_3CH_2CH_2^+$ (propyl cation).

Carbenoid

A carbene like chemical species but with properties and reactivity differing from the free carbene itself, e.g. $R^1R^2C(Cl)M$ (M = metal)

Carbocation

A cation containing an even number of electrons with a significant portion of the excess positive charge located on one or more carbon atoms. This is a general term embracing carbenium ions, all types of carbonium ions, vinyl cations, etc. Carbocations may be named by adding the word "cation" to the name of the corresponding radical Such names do not imply structure (e.g. whether three-coordinated or five-coordinated carbon atoms are present).

Carbon

Carbon has been known since ancient times. The origin of the name comes from the Latin word carbo meaning charcoal. Graphite form of carbon is a black, odourless, slippery solid. Graphite sublimes at 3825 °C. Diamond form is a clear or coloured; an extremely hard solid. C60 is Buckminsterfullerine. Carbon black burns readily with oxidants. Carbon is made by burning organic compounds with insufficient oxygen. There are close to ten million known carbon compounds, many thousands of which are vital to organic and life processes. Radiocarbon dating uses the carbon-14 isotope to date old objects.

Carbon 14

^{14}C, an isotope of carbon-12 (^{12}C). ^{14}C contains two more neutrons and is radioactive and used in carbon dating. While carbon-12 is not radioactive, the half life of ^{14}C is 5730 years. This relatively short half life allows the ratio of carbon-12 to carbon-14 to be used to date objects containing carbon to an age of 50,000 years before present time.

Carbon black

Finely divided forms of carbon made by the incomplete combustion or thermal decomposition of natural gas, higher molecular weight hydrocarbons or other carbon-containing compounds.

Carbon cycle

A complex cycle that circulates carbon through the atmosphere, oceans, and land which includes vegetation and soil and carbon is in various forms and oxidation states throughout the cycle.

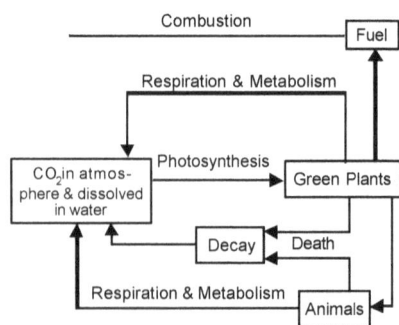

Basic Carbon Cycle Flow Diagram

Carbon dioxide (CO_2)

Colourless, odorless gas which is the major carbon-containing product of combustion of carbon compounds. Its removal in the atmosphere involves the photosynthetic cycle in plants which convert CO_2 into carbohydrate and other organic molecules important in plant growth, as oxygen is released. It is also removed by the oceans where it is converted to carbonate deposits. Its concentration in the atmosphere varies with position on the earth, season, time of day, etc.

Carbon disulphide

CS_2, a compound used to manufacture products such as rayon and cellophane. Carbon disulphide is produced naturally by microbial activity in marshes and in volcanic ash. Since carbon disulphide does not adhere well to sediments, if it comes into contact with soil, it could percolate into groundwater, where it is very soluble. CS_2 can also add to photochemical smog development when it reacts with other organic substances in the atmosphere, such as methane or oxides of nitrogen.

Carbon monoxide

CO, a toxic, odorless, colourless gas produced during fossil fuel or biomass burning. Compound consisting of one carbon and one oxygen. Except for carbon dioxide, it is one of the longest lived naturally occurring atmospheric carbon compounds (this wording is meant to exclude chlorofluorocarbons). The recent change in tropospheric CO content may portend a change in the balance between oxidants and reductants in the atmosphere.

Carbon sequestration

A method of capturing carbon dioxide so that it is not released into the atmosphere. This is a proposed response to the increase of CO_2 in the atmosphere mostly from anthropogenic sources since the industrial revolution. It can be achieved chemically in two obvious ways: carbon dioxide can be captured after a fossil fuel has been combusted in either the concentrated exhaust stream or, for example, carbon dioxide can be generated in fuel consumption/precombustion in the so-called syngas (synthesis gas) process which produces molecular hydrogen and CO from a methane-rich feed gas. That mix reacts with high temperature steam to produce H_2 and CO_2 which is captured. H_2 is burned to produce energy. Even more difficult is collecting CO_2 from the atmosphere at ambient concentrations in tropospheric air. Carbon dioxide produced by hydrocarbon combustion can be pressurized and injected into old salt mines or used in enhanced oil recovery.

Carbon tax
A monetary dividend, which is agreed to be paid in order to emit carbon dioxide from such sources as burning of fossil fuels and biofuels. It acts as a central mechanism for reducing carbon emissions in the Earth's atmosphere. This can be contrasted with cap and trade.

Carbon tetrachloride
CCl_4, a compound consisting of a carbon and 4 chlorines that is active in ozone depletion when the compound is broken down and releases chlorine atoms (radicals). Chlorine reacts with the ozone creating diatomic oxygen and chlorine monoxide which cycles back to chlorine radicals.

Carbon tetrafluoride
CF_4, is known as Freon 14, carbon tetrafluoride is a stable, non-flammable, colourless gas. It absorbs light at 8 mm (in the infrared), is very stable, and

does not react with water. This compound is theoretically considered a likely candidate for warming the earth during the next ice age.

Carbonate mineral
A mineral that is made up of compounds with a carbonate group bonded to a metal. Calcite is a good example of a carbonate mineral.

Carboniferous period
The time period between 280-345 million years ago BP of Earth's geologic history. Characterized by glacial onsets and melting and massive migration and extinctions of species during this period.

Carbonium ion
The term should be used with great care since several incompatible meanings are currently in use. It is not acceptable as the root for systematic nomenclature for carbocations.
(1) In most of the existing literature the term is used in its traditional sense for what is here defined as carbenium ion.
(2) A carbocation, real or hypothetical, that contains at least one five-coordinate carbon atom.
(3) A carbocation, real or hypothetical, whose structure cannot adequately be described by two-electron two-centre *bonds* only.
(The structure may involve carbon atoms with a coordination number greater than five.)

Carbonization
Carbonization begins when you heat organic substances like wood, sugar or meat with no presence of air; they go black because of secreted carbon.

Carbonyl group
A functional group composed of a carbon atom double-bonded to an oxygen atom: C=O.

Carbonyl sulphide

COS, a gas that is very stable and unreactive in the troposphere, but, it is thought, photolyzes to form carbon monoxide, CO, and sulphur, S, in the stratosphere. Through stratospheric chemical reactions, the sulphur atoms are converted to SO_2 and H_2SO_4 which form sulphate aerosol and cloud condensation nuclei, but eventually settle into the troposphere and react to form sulphuric acid, a component of acid rain. Volcanic eruptions contribute some of this COS to the atmosphere. The major biospheric sources of COS are thought to be biological.

Carboxyl group

Carboxyl groups are chemical functional groups with one carbon, one hydrogen, and two oxygen atoms (COOH). You will find these on many of the amino acids. It also makes molecules that are considered weak carboxylic acids. It is also defined as a polyatomic ion.

Carboxylation

A chemical reaction in which a carboxylic acid group is introduced in a substrate.

Carboxylic acids

Carboxylic acids are organic compounds characterized by the presence of one or more RC(=O)OH groups (the carboxyl group). In the systematic chemical nomenclature carboxylic acids names end in the suffix -oic (e.g. ethanoic acids, CH_3COOH). The carbon of the terminal group being counted as part of the chain. They are generally weak acids. Carboxylic acids include a large and important class of fatty acids and may be either saturated or unsaturated. There are also some natural aromatic carboxylic acids (benzoic, salicylic).

Carrier gas

A gas introduced in order to transport a sample for analytical purposes. In gas chromatography it is the gas which is passed continuously through the column and whose passage promotes the elution of the components of the sample. The carrier gas together with the portions of the sample present in this phase constitutes the mobile phase.

Carrier-linked prodrug (Carrier prodrug)

A carrier-linked prodrug is a prodrug that contains a temporary linkage of a given active substance with a transient carrier group that produces improved physicochemical or pharmacokinetic properties and that can be easily removed in vivo, usually by a hydrolytic cleavage.

Carry-over

Substances released from fibers during pulping that fail to be removed during washing.

Cascade prodrug

A cascade prodrug is a prodrug for which the cleavage of the carrier group becomes effective only after unmasking an activating group.

Catabolism

Catabolism consists of reactions involving endogenous organic substrates to provide chemically available energy (e.g., ATP) and/or to generate metabolic intermediates used in subsequent anabolic reactions.

Catabolite

A catabolite is a naturally occurring metabolite.

Catalysis

The alteration of the rate of a chemical reaction (usually increase in the rate) by the addition of some substance (the catalyst) which does not undergo a net chemical change. Cases occur with certain reactants in which the addition of a substance reduces the rate of a particular reaction, for example, the addition of an inhibitor in a chain reaction or a poison in a catalytic reaction. The term "negative catalysis" has been used for these phenomena, but this usage is not recommended; terms such as inhibition or poisoning are preferred.

Catalysis

A catalyst is a compound or element that can increase the rate of a chemical reaction. Catalysts can lower activation energy of a reaction to help a reaction proceed faster and with less energy.

Catalytic converter

An air pollution control device using the exhaust system of cars. The converter helps complete combustion of any fuel that was not burned in the engine and reduce the presence of other harmful emission concentrations. The converter changes the unburned hydrocarbons and carbon monoxide in the exhaust into carbon dioxide and water vapour. The converter use chemical catalysis to create this change.

Cathode

Electrode where electrons are gained (reduction) in redox reactions.

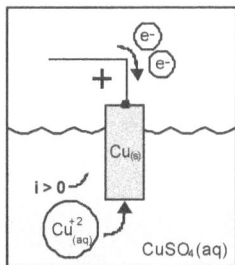

Cation

An ion carrying a positive charge due to the loss of electrons.

Cationic

Having a positive charge (usually balanced by counter-ions in the adjacent solution).

Cationic demand

The amount of positively charged polymer needed to titrate a given aqueous suspension of fibers or colloidal matter to zero zeta potential.

Cationic direct dyes

Dye molecules that are similar to "normal" direct dyes (large and flat), but have positively charged amine groups.

Cationic starch

The most widely used dry-strength chemical for paper machine wet-end addition.

Cations

Ion with a positive charge.

Caustic soda

Sodium hydroxide, a strong base, used in pH adjustment and manufacture of paper & pulp, textiles detugents & drinking water. Chemical formula is $NaOH$.

Ceilometre

An automatic, recording instrument for reading the height of the cloud-base.

Cell, continuous measuring

A measuring cell which operates continuously.

Cell, discontinuous measuring

A measuring cell which operates intermittently and not necessarily at fixed time intervals.

Cell, sequential measuring
A measuring cell which operates according to a succession of operations on the sample or on the sensitive elements (or on both), these operations being carried out according to one or more repetitive programmes. Consisting of hundreds of linked glucose units and is mostly.

Cellulose
A polysaccharide (carbohydrate) found in plants. It is a structural carbohydrate that is an important part of the cell walls. It protects and strengthens the plant. It is a long chain of glucose molecules connected by a different type of glycosidic bond than the one found in starches. Formula $(C_6H_{10}O_5)_n$

Celsius temperature scale
The temperature scale on which the boiling point of water is 100° C and the freezing point, 0°C.

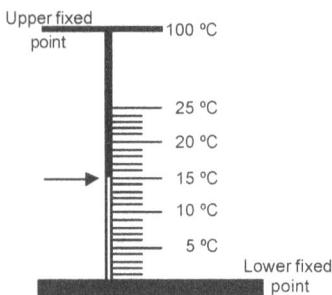

Celsius Scale of Temperature

Central atom
In a Lewis structure, usually the atom that is the least electronegative.

Centrifuging
A method of separating suspensions or emulsions by rapid spinning.

Ceramic filter
A component of a stack sampling system which is suitable for high temperature use; also known as a ceramic thimble.

Cerium
Symbol: "Ce" Atomic Number: "58" Atomic Mass: 140.12amu. Cerium is one of the elements in the lanthanide series of inner transition elements. It may also be classified as a rare earth element. You can find this silvery coloured metal in air conditioners, your computer, and even the oven.

Cesium
Symbol: "Cs" Atomic Number: "55" Atomic Mass: 132.91amu. One of the alkali metal group. This element can be found in many minerals. When pure it is a silvery-white colour and is used in atomic clocks and photoelectric cells. It is one of three metals found in a liquid state at room temperature.

Chain reaction
Chain reactions are characterized by a series of interrelated steps involving initiation, propagation, and termination. If the propagation steps recur a number of times for each initiation step and termination step, the reaction is called a chain reaction.

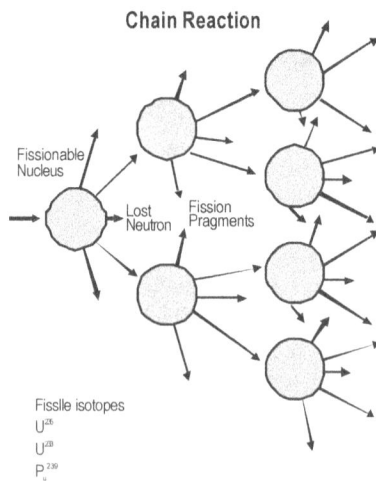

Chain Reaction

Chalk
A calcium carbonate filler comprised of shells of marine organisms (cocoliths).

Chappuis Band of Ozone Absorption
The wavelengths of light absorbed by ozone in the visible region, approximately 380 to 750 nm. Compare to ozone's ultraviolet absorption region, the Hartley-Huggins band.

Charcoal
A carbonaceous solid residue which is formed in the destructive distillation of wood. It has a very high surface area per unit weight which makes it especially useful as an absorber of various gases and vapours.

Charge
Describes an object's ability to repel or attract other objects. Protons have positive charges while electrons have negative charges. Like charges repel each other while opposite charges, such as protons and electrons, attract one another.

Charge demand
The amount of a standard, highly charged polymer required to neutralize the net electrical charges on suspended matter or colloids in an aqueous sample.

Charge neu-tralization
A mechanism of increasing fine particle retention (slightly) by reducing or eliminating like-charge repulsion between solids.

Charge patch
A mechanism of agglomeration of suspended particles based on adsorption of large, oppositely charged polymers, with the effect maximized at approximately 50% coverage.

Charge population
The net electric charge on a specified atom in a molecular entity, as determined by some prescribed definition, e.g. that of MULLIKEN.

Charge-transfer complex
A ground state *adduct* which exhibits an observable charge transfer absorption band.

Charles' law
A scientist named Jacques Charles did many experiments involving gas volumes and temperatures. He determined that the volume a gas needs is directly proportional to the temperature of the system (assuming a constant pressure). The formula goes: V=Tk (where k is a constant).

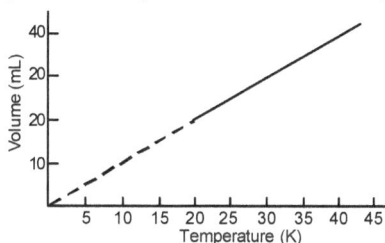

Checkwork
The multiple openings in a refractory wail which promotes turbulent mixing of the products of combustion.

Chelating agents
Molecules having multiple carboxyl groups in close proximity, such that they form very strong complexes with certain metal ions.

Chelation
The formation or presence of bonds (or other attractive interactions) between two or more separate binding sites within the same ligand and a single central atom. A molecular entity in which there is chelation (and the corresponding chemical species)

is called a "chelate". The terms bidentate (or didentate), tridentate, tetradentate... multidentate are used to indicate the number of potential binding sites of the ligand, at least two of which must be used by the ligand in forming a "chelate". For example, the bidentate ethylenediamine forms a chelate with CuI in which both nitrogen atoms of ethylenediamine are bonded to copper. The phrase "separate binding sites" is intended to exclude cases such as $[PtCl_3(CH_2=CH_2)]^-$, ferrocene, and (benzene) tricarbonylchromium in which ethene, the cyclopentadienyl group, and benzene, respectively, are considered to present single binding sites to the respective metal atom, and which are not normally thought of as chelates.

Cheletropic reaction

A form of cycloaddition across the terminal atoms of a fully conjugated system with formation of two new sigma bonds to a single atom of the ("monocentric") reagent. There is formal loss of one pi bond in the substrate and an increase in coordination number of the relevant atom of the reagent. An example is the addition of sulphur dioxide to butadiene:

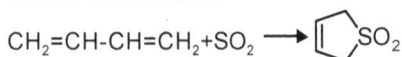

$$CH_2=CH-CH=CH_2+SO_2 \longrightarrow \boxed{}SO_2$$

The reverse of this type of reaction is designated "cheletropic elimination".

Chemical bonds

When atoms of different elements bind together to form a molecule of a substance, the bonds that hold the different atoms together are formed by a electrons being transferred from one atom to another or by two atoms sharing electrons.

The electrons experience a force of attraction from both nuclei. This negative - positive - negative attraction holds the two particles together

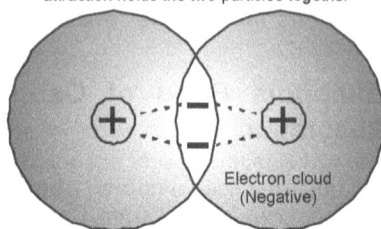

This attraction is called a chemical bond one pair of electrons constitutes ONE Bond

Chemical building block

One of a number of interchangeable reagents which can be used in combinatorial library synthesis, part of the structure of which becomes incorporated into the final product, i.e. its residue.

Chemical change

A change from one form to another which results in the production of at least one new substance. i.e. a chemical reaction. Chemical changes are generally difficult to reverse. They are indicated by a permanent colour change, the production of a gas, precipitate or light.

Chemical cleaning

Chemical cleaning is a removal of fatty and other impurities combined with it from fabrics with the help of organic solvents.

Chemical combination

A chemical reaction in which two elements or compounds are combined to form a more complex compound.

Chemical decomposition

This is the molecular action of the larger process of decomposition. Compounds are broken down into simpler compounds and elements.

Chemical equation

A condensed statement that uses formulas to show the reactants and products in a chemical change.

Chemical equilibrium

A condition in which two chemical changes exactly oppose one another. Equilibrium is a dynamic condition in which concentrations do not change and the rates of opposing reactions are equal.

Chemical forces

Chemical forces act on the bonds of molecules and atoms. They change the chemical makeup of systems. Physical forces are different from chemical forces in that they do not change the chemical makeup of molecules.

Chemical formula

a notation made with numbers and chemical symbols indicating the composition of a compound and the number of atoms of an element in one molecule.

Chemical ionization

The process in which primary ions, commonly formed by electron impact, react with neutral reagent gas molecules (e.g., by electron or proton transfer) to farm reagent ions. The extent of fragmentation of the reagent ion can be controlled through the exothermicity of the transfer reaction. Commonly employed in chemical ionization mass spectrometry.

Chemical kinetics

the branch of chemistry concerned with the rates and mechanisms of chemical reactions.

Chemical lifetime

The length of time a chemical species can survive without reacting, photolyzing, dissociating, or otherwise changing into another chemical species. Highly reactive chemicals have short lifetimes. For instance, if the reaction rate of a target species with an attacking species is very fast then the lifetime of the target species will be short. For example, the reaction of smalls radicals like hydroxyl radical in the troposphere is very fast with many common tropospheric species, and therefore the tropospheric lifetime of hydroxyl radical is measured in seconds.

Chemical properties

Properties that require a chemical reaction to observe.

Chemical property

A property that describes the behaviour of a substance as it changes into other substances. ie. a new substance is formed.

Chemical raw material

Chemical raw material are petroleum fractions used for obtaining organic chemicals, those are mostly refined gas and petroleum or fraction parts of petrol.

Chemical reduction

The chemical separation of a compound resulting in the production of a metal.

Chemical replacement

A chemical reaction where one element is replaced by another. Copper and sulphuric acid combine to create copper sulfate and hydrogen.

Chemical separation

A means of separating compounds into simpler substances based upon the chemical properties of that compound. At least one new substance is formed. eg. electrolysis, chemical reduction, heating.

Chemical species

An ensemble of chemically identical molecular entities that can explore the same set of molecular energy levels on the time scale of the experiment. The term is applied equally to a set of chemically identical atomic or molecular structural units in a solid array. For example, two conformational isomers may be interconverted sufficiently slowly to be detectable by separate NMR spectra and hence to be considered to be separate chemical species on a time scale governed by the radiofrequency of the spectrometer used. On the other hand, in a slow chemical reaction the same mixture of conformers may behave as a single chemical species, i.e. there is virtually complete equilibrium population of the total set of molecular energy levels belonging to the two conformers.

Chemiluminescence analyser

Instrument consisting of a reaction chamber with separate inlets for the sample and reagent gas, an optical filter, a photomultiplier and a signal processing device. The reactive gas is introduced in excess. The quantity of light produced is proportional to the sample flow rate and the concentration of the measured substance in the sample under specified temperature and pressure conditions. The filter limits the wavelength to the region of interest and helps to eliminate interferences.

Chemiluminescent methods of detection (analysis)

Methods which utilize gas or liquid phase reactions between two molecules which produces a third molecule in an excited state. The wavelength distribution of the light emission from the excited molecule is characteristic of the species; in some circumstances this may be used to identify and to determine the concentration of one of the reacting species.

Chemistry

the study of matter, its structures, properties, and composition, and the changes that matter undergoes.

Chemoselectivity

Chemoselectivity is the preferential reaction of a chemical reagent with one of two or more different functional groups. A reagent has a high chemoselectivity if reaction occurs with only a limited number of different functional groups. For example, sodium tetrahydroborate is a more chemoselective reducing agent than is lithium tetrahydroaluminate. The concept has not been defined in more quantitative terms. The term is also applied to reacting molecules or intermediates which e xhibit selectivity towards chemically different reagents.

Chemset

A collection of two or more library members, building blocks or reagents; preferred notation in the Journal of Combinatorial Chemistry and convenient for describing synthetic procedures on pools of compounds.

Chimney (stack)

A vertical flue for conducting cooled combustion products of a process to the atmosphere. This term also includes structures and opening of any kind from or through which smoke, grit, dust or fumes may be emitted.

Chimney effect

A vertical movement of a localized mass of air or other gases which occurs due to local temperature differences.

Chimney height (stack height), effective

A height used for the purposes of calculating the dispersion of emitted gases from a chimney, and which differs from the real chimney height by an amount which depends on such factors as the exit velocity, buoyancy effects and wind speed; it may also be affected by the local topography. It denotes the maximum height of the centre of a plume path above the level of the ground. The effective height may be above or below the actual chimney height, although the former case is most common.

Chiral

A term used to describe an object that is non-superposable on its mirror image

Chiral centre

Chiral centre in organic chemistry is most often an asymmetrically substituted carbon atom (C*).

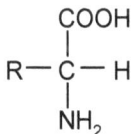

$$
\begin{array}{c}
COOH \\
| \\
R - C - H \\
| \\
NH_2
\end{array}
$$

Chiral molecule

Chiral molecule is a molecule which cannot be superimposed on its mirror image. A common example is an organic molecule containing a carbon atom to which four different atoms or groups are attached. Such molecules exhibit optical activity, i.e., they rotate the plane of a polarised light beam.

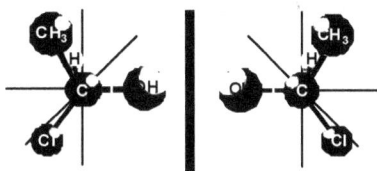

Chirality

Used to describe when symmetric parts of a molecule are not super imposable on one another.

Chloracne

A painful, disfiguring condition similar to common acne that it caused by people being exposed to high concentrations of PCB's (polychlorinated biphenyls). It is a biological response to the exposure of different types of organochlorine compounds.

Chlorination

1. Chlorination is an addition or substitution of chlorine in organic compounds.
2. Chlorination is a sterilisation of drinking and swimming pool water or oxidation of undesirable impurities, using chlorine or its compounds.

Chlorine

Cl_2, molecular chlorine. In the stratosphere, atomic (radical) chlorine is very destructive because it depletes the greatly needed ozone layer which protects the earth from ultraviolet radiation from the sun. In the Antarctic stratosphere, molecular chlorine along with nitric acid are formed by the reaction of hydrogen chloride and chlorine nitrate both stratospheric chlorine reservoir species. This process occurs on polar stratospheric clouds which serve as the reaction sites. Once formed, Cl_2 vapourizes into the surrounding air as nitric acid also formed in that process binds with the ice matrix. Cl_2 is then photodissociated in sunlight (lambda <= 450 nm) into chlorine radicals. These chlorine radicals then catalytic destroy ozone.

Chlorine atoms

Cl, the seventeenth element in the periodic table of elements. It has a atomic weight of 35.453 grams per mole. It has 17 protons in its nucleus and 7 electrons in its outer shell, an odd number which makes this neutral atom a radical and a very effective catalyst in the reaction that breaks down ozone in the stratosphere over Antarctica.

Chlorine dioxide

ClO_2, a radical, undergoes photodecomposition in the stratosphere where the products of this reaction react with ozone. Since this is a photochemical reaction it only takes place while the sun is up. Experiments over Antarctica have shown a direct relation between polar ozone loss and the increase in halocarbon chemistry, which comes from anthropogenic sources. Scientist are currently looking at the molecular behaviour of chlorine dioxide in the atmosphere in order to understand its role in depletion of ozone more thoroughly.

Chlorine monoxide

ClO, a radical species (with an odd number of electrons in its outer shell) which plays an important role in the breakdown of stratospheric ozone over Antarctica. Formed by the photolysis of CFCs in the stratosphere and the subsequent destruction of an ozone molecule, these radicals can act as a catalyst in the destruction of ozone while not being destroyed themselves.

Chlorine nitrate

$ClNO_3$, this is a stratospheric reservoir species for chlorine and nitrogen, two of the catalysts in the breakdown of ozone. Frankly, it is named in a confusing manner; it is formed from the reaction of chlorine monoxide and nitrogen dioxide (not chlorine atoms with nitrate). It reacts with HCl at low temperatures on the surfaces of polar stratospheric clouds (PSCs over Antarctica and probably also in the stratosphere over the Arctic). That normally slow reaction heterogeneously produces molecular chlorine and nitric acid. The former outgases from the PSC surface and is quickly photolyzed by 450 nm or shorter wavelength light to form chlorine radicals which rapidly catalyze the breakdown of ozone.

Chlorobenzene

C_6H_5Cl, a colourless liquid that is manufactured for use as a solvent. It quickly evapourates in the air and is degraded by hydroxyl radicals that are produced photochemically. The gas acts as a source of ClO, which helps in the breakdown of stratospheric ozone.

Chlorodifluoromethane (HCFC-22)

$CHClF_2$, this chemical is an intermediate replacement for the old CFCs because it contains a hydrogen atom, making a molecule that is easily attacked by hydroxyl radical in the atmosphere, therefore causing it to have a shorter atmospheric lifetime compared to the CFCs it replaces.

Chloroethane

This manmade VOC is highly reactive in the atmosphere. It is a gas at room temperature and when released, it readily reacts with oxidizing agents, most quickly with hydroxyl radical, half life ~ 40 days. The subsequent products are removed via sedimentation, precipitation, or rainout. Chloroethane has been used in the manufacturing and production of insecticides, dyes and drugs; as a solvent; and as a fugitive emission from landfills. Its molecular formula is C_2H_5Cl.

Chlorofluorocarbons-cfcs

Very stable chemical compound, used in refrigerants, solvent, and aerosols, which release chlorine (important) and fluorine (less important) into the upper atmosphere. In the stratosphere, CFCs are photolyzed (by incoming solar UV) to form carbon dioxide, hydrogen fluoride, HF, and ultimately (after multiple UV absorption events) chlorine radicals.

Chloroform

$CHCl_3$, a colourless liquid that evaporates easily into the air. The compound is released into the air by direct and indirect sources and breaks down in the lower atmosphere into carbon dioxide, phosgene (carbonic dichloride), and hydrogen chloride. The degradation occurs in the troposphere by the reaction of the compound with hydroxyl radicals.

Chloromethane

A colourless gas with a sweet odor. It was once used as a refrigerant in consumer products, but is no longer used because of its toxicity. It is central nervous system irritant, and in high doses can cause paralysis, seizures, and coma. Chloromethane was first synthesized by Peligot in 1835. Its chemical formula is CH_3Cl, and it has a melting point of -97°C, a boiling point of -24°C, and is naturally produced by sunlight reacting with biomass and chlorine in the oceans. It was used industrially as a refrigerant.

Chlorophyll

Molecular formula $C_{55}H_{72}O_5N_4Mg$ & $C_{55}H_{70}O_6N_4Mg$ Chlorophyll is the pigment in plants that absorbs light rays. The organic compound found in plants that captures the energy from the sun and releases the energy to form chemical bonds. The capture of light is the first step of photosynthesis. Chlorophyll is found in the chloroplasts of plants and there are many different types of the compound. Chlorophyll has many forms and gives plants their green colour. The key element in chlorophyll is magnesium (Mg).

Chromatogram in chromatography

A graphical presentation of detector signal against time, having a baseline and peaks.

Chromatographic analysis

A method of separation of different chemical species based upon selective adsorption. Gas chromatography involves the separation of components (gases or vapours) in a gaseous stream (carrier gas) on a column of some suitable sorbent (stationary phase). Nonvolatile components are often separated by liquid chromatography where a solution of the components is separated by partition between a liquid mobile phase and a "solid" stationary phase.

Chromatography

A chemical analysis method based on the different rates at which different chemicals pass through a column.

Chromium

Symbol: "Cr" Atomic Number: "24" Atomic Mass: 52.00amu. Chromium is one of the transition elements. You can find chromium in rubies and other minerals, in utensils, and in the process of making chrome parts for cars and motorcycles.

Chromophore

The part (atom or group of atoms) of a molecular entity in which the electronic transition responsible for a given spectral band is approximately localized. The term arose in the dyestuff industry, referring originally to the groupings in the molecule that are responsible for the dye's colour.

CIDNP

Non-Boltzmann nuclear spin state distribution produced in thermal or photochemical reactions, usually from colligation and diffusion, or disproportionation of radical pairs, and detected by NMR spectroscopy by enhanced absorption or emission signals.

Cine-substitution

A substitution reaction (generally aromatic) in which the entering group takes up a position adjacent to that occupied by the leaving group. For example:

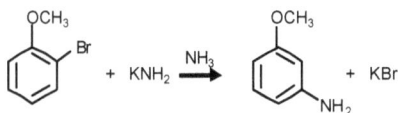

Circuit

The path through which electrons flow.

Cirrus clouds

High clouds that are formed entirely from ice crystals. They appear delicate and wispy and can reach a height of 35,000 feet (10,700 metres). Other types of cirrus clouds include cirrostratus and cirrocumulus. Cirrostratus is a thin sheet of cloud that often causes a halo to appear around the sun or moon. Cirrocumulus look like many small tufts of cotton; however, these clouds rarely form.

Clathrates

Also called gas hydrates, formed by or having molecules which are interlaced in a lattice-like geometrical pattern.

Clay

A platey mineral filler composed of aluminium silicate, formally known as kaolinite (except that other minerals, such as montmorillonite, also can be called "clays").

Clean air act

The Clean Air Act passed in 1970 and later in November of 1990 made into law established nationwide levels of acceptable air pollution from automobiles, individuals, and industry. The Environmental Protection Agency is responsible for enforcement of standards and regulations of the Clean Air Act.

Cleaners

Hydrocyclone equipment designed to remove grit from thin-stock furnish by a centrifugal action of rotating liquid.

Cleavage

Process of releasing a compound from a solid support, thereby permitting assay or analysis of the compound by solution-phase methods. Dissolution of the compound following cleavage, rather than the cleavage step itself, may be rate-limiting.

Climate

Determined by the daily weather interactions over many years. Characteristics used in determining climate are temperature, precipitation, humidity, sunshine, and cloudiness, wind, and air pressure. Climatologists describe climate in terms of average temperature and precipitation amounts.

Clone

A clone is a population of genetically identical cells produced from a common ancestor. Sometimes, "clone" is also used for a number of recombinant DNA (deoxyribonucleic acid) molecules all carrying the same inserted sequence.

Closed water system
A papermaking process in which the amount of liquid effluent has been decreased, sometimes to zero (totally closed).

Closure
A mathematical term which says that if you operated on any two real numbers A and B with +, -, * or /, you get a real number.

Cloud
Condensed water vapour floating in air. They can take many different shapes due to wind patterns and moisture content. They play an important part in the world's weather because of the water they bring and because of their radiative properties vis a vis global warming.

Cloud condensation nuclei (ccn)
Condensed water vapour that is so small that it can only be seen through a microscope. CCN are actually the center of the droplet. Many of these nuclei are tiny salt particles, sulfate or nitrate aerosol, or small particles present in smoke.

Clouds, altocumulus
A dappled layer of patch or cloud composed of flattened globules that may be arranged in groups, lines or waves collectively known as billows; 2 000-6 000 m; vertical velocities of 0.05-0.1 m s^{-1}.

Clouds, altostratus
A grey, uniform, striated or fibrous sheet but without halo phenomena,

and through which the sun is seen only as a diffuse, bright patch or not at all; usually at elevations 2 000-6 000 m; vertical velocities of 0.05-0.1 m s^{-1}.

Clouds, cumulonimbus
Heavy masses of dense cloud whose cumuliform summits rise in the forms of towers, the upper parts having a fibrous texture and often spreading out into the shape of an anvil; these clouds generally produce showers of rain and sometimes of snow, hail or soft hail, and often develop into thunderstorms; up to 12000 m; summits may be as cold as -50 °C; strong convective motions with vertical velocities of 3 to greater than 30 m s^{-1}.

Clouds, cumulus
Detached, dense clouds with a dome-shaped upper surface with sharp-edged, rounded protuberances and a nearly horizontal base; 600-6 000 m or more; convective motion with rising, large bubbles of warm air with vertical speeds of 1-5 m s^{-1}.

Clouds, stratocumulus
A layer of patches composed of laminae or globular masses arranged in groups, lines, or waves and having a soft, grey appearance; very often the rolls are so close together that their edges join and give the undersurface a wavy character; the process of formation (cumulogenesis) involves the spreading out of the tops of cumulus clouds, the latter having disappeared; <2 000 m; usually warmer than -5 °C; vertical velocities usually <0.1 m s^{-1}.

Clouds, stratus
A uniform featureless layer of cloud resembling fog but not resting on the ground; when this very low layer is broken up into irregular shreds, it is designated as fractostratus; 300-600

m; widespread irregular stirring and lifting of the shallow layer of cool, damp air near the ground.

Cluster

Group of compounds which are related by structural or behavioural properties. Organizing a set of compounds into clusters is often used in assessing the diversity of those compounds, or in developing SAR (structure-activity relationship) models.

Coagulation

The coming together and sticking of small, suspended particles, brought about by addition of salt, change of pH, or chemical additions that reduce or eliminate like-charge repulsion.

Coagulation (flocculation)

Process of converting a finely divided or colloidally dispersed suspension of one substance (usually a solid) in a liquid into larger-size particles which do settle or precipitate under the influence of gravity. Aluminium sulfate or other salt which contains a trivalent or divalent metal ion is sometimes used for this purpose.

Coal desulphurization

Processes by which sulphur compounds are removed from coal. Some of the sulphur content of coal is composed of iron pyrites (FeS) which has a density (about 5 g cm^{-3}) very different from that of coal (1.25-1.45 g cm^{-3}) and can be removed by mechanical cleaning processes.

Coal tar

Coal tar is a material obtained from the destructive distillation of coal in the production of coal gas. The crude tar contains a large number of organic compounds (e.g. benzene, naphthalene, methylbenzene, etc.),

which can be separated by fractional distillation.

Coarse mode particles

Particles that are larger than two micrometers in diameter. They come form sea sprays, volcanoes, crushing or grinding of rocks, wind blown soil, and account for about 95% of the aerosol particles in ambient air.

Cobalt

Symbol: "Co" Atomic Number: "27" Atomic Mass: 58.93amu. Cobalt is one of the transition elements. You can find cobalt in magnets, stainless steel, pottery, and Vitamin B-12.

Codon

A codon is the sequence of three consecutive nucleotides that occurs in mRNA which directs the incorporation of a specific amino acid into a protein or represents the starting or termination signals of protein synthesis.

Coefficients

A number preceding formula units (atoms, ions, molecules) in balanced chemical equations, indicating the relative number of units involved in the reaction.

Coenzyme

A coenzyme is a dissociable, low-molecular weight, non-proteinaceous organic compound (often nucleotide) participating in enzymatic reactions as acceptor or donor of chemical groups or electrons.

Cof

Coefficient of friction, the ratio of force required to initiate (static) or sustain (dynamic) sliding, versus the perpendicular force pushing the surfaces together.

COH, coefficient of haze

One technique of measurement of the amount of filterable particulate matter suspended in air which has been used in the past depends upon drawing a measured sample of air (usually 1000 linear feet) through a paper or membrane filter. A measurement is made of the intensity of light transmitted through the dust spot formed relative to that transmitted through an identical clean filter. The dirtiness of the air is reported in terms of the COH unit.

Cohesion

Cohesive forces of attraction happen between molecules of the same type. Two water droplets that are close to each other will combine into one because of cohesive forces.

Collagen

Collagen is the primary organic constituent of bone, cartilage, and connective tissue (becomes gelatine through boiling).

Collection efficiency

A term which characterizes an entire sampling and sample pretreatment procedure, usually represented as a percentage of the original amount of the analyte which is left for measurement (signal formation) after having passed through this procedure. This term also applies to the effciency of collection of an air pollutant by an arrestment plant.

Collector

A device for removing and retaining contaminants from air or other gases. Term which is often applied to cleaning devices in exhaust systems. Also used to designate a device for removing and retaining samples from media in different environmental compartments to be investigated. A collector is sometimes used to describe a scavenger. GB—A solid substance added to or formed within a solution to collect a micro- or macro-component.

Colligative properties

Properties of a solution that depend only on the number of particles dissolved in it, not the properties of the particles themselves. The main colligative properties addressed at this web site are boiling point elevation and freezing point depression.

Colloidal

Having to do with finely divided substances in which at least one dimension is within the range of about 0.001 to 1 micrometers.

Colloidal silica

A type of microparticle product that is usually used in sequential addition with either cationic starch or a PAM retention aid product to achieve enhanced dewatering and retention.

Colloidal titration

A method of determining the charge demand of an aqueous sample by addition highly charged polymer to a neutral endpoint, usually with a charge-sensitive dye endpoint.

Colour

Colour is a measure of reflected wavelengths of light. Colours are also only useful to organisms that can see with the visible spectrum of light. An element like gold may have a yellow colour while mercury will be highly reflective and silvery (like silver colour).

Colourimetre

An instrument used for colour measurement based on optical comparison with standard colours.

Column ozone

The total amount of ozone that is found in a column of air. The majority of this amount of O_3 is typically found in the stratosphere.

Combinatorial chemistry

The use of chemical methods to generate all possible combinations of chemicals starting with a subset of compounds. The building blocks may be peptides, nucleic acids or small molecules. The libraries of compounds formed by this methodology are used to probe for new pharmaceutical reagents.

Combinatorial library

A set of compounds prepared by combinatorial chemistry. May consist of a collection of pools or sub-libraries.

Combinatorial organic synthesis

A key feature of combinatorial techniques is that compound synthesis can be designed such that a range of structures can be produced simultaneously as mixtures in the same reaction vessel or individually in parallel using semi-automated synthesis. The repetitive nature of the synthetic processes involved in most combinatorial applications lends itself to automation or semi-automation. This key feature means that the bench chemist can single-handedly prepare tens, hundreds, or thousands of compounds of known structures in the time that it would take to prepare only a few pure entities by orthodox methodology.

Combinatorial synthesis

Combinatorial synthesis is a process to prepare large sets of organic compounds by combining sets of building blocks.

Combined gas law

There came a time when scientists combined the ideas in Boyle's Law and Charles' Law. The result was the combined gas law that worked for pressure, temperature, and volume. The formula goes: $(P_1V_1)/T_1=(P_2V_2)/T_2$. From this formula you can determine the values of pressure, volume, or temperature when you know the values of one system and all but one of the values for a second system.

Combustion

When a compound is changed into water, heat, and CO_2 as a result of combining with oxygen.

Combustion chamber

The region within which solids, vapours and gases from the primary chamber are burned and the some settling of fly ash takes place.

Combustion gases

Gases and vapours produced in furnaces, combustion chambers or in open burning.

Common-ion effect

the dissociation of a slightly soluble ionic compound is decreased by adding to the solution a readily soluble ionic compound that has an ion in common with the slightly soluble compound.

Commutativity

A math property which states:
A + B = B + A and A * B = B * A.

Comparative molecular field analysis

Comparative molecular field analysis (CoMFA) is a 3D-QSAR method that uses statistical correlation techniques for the analysis of the quantitative relationship between the biological activity of a set of compounds with a specified alignment, and their three-dimensional electronic and steric properties. Other properties such as hydrophobicity and hydrogen bonding can also be incorporated into the analysis.

Compass

A compass is a scientific instrument that tells the user the direction of magnetic north. South is directly opposite north, east is to the right, and west is to the left.

Complementary gas

Generally the most abundant component (pure gas or gas mixture) which makes up the mixture intended for the calibration.

Complex

A molecular entity formed by loose association involving two or more component molecular entities (ionic or uncharged), or the corresponding chemical species. The bonding between the components is normally weaker than in a covalent bond. The term has also been used with a variety of shades of meaning in different contexts: it is therefore best avoided when a more explicit alternative is applicable. In inorganic chemistry the term "coordination entity" is recommended instead of "complex".

Complexation

1. Interaction between small molecules (ligands) and an ion to form a chemical complex.
2. Interaction between a soluble polymer and something else to form a polyelectrolyte complex that may precipitate.

Composite reaction

A chemical reaction for which the expression for the rate of disappearance of a reactant (or rate of appearance of a product) involves rate constants of more than a single elementary reaction.

Examples are "opposing reactions" (where rate constants of two opposed chemical reactions are involved), "parallel reactions" (for which the rate of disappearance of any reactant is governed by the rate constants relating to several simultaneous reactions to form different respective products from a single set of reactants), and stepwise reactions.

Composition percentage

This value tells the percentage of a solution that could be a percentage of mass or percentage by volume. It is determined by dividing the value for the solute by the value for the solution and then multiplying by 100 to get the percentage. Seven milliliters of HCl divided by 100 milliliters of water creates a 7 percent by volume solution.

Compound

A pure substance made up of two or more elements that are joined together by chemical bonds. Compounds can be broken down into simpler substances by chemical separation. ie. electrolysis, chemical reduction producing metals and by thermal decomposition.

Comproportionation

The reverse of disproportionation. The term "symproportionation" is also used.

Computational chemistry

Computational chemistry is a discipline using mathematical methods for the calculation of molecular properties or for the simulation of molecular behaviour.

Computer-assisted drug design

Computer-assisted drug design involves all computer-assisted techniques used to discover, design and optimize biologically active compounds with a putative use as drugs.

Concentrated

A solution containing a large amount of solute

Concentrated solution

A solution (liquid mixture) that has a large amount of solute dissolved. As you add more sugar to a glass of water, the sugar solution becomes more concentrated.

Concentration

Concentration is the amount of one substance in a system relative to the amount of other substances. If you have a glass of water, the concentration of water in the glass is 100%. A glass of salt water will have a specific concentration of salt in the water.

Concentration, gas and liquid solutions

This represents the quantity of matter (mol, g, molecules, or other) per unit of volume (cm^3, L, m^3, or other). The IUPAC designation of this quantity is the amount of substance concentration (with the SI base unit of mol m^{-1}, but practical units of mol dm^{-3} or mol L^{-1}). For a gas phase species it is common to describe the concentration as the number of molecules of the particular species per cm^3 of air; this unit is most common in gas phase kinetics and in calculations involving chemical changes in the atmosphere. The number concentration or number density, often employed in physics and in physical chemistry, describes the number of molecules per cm^3; however in writing the units for this quantity, molecules are understood but omitted; only cm" is written.

Concentration, ground level

The concentration of a chemical species, normally a pollutant, in air; usually measured at a specific height above the ground.

Concentration, particle

Commonly expressed in several ways: mass concentration or number concentration (number of particles cm^{-3}); modern instrumentation allows measurement of the number of particles as a function of size as well as the total number present in a given air volume. For atmospheric aerosols, this is a complex distribution for which diameters range from below 0.01 to above 100m; the particles making the highest contribution to the total number density are in the size range below 0.1m, those contributing most to the total surface area are in the 0.1 to 1.0m range, while those with the highest contribution to the volume or mass of the aerosol come from both the 0.1 to 1.0 and 1.0 to 100m ranges.

Concerted process

Two or more primitive changes are said to be concerted (or to constitute a concerted process) if they occur within the same elementary reaction. Such changes will normally (though perhaps not inevitably) be "energetically coupled". (In the present context the term "energetically coupled" means that the simultaneous progress of the primitive changes involves a transition state of lower energy than that for their successive occurrence.) In a concerted process the primitive changes may be synchronous or asynchronous.

Condensate

A condensate is an example of moisture that has condensed. Condensate might be created during the process of distillation. When you boil water and it condenses on the lid of the pot, you have created a condensate.

Condensation

The physical process of converting a material from a gaseous or vapour phase to a liquid or solid phase; this commonly results when the temperature is lowered and/or the vapour pressure of the material is increased. The tendency exists for condensation to occur when the partial pressure of a given component of a gaseous mixture at a given temperature exceeds the vapour pressure of the liquid or solid form of that component at the given temperature.

Condensation nuclei (sometimes symbolized as CN)

A particle, either liquid or solid, or an ion upon which condensation of water vapour (or other substances) begins in the atmosphere. Condensation nuclei are usually very small hygroscopic aerosols (0.001 to 0.1m in diameter), but these are not as abundant as the smaller particles. The number of CN which are active (initiate condensation) in a given air mass may be a function of the relative humidity.

Condensation point

The condensation point is when a gas reaches a temperature to become a liquid. Energy is taken out of the atoms in the gas state and they condense, forming drops of liquid. You can also think of the point in nature when water vapour cools and forms small droplets, such as dew in the morning.

Condensation reaction

A (usually stepwise) reaction in which two or more reactants (or remote reactive sites within the same molecular entity) yield a single main product with accompanying formation of water or of some other small molecule, e.g. ammonia, ethanol, acetic acid, hydrogen sulfide.

Condensed structural formulas

Condensed structural formulas are shortened and easier layout of structural formulas of organic compounds (butane, $CH_3(CH_2)_2CH_3$).

Conductivity

Ease with which an aqueous solution conducts electricity; conductivity increases with salt, acid, or base concentrations.

Configuration

the permanent geometry of a molecule that results from the spatial arrangement of its bonds.

Configuration (molecular)

In the context of stereochemistry, the term is restricted to the arrangements of atoms of a molecular entity in space that distinguishes stereoisomers, the isomerism of which is not due to conformational differences.

Conformation

The spatial arrangements of atoms affording distinction between stereoisomers which can be interconverted by rotation about formally single bonds. Some authorities extend the term to include inversion at trigonal bipyramidal centres and other "polytopal rearrangements".

Congener

A congener is a substance literally con- (with) generated or synthesized by essentially the same synthetic chemical reactions and the same procedures. Analogs are substances that are analogous in some respect to the prototype agent in chemical structure.

Conjugate acid

A conjugate acid is a molecule that is created when you start with a base and add a proton.

Conjugate acid-base pair

The Brønsted acid BH^+ formed on protonation of a base B is called the conjugate acid of B, and B is the conjugate base of BH^+. (The conjugate acid always carries one unit of positive charge more than the base, but the absolute charges of the species are immaterial to the definition.) For example: the Brønsted acid HCl and its conjugate base Cl^- constitute a conjugate acid-base pair. The mechanism of many condensation reactions has been shown to comprise consecutive addition and elimination reactions, as in the base-catalysed formation of (E)-but-2-enal (crotonaldehyde) from acetaldehyde, via 3-hydroxybutanal (aldol). The overall reaction in this example is known as the aldol condensation.

Conjugate base

A conjugate base is a molecule that is created when you start with an acid and remove a proton.

Conjugate pair

an acid and a base that may be formed reversibly from one another. The conjugates differ from one another in composition by only a single hydrogen atom.

Conjugated double bond

Conjugated double bond in organic compounds is a system of double bonds between atoms which are separated by one single bond (1,3-butene, $H_2C=CH-CH=CH_2$).

Conjugation

A system of atoms covalently bonded with alternating single and multiple (e.g. double) bonds (e.g., C=C-C=C-C).

Connectivity

In a chemical context, the information content of a line formula, but omitting any indication of bond multiplicity.

Conservation of Matter

Name of the concept that explains how mass cannot be created or destroyed during a chemical reaction.

Consistency

The mass fraction (or percentage) of solid, filterable material in a given slurry sample.

Constituent (with reference to an air sample)

A component of the air sample for which a specified quantity is to be determined by measurement or analysis; see air quality characteristic.

Constitution

The description of the identity and connectivity (and corresponding bond multiplicities) of the atoms in a molecular entity (omitting any distinction from their spatial arrangement).

Contact angle

The angle, drawn through the liquid phase, between a flat solid and an air-liquid interface when a drop is placed on a surface.

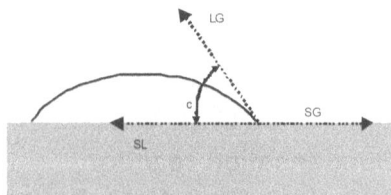

Contact Angle

Contact metamorphism

Metamorphic rocks that have been formed in areas where volcanic activity has occurred. The heat from the lava directly heats the neighboring rocks and causes them to reform. There are more crystals in this type of metamorphic rock.

Contaminant, air

A substance, gaseous material or aerosol, which is present in an air mass at levels greater than in clean air. An air contaminant has been added commonly by anthropogenic activity; see also air pollutant.

Continental drift

A term applied to early theories supporting the possibility that the continents are in motion over the Earth's surface.

Continuous air monitoring programme (CAMP)

In the United States the CAMP programme represents a series of monitoring stations which were established near large cities for the continuous monitoring of gaseous pollutants, SO_2, NO, NO_2, CO, hydrocarbons, and O_3.

Continuous spectrum

A spectrum all the colours of light.

Control agencies

Air pollution control agencies, established nationally or locally, which are designated to monitor and control air pollution in their designated areas through the enforcement of air pollution control legislation.

Controlled atmosphere

A synthetic gaseous sample of pure air which may contain carefully determined amounts of certain contaminants; this may be used as a standard for the calibration of analytical techniques, as a simulated environment for the study of biological responses, or for other purposes.

Convection

Process by which, in a fluid being heated, the warmer part of the mass will rise and the cooler portions sink. This is also a component of the theory for continental drift, in that the circulating movements of crystal materials push the continents apart. Convection (as applied to air motion) Vertical motion of the air induced by the expansion of the air heated by the earth's surface and its resulting buoyancy.

Conversion factors

numbers that are used to change, or convert, from one unit to another.

Converting

Processes involved with changing paper into end-products such as cut-size paper, envelopes, boxes, etc.

Cooperativity

Cooperativity is the interaction process by which binding of a ligand to one site on a macromolecule (enzyme, receptor, etc.) influences binding at a second site, e.g. between the substrate binding sites of an allosteric enzyme. Cooperative enzymes typically display a sigmoid (S-shaped) plot of the reaction rate against substrate concentration.

Coordination

The formation of a covalent bond, the two shared electrons of which have come from only one of the two parts of the molecular entity linked by it, as in the reaction of a Lewis acid and a Lewis base to form a Lewis adduct; alternatively, the bonding formed in this way. In the former sense, it is the reverse of unimolecular heterolysis. "Coordinate covalence" and "coordinate link" are synonymous (obsolescent) terms. The synonym "dative bond" is obsolete. The term is also used to describe the number of ligands around a central atom without necessarily implying two-electron bonds.

Coordination number

The coordination number of a specified atom in a chemical species is the number of other atoms directly linked to that specified atom. For example, the coordination number of carbon in methane is four, and it is five in protonated methane, CH_5^+.

Coordinatively saturated

A transition metal complex that has formally 18 outer shell electrons at the central metal atom.

Coordinatively unsaturated

A transition metal complex that possesses fewer ligands than exist in the coordinatively saturated complex. These complexes usually have fewer than 18 outer shell electrons at the central metal atom.

Copolymer

A long-chain molecule composed of two different types of monomer units.

Copper

Symbol: "Cu" Atomic Number: "29" Atomic Mass: 63.55amu. Copper is one of the transition elements. Copper is one of the most well known metals. Humans have used it for thousands of years. It is a reddish colour and can be found alone or in many different minerals. You might find copper in pipes, coins, alloys, and electronics.

Coriolis force

A fictional source associated with the earth's rotation. It results in the deflection of all objects not at the equator to the right in the direction of motion in the northern hemisphere and to the left in the southern hemisphere.

Correlation analysis

The use of empirical correlations relating one body of experimental data to another, with the objective of finding quantitative estimates of the factors underlying the phenomena involved. Correlation analysis in organic chemistry often uses linear free-energy relations for rates or equilibria of reactions, but the term also embraces similar analysis of physical (most commonly spectroscopic) properties and of biological activity.

Corrosion

The deterioration and wearing away of metals.

Couch roll

A roll that applies vacuum through a forming fabric, by means of perforations, just before paper leaves the forming section.

Counter-ion

Ion in solution adjacent to a charged surface, so that the net charge of the system is zero.

Coupling constant (spin-spin coupling constant), J (SI unit: Hz (NMR))

A quantitative measure for nuclear spin-spin, nuclear-electron (hyperfine coupling) and electron-electron (fine coupling in EPR) coupling in magnetic resonance spectroscopy. The "indirect" or scalar NMR coupling constants are in a first approximation independent of the external magnetic field and are expressed in Hz.

Covalence

Covalence is the ability of an element to bond with other elements by sharing electrons across a bond. Covalent compounds can be made with single, double, and triple bonds. These bonds are not as easily broken in solution as electrovalent compounds. Two covalent bonds happen between carbon and two oxygen atoms in carbon dioxide.

Covalent

A type of strong molecular bonding that involves sharing of electrons by different atoms.

Covalent bonds

When atoms of different elements bind together to form a molecule of a substance by sharing electrons, the type of bond formed is called a Covalent Bond. The Covalent Bond is a very strong bond that is the main type of bond occurring in Organic Compounds. These bonds are referred to as Co-valent because each of the atoms participating in the sharing of electrons Co-operates to achieve the chemical goal of having an outer shell being full of electrons.

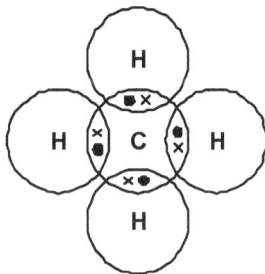

Cracking

The process whereby complex organic molecules such as heavy hydrocarbons are broken down into simpler molecules (e.g. light hydrocarbons) by the breaking of carbon-carbon bonds.

Critical mass

The amount of a specific radioactive material it takes to create a chain reaction.

Critical point

The temperature and pressure at which the liquid and vapour intensive properties (density, heat capacity, etc.) become equal. It is the highest temperature (critical temperature) and pressure (critical pressure) at which both a gaseous and a liquid phase of a given compound can coexist.

Critical pressure

Pressure needed to force a gas into a liquid state when the gas is at its critical temperature.

Critical temperature

A temperature beyond which a gas cannot be turned into a liquid no matter how much pressure is applied. The process of liquefaction cannot occur above the critical temperature.

Crosslinking

Property of a solid support prepared from polymeric materials with interconnected strands. Often results from the inclusion of multifunctional monomers in the polymerization reaction, e.g. divinylbenzene in polystyrene production. In such cases, the degree of crosslinking is often quoted as the proportion of the multifunctional monomer in the reaction mixture. The extent of crosslinking is important for physical properties of the solid support, such as the propensity to swell in different solvents.

Crown

A molecular entity comprising a monocyclic ligand assembly that contains three or more binding sites held together by covalent bonds and capable of binding a guest in a central (or nearly central) position. The adducts formed are sometimes known as "coronates". The best known members of this group are macrocyclic polyethers, such as "18-crown-6", containing several repeating units -CR_2CR$_2$O- (where R is most commonly H), and known as crown ethers.

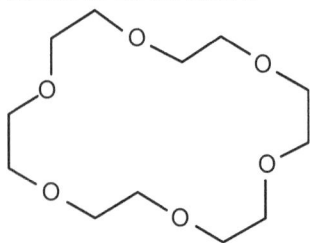

"18-crown-6"

Cryogenic
Term used to describe low temperature processes, apparatus, etc.; usually applied to systems operated at the temperature of liquid nitrogen, helium or other condensed gas which boils at a very low temperature (at atmospheric pressure).

Cryosphere
The portion of the earth which consists of the ice masses and snow deposits which include continental ice sheets, mountainous glaciers, sea ice, surface snow cover and lake/river ice. Alterations in the extent of snow cover are due to seasonal fluctuations and are interrelated with atmospheric circulation. Sea level and hydrologic cycle variations can affect the volume of water tied up in the glaciers and ice sheets.

Cryptand
A molecular entity comprising a cyclic or polycyclic assembly of binding sites that contains three or more binding sites held together by covalent bonds, and which defines a molecular cavity in such a way as to bind (and thus "hide" in the cavity) another molecular entity, the guest (a cation, an anion or a

neutral species), more strongly than do the separate parts of the assembly (at the same total concentration of binding sites). The adduct thus formed is called a "cryptate". The term is usually restricted to bicyclic or oligocyclic molecular entities. Example:

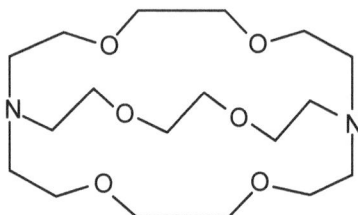

Corresponding monocyclic ligand assemblies (crowns) are sometimes included in this group, if they can be considered to define a cavity in which a guest can hide. The terms "podand" and "spherand" are used for certain specific ligand assemblies. Coplanar cyclic polydentate ligands, such as porphyrins, are not normally regarded as cryptands.

Crystal
A solid that has a definite geometric shape or pattern because the particles are arranged in an orderly manner. eg. table salt is cubic.

Crystal cleavage
Cleavage is the way a crystal breaks when it is fractured. A crystal usually breaks along points of molecular weakness leaving a smooth break between two surfaces. The fresh surface is not as smooth as the naturally occurring surfaces of the crystal. There are four types of cleavage: none, distinct, indistinct, and perfect. Diamond cutters hope for perfect cleavage when they cut diamonds.

Crystal fracture
Crystals fracture in the same way anything would fracture. It is an uneven

break. If you were to hit an ice cube with a hammer, it would fracture in an uneven manner.

Crystal habit
The general form a crystal takes. This is a larger formation than the actual shape of a crystal. While a crystal shape can be cubic, groups of crystals can form a shape that is bladed or prismatic.

Crystal lattice
A crystal lattice is a very exact organization of atoms that allows for a specific place for every molecule or atom in the solid. If a solid is made up of pure elements or compounds, it can create a very specific structure. A good example of a crystal lattice is a diamond. Salt (NaCl) has a specific cube shape for the crystal. One sodium atom connects to one chlorine atom and that combination repeats. The final structure is a cube.

Crystal modifier
An additive that tends to make scale deposits weaker or less able to adhere to surfaces.

Crystal twinning
Crystal twinning occurs when two crystals grow in different directions and eventually intersecting. There are two basic types: penetration and contact. Penetration twin crystals intersect. Contact twin crystals meet at a center point.

Crystalline solid
A crystalline solid has a specific organization of molecules and atoms. These are the classic crystals of the world such as diamonds and all gemstones. They are often made up of specific molecules and have very structured geometric shapes. These

solids also have more clearly defined melting points. Table salt would be a good example of a crystalline solid.

Crystallization
Physical or chemical process or action which results in the formation of regularly-shaped, -sized, and -patterned solid forms known as crystals.

CTMP
Chemi-thermomechanical pulp, a type of high-yield fiber that contributes bulk to paper.

Cubic crystal
A crystal shaped like a cube. A cube has six sides and might look like a die from a board game.

Cumulated double bond
Cumulated double bond in organic compounds is a system of two double bonds on the same atom of carbon (C=C=C)

Cumulative sample
A sample collected over an extended period of time.

Cumulus clouds
Clouds forming in the troposphere which are vertically formed with flat bases and fluffy, rounded tops. They have often been described as cauliflower-like in structure. They occur at heights of 500-6000 metres in elevation from the earth and most often occur scattered or in dense heaped packs. They are formed due to buoyant upward convection during warm, anti-cyclonic summer weather.

Cupola
A vertical shaft furnace used for melting metals; the melting of ores is accomplished in a blast furnace.

Curing

Reactions of certain sizing agents and wet-strength agents that occur during the drying of paper.

Curium

Symbol:"Cm" Atomic Number:"96" Atomic Mass: (247)amu. Curium is one of the elements in the actinide series of inner transition elements. It may also be classified as a rare earth element. It is a very radioactive element but has been used in satellites and space exploration.

Custom synthesis

Used for the production of organic drug compounds to the specification of the client for the their specific development and research needs.
Cut off (as applied to aerosol sizes) The size of particles at which the retention efficiency of an instrument device drops below a specified value under defined conditions.

Cyclative cleavage

Cleavage resulting from intramolecular reaction at the linker which results in a cyclized product. The cleavage may also act as a purification if resin-bound side-products are incapable of cyclizing, and thus remain attached to the solid support on release of the desired material.

Cycle

In the atmosphere or biosphere a sequence of events in repetitive motion in which the final output feeds back into the initial input. Examples of this include biogeochemical cycles, including the nitrogen, carbon, and sulphur cycles in which these species are chemically processed in gas, solid, and solution phase by physical and biological processes which change their form, oxidation state, and physical state.

Cycloalkane

An alkane that has one or more rings of carbon atoms in the chemical structure of its molecule. Chemical formula $C_nH_2(n+1-g)$ when n = number of C atoms g = number of rings in the molecule.

Cyclone (collector)

A dust, grit, or droplet separator utilizing essentially the centrifugal force derived from the motion of the gas. The flow of gases containing suspended particles into the device is transformed into a confined vortex from which centrifugal forces tend to drive the suspended particles to the wall of the cyclone body. The agglomerated particles are subsequently removed from the cyclone by gravitational action.

Cyclone (meteorology)

A large circulatory wind system around a region of low atmospheric pressure; rotation is counterclockwise (viewed from above) in the northern hemisphere and clockwise in the southern hemisphere.

D

Dalton

Atomic mass is not measured in pounds or grams. Scientists used something called Daltons. One Dalton is equal to one-twelfth the mass of a carbon atom. Scientists also call a Dalton an Atomic Mass Unit.

Daniell cell

an electrochemical cell in which zinc metal reacts with aqueous copper ions

Dark reaction (darkness reaction)

A chemical reaction that does not require or depend on the presence of light. Contrasts with a photochemical reaction which is initiated by light absorption by one or more of the reactants.

Daughter isotope

In a nuclear equation the compound remaining after the parent isotope (the original isotope) has undergone decay. A compound undergoing decay, such as alpha decay, will break into an alpha particle and a daughter isotope.

Dcs

Dissolved and colloidal substances, usually derived from wood and usually having a negative charge, tending to interfere with retention aids and other papermaking additives.

De novo design

De novo design is the design of bioactive compounds by incremental construction of a ligand model within a model of the receptor or enzyme active site, the structure of which is known from X-ray or nuclear magnetic resonance (NMR) data.

Decanting

The separation of an insoluble solid from a liquid by carefully pouring off the liquid leaving the solid sediment behind.

Decay

Change of an element into a different element, usually with some other particle(s) and energy emitted.

Decay rate

The rate at which a pollutant is removed from the atmosphere either by reaction with reactive transient species such as the HO-radical, O_3, etc., by photodecomposition initiated by light absorption by the impurity, or by loss at the surface of aerosols, the earth, etc. The decay rate as applied to radioactive materials is related to the radioactive half-life ($t_{1/2}$) of the particular isotopic species A and its concentration $[A]_t$ at the given time (t) Rate = $[A]_t(\ln 2)/t_{1/2}$.

Decimal

The number of digits to the right of the decimal point in a number.

Decode

Use of a surrogate analyte to define the reaction path to which the solid support was exposed, and hence imply the structure of a member of a combinatorial library or the reaction sequence for its preparation.

Decomposition

Chemical decomposition, analysis or breakdown is the separation of a chemical compound into elements or simpler compounds. It is sometimes defined as the exact opposite of a chemical synthesis. Chemical decomposition is often an undesired chemical reaction. The stability that a chemical compound ordinarily has is eventually limited when exposed to extreme environmental conditions like heat, radiation, humidity or the acidity of a solvent. The details of decomposition processes are generally not well defined, as a molecule may break up into a host of smaller fragments. Chemical decomposition is exploited in several analytical techniques, notably mass spectrometry, traditional gravimetric analysis, and thermogravimetric analysis. A broader definition of the term decomposition also includes the breakdown of one phase into two or more phases

Decomposition of organic matter

The breaking down (mineralization) of organic matter to produce reduced or oxidized products such as NH_3, NO_x and CO_2 (g) and their subsequent release into the atmosphere; however, much of these decomposition products remain in the soil.

Decomposition reaction

A chemical change in which a substance is broken down into two or more simpler substances.

Deculator

A device that removes entrained and dissolved air from thin-stock furnish by applying vacuum as the stock is sprayed into an open chamber, usually at the outlet of hydrocyclone cleaners.

Definite proportions

This is a concept that explains how formulas of similar compounds are identical no matter where you are in the universe. Sodium chloride will always be made of one sodium and one chloride atom. Water will always be made of one oxygen and two hydrogen atoms.

Defoamer

An additive mixture, usually containing a water-insoluble surfactant and often containing hydrophobic particles, that destabilizes foam bubbles.

Deforestation

Type of "forestry practice" which involves the permanent removal of forests and their undergrowth so that the land can serve another purpose. This practice has had a profound effect on global environmental problems (air pollution, global warming), soil erosion, desertification, sedimentation of water courses, alteration of climate and hydrological cycles, alteration of the atmospheric oxygen and carbon dioxide balance and has caused many species to become extinct, reducing worldwide biodiversity. A common deforestation practice is to simply burn the forest while clearing the land for a seasonal crop.

Degenerate rearrangement

A molecular rearrangement in which the principal product is indistinguishable (in the absence of isotopic labelling) from the principal reactant. The term includes both "degenerate intramolecular rearrangements" and reactions that involve intermolecular transfer of atoms or groups ("degenerate intermolecular rearrangements"): both are degenerate isomerizations. The occurrence of degenerate rearrangements may be detectable by isotopic labelling or by dynamic NMR techniques. For example: the [3,3]sigmatropic rearrangement of hexa-1,5-diene (Cope rearrangement),

Synonymous but less preferable terms are "automerization", "permutational isomerism", "isodynamic transformation", "topomerization".

Dehydrogenation

Dehydrogenation is a chemical reaction in which hydrogen is removed from a compound. Dehydrogenation of organic compounds converts single carbon-carbon bonds into double bonds. It is usually affected by means of a metal catalyst or in biological systems by enzyme dehydrogenases.

Delaminated clay

A kaolin product formed by processing in a ball mill, rubbing the clay between small porcelain spheres, separating them into thin platelets.

Deliquescence

The process that occurs when the vapour pressure of the saturated aqueous solution of a substance is less than the vapour pressure of water in the ambient air. When water vapour is collected by the pure solid compound, a mixture of the solid and liquid, or an aqueous solution of the compound forms until the substance is dissolved and is in equilibrium with its environment; at this time the vapour pressure of water over the aqueous solution will equal the partial pressure of water in the atmosphere in contact with it.

Delocalisation

A quantum mechanical concept most usually applied in organic chemistry to describe the pi bonding in a conjugated system. This bonding is not localized between two atoms: instead, each link has a "fractional double bond character" or bond order. There is a corresponding "delocalization energy", identifiable with the stabilization of the system compared with a hypothetical alternative in which formal (localized) single and double bonds are present. Some degree of delocalization is always present and can be estimated by quantum mechanical calculations. The effects are particularly evident in aromatic systems and in symmetrical molecular entities in which a lone pair of electrons or a vacant p-orbital is conjugated with a double bond (e.g. carboxylate ions, nitro compounds, enamines, the allyl cation). Delocalization in such species may be represented by partial bonds or as resonance (here symbolized by a two-headed arrow) between contributing structures.

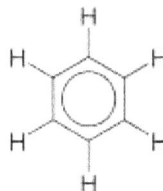

Demister

Apparatus made of wire mesh or glass fibre which is used to help remove acid mist as in the manufacture of sulphuric acid. Demisters are also components of wet arrestment plants.

Denature

When the structure of proteins beak down from exposure to heat.

Dendrimer

A polymer having a regular branched structure. If suitably functionalized (such as the benzyl alcohol-substituted it may be used as a soluble support, in which case the desired, dendrimer-supported, material may be isolated by size-exclusion chromatography. Dendrimers may also be attached to a polymer and used as a solid support, with significantly increased loading over the initial resin.

Dendritic habit

A dendritic habit describes the shape of a large group of crystals that looks like the branching of veins or a plant.

Denitrification

A step in the earth's nitrogen cycle which involves the reduction of nitrates (oxidized N) into nitrite, nitrous oxide, ammonia or elemental nitrogen (more reduced N), that is, the conversion of species most often in the liquid or solid phase to chemical species most commonly gaseous. It is carried out by certain forms of denitrifying bacteria in the soil and serves as an important part of the breakdown of dead organisms and the ultimate source of most of the N_2 in the atmosphere. It is also responsible for the loss of much of the soil's natural nitrogen and that of synthetic fertilizers.

Dense

A compact substance or a substance with a high density.

Density

The mass per unit volume of a gas, liquid, or solid under specified conditions (temperature, pressure, etc.).

Density, number

The number of atoms, molecules or aerosol particles per unit volume of gas (commonly in units of molecules cm^{-3}).

Denuder system (tube or assembly)

An apparatus used to separate gases and aerosols (over a given diameter) which is based upon the difference in diffusion velocity between gases and aerosol particles. Usually a tube containing a selective internal wall coating which removes the gaseous compounds at the wall.

Deodorizer

Equipment for the removal of noxious gases and odors, which may consist of combustion, absorption, or adsorption units; see emission control equipment.

Deposition

Deposition is normally considered to be one of two types: dry deposition is the process by which aerosols and gases in the air are deposited on the surface of the earth (soil, water, rock, plants, etc.); this is termed "dry" deposition even when the receptor surface is moist. Wet deposition is that process which involves the transport of chemicals to the surface of the earth by water droplets or snow crystals which scavenge pollutants as they form and fall through the atmosphere.

Deposition velocity

The ratio of flux density (often given in units of $g\ cm^{-2}\ s^{-1}$) of a substance at a sink surface to its concentration in the atmosphere (corresponding units of g cm^{-3}). While the units of this ratio are clearly those of velocity (in this case $cm\ s^{-1}$), the ratio is not a flow velocity in the normal sense of the word.

Deposits
Accumulations of material, coming from the water or suspended particles, onto wetted surfaces within a paper machine system.

Derivative
A chemical product that is formed by modification of a base material, as in the case of cationic starch made from natural starch.

Descriptor
Numerical representation of a molecular property, including bulk properties (e.g. log P, molecular weight), two-dimensional (2-D) features (atom connectivity's) or three-dimensional (3-D) features (molecular shape). A complete set of descriptors comprises a fingerprint.

Desertification
Simply the change of useful land into a desert environment as cause by natural and/or anthropogenic causes. Factors effecting desertification include droughts; land use, such as grazing and crop use; and climate variations. Desertification influences atmospheric chemistry because the humidity and biospheric gas emissions from the modified biome are also changed by this process.

Desiccant
A desiccant goes through a process of deliquescence to dry an area or volume of air. Desiccants are often found in small packs when humidity needs to be decreased.

Desorption
The removal of a substance from a surface on which it has become absorbed. Desorption is accelerated by heating and exposure of the surface to a low pressure (or vacuum). GB: The converse of adsorption, i.e. the decrease in the amount of adsorbed substance.

Desulphurisation
The process by which sulphur is removed from a material such as coal or oil. It may involve one of many techniques including elutriation, froth flotation, laundering, magnetic separation, chemical treatment, etc.

Detachment
The reverse of an attachment.

Detackifier
A mineral (e.g. talc) or polymer having the ability to adsorb onto tacky materials and reduce their tendency to adhere.

Detection
The process of establishing the presence of air pollutants by means of specific instrumentation and sampling.

Detection limit (threshold)
The minimum concentration of substance which produces an observable response.

Detection limit, lower
The minimum concentration of a compound in an air sample which can be determined by an analytical method with a given statistical probability. Usually the lower detection limit is defined as three-times the standard deviation of the noise of an analytical method under the assumption that its distribution is Gaussian.

Detection limit, relative
Smallest amount of material detectable (with 99.7% probability) in a matrix relative to the amount of material analysed - given in atomic, mole or weight fractions.

Detector
An instrument or part of an instrument which indicates the presence of air quality characteristic by means of some specific spectroscopic or chemical property of the pollutant.

Dew point
The temperature at which air is cooled enough to reach its saturation point (100% humidity) for a given volume of water vapour in the air. If the air cooling occurs because of adiabatic expansion, clouds are formed; if it is due to contact of the air with a colder object, condensation (known as dew) is formed on the object; and if it is due to mixing of a warmer, moist air parcel with a cooler, dry parcel, fogs and condensation trails are created. Unlike humidity, the dewpoint is not based upon the temperature or pressure of the air, but solely upon the water vapour content.

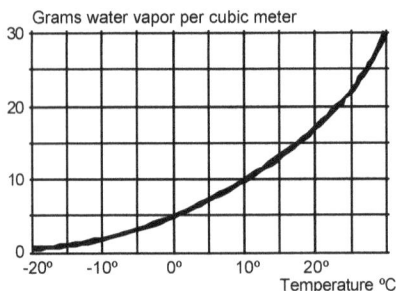

Grams water vapor per cubic meter

Temperature ºC

Diamagnetic
Substances having a negative magnetic susceptibility are diamagnetic. They are repelled out of a magnetic field.

Diameter, equivalent
The diameter of a spherical particle which will give identical geometric, optical, electrical or aerodynamic behaviour to that of the particle (non-spherical) being examined; sometimes referred to as the Stokes

diameter for particles in non-turbulent flows.

Diastereoisomerism
Stereoisomerism other than enantiomerism. Diastereoisomers (or diastereomers) are stereoisomers not related as mirror images. Diastereoisomers are characterized by differences in physical properties, and by some differences in chemical behaviour toward achiral as well as chiral reagents.

Diastereomers
Two or more isomers of a molecule which are not enantiomers of one another.

Diatomic
molecules consisting of two atoms. The seven diatomic molecules are H, N_2, O_2, F_2, Cl_2, Br_2, I_2

Dibromotetrafluoroethane
A chemical also known as Halon-2402 which has the chemical formula $C_2F_4Br_2$. It is a known ozone depleting chemical and is listed as a Class I ozone depleting chemical in the United States Clean Air Act amendments of 1990. It is commonly used as a fire extinguishing agent. The reason it has so much ozone depleting potential is because it contains bromine, which has many times the ozone depleting potential of chlorine.

Dichlorodifluoromethane
CCl_2F_2, This compound, also known as Freon® 12 or CFC-12, is the primary CFC that has been linked to the catalytic destruction of ozone. Even though the compound is found in very small concentrations, its properties make it a significant factor in stratospheric chemistry. CCl_2F_2 absorbs UV light in the upper

stratosphere where it arrives decades after being released in the troposphere. CFCs, which were originally created by Dupont corporation, were used as refrigerants for everything from air conditioning to home refrigerators because they are non-toxic and extremely unreactive (in the troposphere). It is this unreactivity that makes them such a problem for the atmosphere, because they are able to last long enough to make it to the stratosphere, where they cause so many problems. CCl_2F_2 production, along with all CFCs, has been banned since the mid 1990s, but some scientists believe that the damage has already been done.

Dichloromethane

CH_2Cl_2, a clear, colourless organic solvent that has a sweet but mild odor and does not occur naturally in the environment. Its principle use is as a solvent in paint removers and as an aerosol propellant in paints and automotive spray products. In addition, it is used as a blowing and cleaning agent of metal, as a solvent in the production of polycarbonate resins, and in film processing, as well as many other industrial applications. In the food industry, it is used as an extraction solvent for caffeine, spices, and hops. All of these applications result in the release of dichloromethane into the environment, with the primary sources being the industries that manufacture the chemical or use it in production, such as the plastic and synthetics manufacturers, as well as the electronics industry.

Dielectric constant

A measure for the effect of a medium on the potential energy of interaction between two charges. It is measured by comparing the capacity of a capacitor with and without the sample present.

Dienes

Dienes are unsaturated organic compounds that contain two fixed double bonds between carbon atoms. Dienes in which the two double-bond units are linked by one single bond are termed conjugated.

Dienophile

The olefin component of a Diels-Alder reaction.

Diethyl ether (ethoxy ethane)

A colourless liquid that was first used in 1842 as an anesthetic in surgeries by inhalation. This liquid is highly flammable and has volatile properties. It is commonly referred to simple as ether. Ethoxy ethane is prone to peroxide formation, and can form explosive diethyl ether peroxide, especially in old storage vessels. Ether peroxides are higher boiling and are contact explosives when dry. Symptoms of severe exposure may include coughing, chest pains, difficulty in breathing, nausea, headache, vomiting, or death. Formula $(C_2H_5)_2O$

Diffraction

A modification which light (or electron, neutron beams, etc.) undergoes in passing by the edges of opaque bodies or through narrow slits or in being reflected from ruled surfaces (or crystalline materials). The light waves, owing to their wave-like nature appear to be deflected and produce fringes of parallel light and dark bands corresponding to regions of constructive reinforcement or destructive interference, respectively, of the waves.

Diffraction analysis

The application of diffraction techniques (X-rays, electrons, neutrons) which are sometimes used to identify the presence of certain solid aerosols and dust particles through the characteristic diffraction patterns which result from each unique crystal structure.

Diffuser

A porous plate or tube, commonly made of carborundum, alundum, or silica sand, through which air is forced and divided into minute bubbles for diffusion in liquids.

Diffusion

The spreading or scattering of a gaseous or liquid material. Eddy diffusion in the atmosphere is the process of transport of gases due to turbulent mixing in the presence of a composition gradient. Molecular diffusion is the net transport of molecules which results from their molecular motions alone in the absence of turbulent mixing; it occurs when the concentration gradient of a particular gas in a mixture differs from its equilibrium value.

Diffusion battery

An aerosol sizing instrument for particles with diameters below 0.2m. The fractionation is based on different diffusivities of the small particles and their deposition on the walls of the long parallel or circular channels, formed by equally spaced plates, bundles of small bore parallel tubes or sets of stainless wire screens.

Diffusion-controlled rate

See encounter-controlled rate, microscopic diffusion control.

Diluent gas

A gas of known quality introduced for analytical purposes so that it quantitatively lowers the concentration of the components of a gaseous

sample; this may also be the complimentary gas.

Dilute

A solution containing a small amount of solute

Dilute solution

A solution (liquid mixture) that has a small amount of solute dissolved. As you add more water to a sugar solution the solution, becomes more and more dilute.

Dilution

Dilution occurs when a solution with a known concentration (standard solution) has more solvent added. As the solvent is added, the molarity may change, but the number of equivalents will not.

Dimension analysis

A problem solving technique that uses the units that are part of a measurement to help solve a problem. Also called factor analysis or unit analysis

Dimethyl sulphide

CH_3SCH_3, released by bacteria on the continents and in the oceans. Oxidized in the marine atmosphere to partially form cloud condensation nuclei and this may effect the formation of clouds over the oceans.

Dinitrogen pentoxide

N_2O_5, a compound that contributes to ozone depletion during springtime in the Antarctic. This occurs because ozone converts some nitrogen dioxide radical to nitrogen trioxide radical, which combines with other dinitrogen radicals to produce dinitrogen pentoxide. The reaction is reversible except in the presents of stratospheric liquid droplets where nitric acid occurs. This reaction ties up the nitrogen dioxide radical allowing more chlorine atoms to be present in the active form.

Dioxins

Family of 75 different toxic chlorinated hydrocarbons formed as by-products in chemical reactions involving chlorine and hydrocarbons, usually at high temperatures. The "premier" and probably most toxic member of the dioxin family is 2, 3, 7, 8-Tetrachlorodibenzo-p-dioxin. Though these compounds have relatively low vapour pressures and poor solubility in water, they cycle from aquatic environments—where they have been deposited from waste incineration, wood burning, pulp bleaching, smelting, etc.

Dip

De-inked pulp, wastepaper from which ink has been floated, screened, or washed.

Dipolar aprotic solvent

A solvent with a comparatively high relative permittivity (or dielectric constant), greater than ca. 15, and a sizable permanent dipole moment, that cannot donate suitably labile hydrogen atoms to form strong hydrogen bonds, e.g. dimethyl sulfoxide. The term (and its alternative "polar aprotic solvent") is a misnomer and is therefore discouraged. Such solvents are usually not aprotic, but protophilic (and at most weakly protogenic). In describing a solvent it is better to be explicit about its essential properties, e.g. dipolar and non-protogenic.

Dipolar bond

A bond formed (actually or conceptually) by coordination of two neutral moieties, the combination of which results in charge-separated structures, e.g., R_3N: + O R_3N^+-O^- The term is preferred to the obsolescent synonyms "coordinate

link", "co-ordinate covalence", "dative bond", "semipolar bond".

Dipole-dipole forces

Intermolecular forces that exist between polar molecules. Active only when the molecules are close together. The strengths of intermolecular attractions increase when polarity increases.

Direct dyes

Dye molecules that are sufficiently large and planar that they tend to remain on a fiber surface without need of a fixative.

Directed library

Library which uses a limited number of building blocks chosen on the basis of pre-existing information or hypothesis which defines the type of functionalities deemed important to obtain a particular activity.

Directed sorting

Technique for organizing a mixture of solid-supported samples by identifying each particle (for instance, on the basis of its shape, marking or by reading a radiofrequency code) and transferring it to an appropriate position in an array.

Directionality

Dependency of a given paper property on the orientation of the sample, especially in relation to the direction of manufacture (machine direction).

Dirt

Visible blemishes, different in colour from the paper, especially when they are dark and numerous.

Disaccharide

A carbohydrate that is made up of two monosaccharides. Chemical formula $C_{12}H_{22}O_{11}$

Discomfort threshold

The lowest value (e.g., concentration of an impurity, etc.) at which a sensation of discomfort is perceived; a measure which varies from person to person.

Dispersants

Substances such as phosphates or acrylates that cause finely divided particles to come apart and remain separate from each other in suspension.

Dispersed rosin size

Rosin or fortified rosin acid that has been emulsified at high temperature and cooled.

Dispersion

The dilution of a pollutant by spreading in the atmosphere due to diffusion or turbulent action (eddy diffusion).

Dispersion forces (also called London dispersion forces)

Dispersion is an intermolecular attraction force that exists between all molecules. These forces are the result of the movement of electrons which cause slight polar moments. Dispersion forces are generally very weak but as the molecular mass increases so does their strength.

Disproportionation

A reaction in which an element is oxidized and reduced. This is how stable molecules are made from radicals.

Dissociation

Process in which large chemical species break down into smaller, usually charged subunits, like a molecule breaking down into the ions that form it.

Dissolution

The transfer of gas to the surface of a water droplet from the bulk atmosphere, and the gas mixing within the droplet.

Dissolved air

Molecules of nitrogen, oxygen, CO_2, and other gases that are part of the liquid phase.

Dissolving

The separation of the particles of a solid by a liquid.

Distillation

Distillation is a process in which one substance is boiled away from another and then collected. It is a process that purifies mixtures and solutions. Scientists often use lab equipment such as a distillation flask and a condenser. The boiled off vapour is cooled and "condensed".

Distilled water

Distilled water is pure water. Tap water contains all sorts of impurities. When all of those impurities are removed, you have distilled water. You can get it by boiling water and collecting the steam.

Distomer

A distomer is the enantiomer of a chiral compound that is the less potent for a particular action. This definition does not excude the possibility of other effect or side effect of the distomer.

Distributivity

A math property which states:
$$A*(B + C) = (A*B) + (A*C).$$

Disulphide bond

Covalent disulfide bonds form during the tertiary structure of protein synthesis. It involves two sulphur atoms bonded to cysteine amino acids in the polypeptide chains.

Diurnal ozone concentration

The ozone concentration in the troposphere is directly related to the pollutants that are in the air and the time of day. For example, during the early hours of the day many pollutants are released into the air. As the day progresses, the sun becomes more overhead and the concentration of the sunlight increases.

Diurnal variation

Indicates variations which follow a distinctive pattern which recurs with a daily cycle.

Diversity

The "unrelatednes" of a set of, for example, building blocks or members of a combinatorial library, as measured by their properties, such as atom connectivity, physical properties, computational measurements or bioactivity.

Diversity reagent

One of a set of reagents which introduces diversity into the library products, as opposed to one which results in an identical conversion for each member of the library. Similar to building block but may be useful to distinguish from other (i.e. "non-diversity") reagents.

Dobson units

Measurement unit for determining the total amount of ozone present in a vertical column of air above the surface of the earth. An air layer at atmospheric pressure of 10^{13} hPa and temperature of 298 K which measures 1 mm in thickness and is equivalent to 100 dobson units.

Docking studies

Docking studies are molecular modeling studies aiming at finding a proper fit between a ligand and its binding site.

Dodecahedral crystal

A crystal that has twelve sides. A twelve-sided object is called a dodecahedron.

Doldrums

Calm, light winds, or squalls lying along the length of the equator. Winds which are part of the general circulation of the atmosphere, which are driven by the input of solar energy and modified by the rotation of the Earth. It is here that 17th and 18th century sailing ships had the most trouble making way and lack of fresh water or food sometimes spelled disaster.

Dosage

As applied to an air pollutant in an exposure chamber, dosage is commonly defined as the concentration of the pollutant times the duration of exposure.

Double bonds

When two atoms participate in a Covalent Bond and share two electrons with each other, the Covalent Bond formed is referred to as a Double Covalent Bond or just Double Bond. A common example of an organic compound containing a double bond is ethylene ($H_2C{=}CH_2$).

Double prodrug (or pro-prodrug)

A double prodrug is a biologically inactive molecule which is transformed in vivo in two steps (enzymatically and/or chemically) to the active species.

Double replacement

A chemical reaction where two compounds are mixed and they exchange parts of their compounds with each other. Think about the mixing of an acid and a base. You start with an acid and base and finish with water and a salt.

Double-blind study

A double-blind study is a clinical study of potential and marketed drugs, where neither the investigators nor the subjects know which subjects will be treated with the active principle and which ones will receive a placebo.

Downfield

A term used to describe the left direction on NMR charts. A peak to the left of another peak is described as being downfield from the peak.

Downwash

As applied to the action of chimney gases, it is the downward motion of the chimney gases brought on by eddies which form in the lee of a chimney when the wind is blowing. It may result in bringing the flue gases to the ground prematurely.

Drainage

The ease with which water is released from among fibers during the formation of paper.

Droplet

A small liquid particle. The size of droplets encountered in the atmosphere extends over a wide range; e.g., liquid aerosol solutions which make up the fine particle fraction of continental tropospheric aerosol are usually <2 m in diameter. Cloud water droplets usually have diameters in the range of 5 to 70m, while rain droplets commonly have diameters ranging from 0.1 to 3 mm.

Droughts

Extensive periods of time where a region suffers from lack of rain, causing dehydration for animals and plants, often resulting in crop failure. Sequential droughts during the 1930s in the United States were extremely damaging to the Great Plains, made worse by poor land management practices.

Drug

A drug is any substance presented for treating, curing or preventing disease in human beings or in animals. A drug may also be used for making a medical diagnosis or for restoring, correcting, or modifying physiological functions (e.g., the contraceptive pill).

Drug disposition

Drug disposition refers to all processes involved in the absorption, distribution metabolism and excretion of drugs in a living organism.

Drug latentiation

Drug latentiation is the chemical modification of a biologically active compound to form a new compound, which in vivo will liberate the parent compound. Drug latentiation is synonymous with prodrug design.

Drug targeting

Drug targeting is a strategy aiming at the delivery of a compound to a particular tissue of the body.

Dry adiabatic lapse rate

Rate at which unsaturated air cools as it travels vertically, provided that all temperature change is adiabatic (without heat exchange), and no condensation occurs. In dry air it can be approximated as 9.8 degrees Celsius per km of rise. It can be used as a basis of comparison for actual temperature profiles of air and can help predict smoke stack gas dispersion characteristics. Contrast with saturated adiabatic lapse rate which is something less than 9.8 degrees/km of rise because of the release of heat at the air packet cools and water vapour condenses.

Dry bulb temperature
In psychrometry, the temperature of the gas measured by a dry bulb thermometer; see psychrometry.

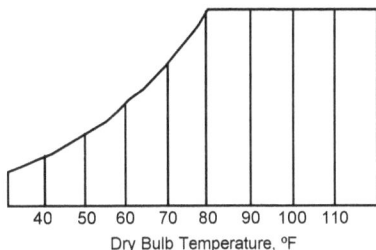

Dry Bulb Temperature, °F

Dry deposition
The transfer of trace species (gases or particles) from the atmosphere to surfaces as a consequence of molecular diffusion, brownian diffusion, or gravitation settling, in the absence of active precipitation. The term refers to the transfer process and not to the surface themselves, which may be moist.

Dry strength
The force or energy required to break a paper sample, by one of various procedures, after equilibration in a standard atmosphere.

Dual action drug
A dual action drug is a compound which combines two desired different pharmacological actions at a similarly efficacious dose.

Dubnium
Symbol: "Db" Atomic Number: "105" Atomic Mass: (262)amu Dubnium is one of several postactinide elements.

Scientists have created these in labs and may have only found a few atoms of the element. You will not find these in use anywhere.

Ductile
Able to be drawn out into a thin wire.

Dust
Small, dry, solid particles projected into the air by natural forces, such as wind, volcanic eruption, and by mechanical or manmade processes such as crushing grinding milling, drilling, demolition, shovelling, conveying, screening, bagging, and sweeping. Dust particles are usually in the size range from about 1 to 100m in diameter, and they settle slowly under the influence of gravity.

Dust collector
A device for monitoring dust emissions. Also the equipment used to remove and collect dust from process exhaust gases; this may employ simply sedimentation (dustfall jars, coated slides, papers, etc.), inertial separation (cyclones, impactors, impingers, etc.), precipitation (thermal and electrostatic) or filtration.

Dust fall
Solid particles in the air which fall to the ground under the influence of gravity.

Dye
Dyes are substances used to impart colour to textiles, leather, paper, etc. Compounds used for dyeing are generally organic compounds containing conjugated double bonds. In practice dyes are classified according to the way in which the dye is applied or is held on the substrate.

Dynamic library
Collection of compounds in dynamic equilibrium. If the composition of the

library is altered, for instance by the presence of a receptor which selectively binds certain library members, then shifting of the equilibrium will lead to an increase in the amount of those components which bind to the target with relatively high affinity.

Dynamic range of an analyser

The ratio between the maximum usable indication and the minimum usable indication (detection limit). A distinction may be made between the linear dynamic range, where the response is directly proportional to concentration, and the dynamic range where the response may be non-linear, especially at higher concentrations.

Dyotropic rearrangement

An uncatalyzed process in which two sigma bonds simultaneously migrate intramolecularly.

Dysprosium

Symbol: "Dy" Atomic Number: "66" Atomic Mass: 162.50amu. Dysprosium is one of the elements in the lanthanide series of inner transition elements. It may also be classified as a rare earth element. You may find this element in lasers, many alloys, and even nuclear reactors.

E

Ebs

Ethylene-bis-stearamide, a common component of pulp mill defoamers that often is found in deposits in paper machine systems.

Ecology

Branch of biology which focuses on the relationships among various species and among the species and their environments. The basic units for study are the species (all the organisms which are capable of interbreeding), population (all of the members of a species occupying a certain geographical area) and community (number of populations interacting within a certain area).

Eddy

In turbulent fluid motion, a blob of the fluid that has some definitive character and moves in some way differently from the main now.

Eddy diffusion

The exchange of gaseous components of the atmosphere in a turbulent flow by rapid mixing of fluid eddies.

Eddy dispersion (diffusion)

The process by which substances are mixed in the atmosphere or in any fluid system due to eddy motion.

Eductor

A liquid pump for mixing air with water which operates under a jet principle using the liquid under pressure as the operating medium.

Effective charge

Change in effective charge is a quantity obtained by comparison of the polar effect of substituents on the free energies of rate or equilibrium processes with that on a standard ionization equilibrium. Provided the effective charge on the states in the standard equilibrium are defined, then it is possible to measure effective charges for states in the reaction or equilibrium under consideration.

Effective molarity (or effective concentration)

The ratio of the first-order rate constant of an intramolecular reaction involving two functional groups within the same molecular entity to the second-order rate constant of an analogous intermolecular elementary reaction. This ratio has the dimension of concentration. The term can also apply to an equilibrium constant.

Efficacy

Efficacy describes the relative intensity with which agonists vary in the response they produce even when they occupy the same number of receptors and with the same affinity. Efficacy is not synonymous to Intrinsic activity.

Efflorescence

The reverse of deliquescence the drying of a salt solution when the vapour pressure of water in the saturated solution of a substance is greater than the partial pressure of water in the ambient air. Also refers to the loss of water of crystallization from a solid salt such as $Na_2CO_3 \cdot 10H_2O$.

Effluent

Any spent liquors or other waste material which are emitted by a source (waste from plating shops, pickling tanks, sewage treatment plants, chemical manufacturing plants, etc.).

Effusion

The movement of gas molecules through an opening that has relatively large holes.

E-folding lifetime

The time required for the concentration of a gas to decrease by 1/e of its original concentration due to a chemical reaction or other sink.

Eighteen-electron rule

An electron-counting rule to which an overwhelming majority of stable diamagnetic transition metal complexes adhere. The number of nonbonded electrons at the metal plus the number of electrons in the metal-ligand bonds should be 18. The 18 electron rule in transition metal chemistry is a full analogue of the "Lewis octet rule".

Einsteinium

Symbol: "Es" Atomic Number: "99" Atomic Mass: (252)amu. Einsteinium is one of the elements in the actinide series of inner transition elements. It may also be classified as a rare earth element. It is a radioactive and unstable element and you will not find it in use anywhere. It was named after the physicist Albert Einstein.

99: Einsteinium   2,8,18,32, 29,8,2

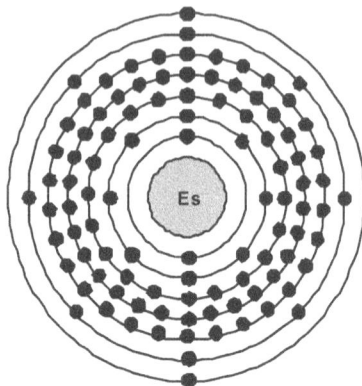

El nino

A condition caused by the decrease in atmospheric pressure over the Eastern Pacific Ocean, weakening the prevailing westerly winds and resulting in warm waters and less nutrient replacement from cold, deeper waters into the Eastern Pacific along the coast of South America.

El nino-southern oscillation (enso)

The relationship of the El Nino conditions and the Southern Oscillation pattern (The Walker Circulation). A high pressure over the Pacific Ocean and low pressure over the East Indies causes heavy rainfall across the Pacific, rise in the sea level and increased surface temperatures.

Elastic

Elastic describes a property of rebound. You may have heard of the elasticity of a rubber band. Rubber bands can stretch and return to their original shape. Elasticity of a collision describes how much energy is lost when an object hits. A very elastic surface absorbs little energy and the object will bounce off. A non-elastic

surface absorbs a lot of energy and the objects involved in the collision lose energy.

Electrical conductivity

A measure of the amount of electricity that can flow through a substance.

Electrochemical cell

An apparatus that uses a spontaneous redox chemical reaction to produce electrical energy.

Electrochemical methods of detection (analysis)

Methods in which either current or potential is measured during an electrochemical reaction. The gas or liquid containing the trace impurity to be analysed is sent through an electrochemical cell containing a liquid or solid electrolyte and in which an electrochemical reaction specific to the impurity takes place.

Electrochemical methods, amperometric detection

The current is proportional to the concentration of the species generating the current.

Electrochemical methods, coulometric detection

The current is directly proportional to the flow rate of the substance involved in the electrochemical reaction, and the amount of charge which flows is proportional to the amount of substances taking part in the reaction.

Electrochemical methods, potentiometric detection

The potential of a cell is related to the concentration (activity) of a reactant which is a component of the cell fluid.

Electrochemistry

The branch of chemistry that deals with the relation of the flow of electric current to chemical changes and with the conversion between chemical and electrical energy.

Electrodes

Device that moves electrons into or out of a solution by conduction.

Electrolysis

A method of using electricity to break chemical bonds or cause electron exchange. An electric current passes through an electrolyte causing ions to move toward the electrodes. The positively charged electrode, called the anode, attracts anions and causes them to be oxidized. The negative electrode is called the cathode. It attracts cations which are then reduced. The electrical energy applied to the ionic solution causes a non-spontaneous process to become spontaneous. Electrolysis of water produces molecular hydrogen and molecular oxygen.

Electrolytes

Molecules that develop a charge when placed in solution (ions).

Electrolytic cell

An apparatus that uses electrical energy to cause a nonspontaneous chemical reaction to occur.

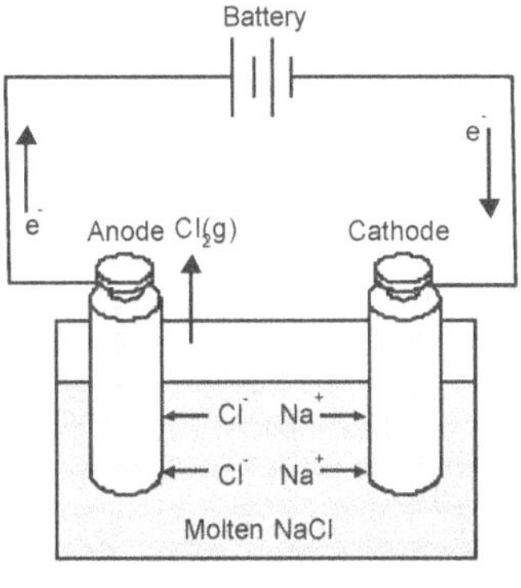

Electrolytic Cell

Electromagnetic spectrum

Complete range of wavelengths which light can have. These include infrared, ultraviolet, and all other types of electromagnetic radiation, as well as visible light.

Electromagnetic wave

A phenomenon that can carry energy through space and is created by the vibration of an electrical charge, which is caused by disturbances in electromagnetic fields. Examples of electromagnetic waves include infrared, visible, microwaves, and x-rays. Forms of electromagnetic waves that can be seen by humans we call light.

Electromotive force (emf)

the voltage difference between two electrodes in an electrochemical cell.

Electron

A negatively charged sub-atomic particle which orbits the nucleus of an atom. The outer electrons are involved in chemical reactions and form chemical bonds with other atoms.

Electron attachment

The transfer of an electron to a molecular entity, resulting in a molecular entity of (algebraically) increased negative charge. (It is not an attachment, as defined in this Glossary.)

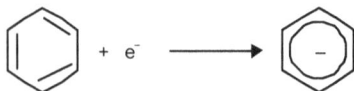

Electron capture detector

One of the most sensitive gas chromatographic detector for halogen-containing compounds like chlorofluorocarbons. James Lovelock's early work with this detector led to the discovery that anthropogenic chlorofluorocarbons used most heavily in the Northern hemisphere were very long-lived and therefore well-mixed throughout the troposphere.

Electron charge

The negative electric charge which appears on the electron or univalent ions [1.602×10^{-19} coulombs or 4.803×10^{-10} electrostatic units (esu)].

Electron configuration

The arrangement of electrons in an atom or molecule.

Electron dot diagram

A diagram that uses dots to represent an element's valence electrons.

Electron geometry

Structure of a compound based on the arrangement of its electrons.

Electron redistribution

Redistribution occurs when electrons in a chemical bond are given up, received, or shared by two or more atoms. The concept accepts that electrons will move around the nuclei of several atoms in a chemical bond.

Electron shell

The orbit followed by electrons around an atomic nucleus. The atom has a number of shells and they are normally labelled K, L, M, N, O, P, and Q.

Electron-deficient bond

A single bond between adjacent atoms that is formed by less than two electrons, as in B_2H_6:

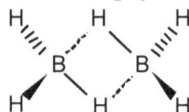

The B-H-B bonds are called a "two-electron three-centre bonds".

Electronegativity

The ability of an atom to attract electrons towards itself in a covalent bond.

Electroorganic reaction

Electroorganic reaction is an organic reaction produced in an electrolytic cell. Electroorganic reactions are used to synthesise compounds that are difficult to produce by conventional techniques. An example of an electroorganic reaction is Kolbe's method of synthesising alkanes.

Electrophile

Literally, electron lover. A positively or neutrally charged reagent that forms bonds by accepting electrons from a nucleophile. Elecrophiles are Lewis Acids.

Electrophoretic mobility

The ratio of velocity to field strength when charged particles in suspension are placed in a known electric field.

Electroplating

A process in which electrolysis is used as a means of coating an object with a layer (plate) of metal.

Electrostatic filter

Filters for which an electrostatic charge is applied to the filter element. A fibrous filter material is often pleated in between V-shaped supports consisting of electrostatically charged, metal rods which are insulated from the supporting frame.

Electrostatic forces

Forces between charged objects.

Electrostatic precipitator

A device which separates particles from a gas stream by passing the carrier gas between pairs of electrodes across which a unidirectional, high-voltage potential is placed. The particles are charged before passing through the field and migrate to an oppositely charged electrode.

Electrovalence

Electrovalence is the ability of an element to bond with other elements by giving or receiving an electron. This state of valence can be positive (positive ions) or negative (negative ions). The created bonds are called electrovalent or ionic bonds. Many salts ($NaCl$) have electrovalent bonds.

Electrovalent bond

A chemical bond that occurs between two atoms when one or more electrons are passed from one atom to another. When they exchange electrons, each of the atoms should have a filled shell. A good example of an ionic bond is the sodium chloride bond. You may also hear the term ionic bond.

Na: 1 Valence e : Cl: 7 Valence e

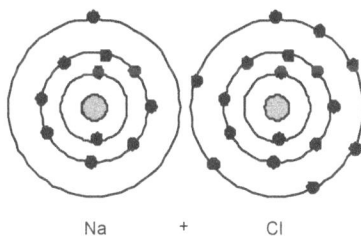

Na   +   Cl

Electro Valent Bond

Element

A pure substance composed of atoms with the same number of protons. Elements may be composed of various isotopes. eg. The element carbon is composed of 98.9% of carbon-12, 1.1 % of carbon-13 and a trace amount of carbon-14. All isotopes of carbon have 6 protons.

Element effect

The ratio of the rate constants of two reactions that differ only in the identity of the element of the atom in the leaving group, e.g., k_{Br}/k_{Cl}. As for isotope effects, a ratio of unity is regarded as a "null effect".

Elementary reaction

A reaction for which no reaction intermediates have been detected or need to be postulated in order to describe the chemical reaction on a molecular scale. An elementary reaction is assumed to occur in a single step and to pass through a single transition state.

Elimination

Elimination is the process achieving the reduction of of the concentration of a xenobiotic including its metabolism.

Elimination reaction

A reaction where atoms and/or functional groups are removed from a reactant.

Elliptic

An object having the shape of an ellipse: a squashed or elongated circle. The sun follows an elliptic path across the sky.

Eluate

The effluent from a chromatographic bed emerging when elution is carried out.

Elute

To remove sorbed materials from a sorbent by means of a fluid called the eluent. To chromatograph by elution chromatography. This term is preferred to the term develop, which has been used in paper chromatography and in thin-layer chromatography. The process of elution may continue until the components have left the chromatographic bed.

Elutriation

The process of separating the lighter particles of a powder from the heavier ones by means of an upward directed stream of fluid (gas or liquid).

Emission

The total rate at which a solid, liquid, or gaseous pollutant is emitted into the atmosphere from a given source; usually expressed as mass per unit time. Primary emissions are those substances which are emitted directly to the atmosphere (e.g., NO, SO_2, etc.), while secondary emissions are formed from the primary emissions through thermal or photochemical reactions (e.g., ozone, aldehydes, ketones, sulphuric acid, nitric acid, etc.). The point or area from which the discharge takes place is called the source; the area in which the emission or its transformed products (e.g., in the case of aerosols, acidic deposition, etc.) may be deposited is called the receptor area or sink. Emission may be applied to noise, heat, etc., as well as pollutants.

Emission control equipment

Air pollution control equipment which either converts the pollutant chemically to a non-polluting substance or collects the pollutant by some means including gravity settling chambers, inertial separators, cyclonic separators, filters, electrical precipitators, scrubbers, (spray towers, jet scrubbers, Venturi scrubbers, inertial scrubbers, mechanical scrubbers and packed scrubbers).

Emission flux

The emission per unit area of the appropriate surface of an emitting source.

Emission inventory

A systematic collection of information concerning the air pollution emissions in a given area. Usually the types of sources (power plants, refineries, etc.) and the height at which the discharge takes place as well as the source contribution (composition and rate of discharge) are summarized. The variation of these emissions with time of day, and month of the year are desired information in inventories as well.

Emission source

Several types of emission sources exist: Point sources of emission include: power plants, incinerators, refineries, steel mills, chemical plants, etc. Often the emissions for these sources are released from elevated stacks. Mobile sources of emission include: automobiles, trucks, buses, ships, airplanes, etc.

Emissivity

The efficiency of a body's ability to absorb and reemit radiation compared to the emissivity of a blackbody at the same temperature. Emissivity ranges from 0 to 1, with one being a blackbody and less than 1 for all other materials. All bodies with a temperature above 0 K emit radiation.

Empirical formula

the formula showing the simplest ratio in which atoms combine to form a compound.

Emulsion

A mixture containing two liquids that cannot mix, one being dispersed throughout the another as very small droplets. eg. oil, water and detergent. The appearance is opaque(cloudy) as light is scattered.

Enantiomer

One of a pair of molecular entities which are mirror images of each other and non-superimposable.

Encoding

Strategy for pool/split synthesis whereby a surrogate analyte is associated with each member of a combinatorial library. This is often achieved by the use of tags attached to the particle of solid support on which the library members are assembled. This allows the determination of the reaction history of an individual particle.

Encounter complex

A complex of molecular entities produced at an encounter-controlled rate, and which occurs as an intermediate in a reaction mechanism. When the complex is formed from two molecular entities it is called an "encounter pair". A distinction between encounter pairs and (larger) encounter complexes may be relevant in some cases, e.g. for mechanisms involving pre-association.

Encounter-controlled rate

A rate of reaction corresponding to the rate of encounter of the reacting molecular entities. This is also known as "diffusion-controlled rate" since rates of encounter are themselves controlled by diffusion rates (which in turn depend on the viscosity of the *medium* and the dimensions of the reactant molecular entities).

End point

the point in a titration at which an indicator shows that neutralization has be reached, when $[H^+] = [OH^-]$.

Endergonic

In an endergonic process, work is done on the system, and $G^0 > 0$, so the process is nonspontaneous. An exergonic process is the opposite: $G^0 < 0$, so the process is spontaneous.

Endothermic

A chemical reaction in which a greater amount of energy is required to break the existing bonds in the reactants than is released when the new bonds form in the product molecules. Energy appears as a reactant in the chemical equation.

Ene reaction

The addition of a compound with a double bond having an allylic hydrogen (the "ene") to a compound with a multiple bond (the "enophile") with transfer of the allylic hydrogen and a concomitant reorganization of the bonding, as illustrated below for propene (the "ene") and ethene (the "enophile"). The reverse is a "retro-ene" reaction.

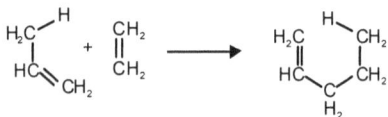

Energy

The ability of a system to do work. Some forms of energy include kinetic (motion), potential (location), thermal (heat), gravitational, and electrical. In chemistry, energy is required to form and break bonds of molecules. Common units of energy are the calorie and joule. According to the Law of Conservation of Energy, energy can neither be created nor destroyed, only transformed.

Energy level

The current level of energy an electron has within an atom.

Enforced concerted mechanism

Variation of reaction parameters in a series of reactions proceeding in non-concerted steps may lead to a situation, where the putative intermediate will possess a lifetime shorter than a bond vibration, so that the steps become concerted.

Enforcement

The act of preventing the discharge into the atmosphere from any source operating without a permit or in violation of the terms of a permit or rules, regulations, or orders of an pollution control agency.

Enhanced greenhouse effect

Increasing the concentration of the trace gases in the air that absorb thermal infrared light, i.e. greenhouse gases, will result in more infrared light redirected to the earth causing an increase in temperatures.

Enol

Enols (also known as alkenols) are alkenes with a hydroxyl group affixed to one of the carbon atoms composing the double bond. Alkenes with a hydroxyl group on both sides of the double bond are called enediols. Deprotonated anions of enols are called enolates.

Entering group

An atom or group that forms a bond to what is considered to be the main part of the substrate during a reaction. For example: the attacking nucleophile in a bimolecular nucleophilic substitution reaction.

Entgegen

German word meaning "opposite". Represented by E in the E/Z naming system of alkenes.

Enthalpy

A thermodynamic variable that is a system's internal energy plus the product of its pressure and volume:
$$H = E + PV.$$

Entrained air

Bubbles that are of intermediate size so that they are carried along with the fibers in a flowing stream of papermaking stock.

Entrainment

The act of forming a mist or fog droplets of a liquid carried off by the vapours of a boiling liquid or from a liquid through which bubbles of gas or vapour are passing rapidly.

Entrainment zone

The layer between the convective mixed layer and the free troposphere that is caused by a temperature inversion. This inversion inhibits the rising of heat and gases, trapping pollutants closer to the ground.

Entropy

The entropy (S) of a system is defined by the equation: $dS \geq dq/T$ where dq is the infinitesimal heat absorbed by the system which is at the thermodynamic temperature, T.

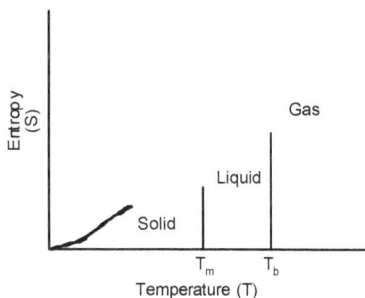

Environmental protection agency

An American federal agency formed in 1970 to protect human health and the environment. The EPA today focuses on the atmosphere, fresh and ocean waters, and soil quality within the United States.

Enzyme

A macromolecule, usually a protein, that functions as a (bio) catalyst by increasing the reaction rate. In general, an enzyme catalyzes only one reaction type (reaction selectivity) and operates on only one type of substrate (substrate selectivity). Substrate molecules are transformed at the same site (regioselectivity) and only one of a chiral substrate or of a racemate is transformed (enantioselectivity).

Enzyme induction

Enzyme induction is the process whereby an (inducible) enzyme is synthesized in response to a specific inducer molecule. The inducer molecule (often a substrate that needs the catalytic activity of the inducible enzyme for its metabolism) combines with a repressor and thereby prevents the blocking of an operator by the repressor leading to the translation of the gene for the enzyme.

Enzyme repression

Enzyme repression is the mode by which the synthesis of an enzyme is prevented by repressor molecules. In many cases, the end product of a synthesis chain (e.g., an amino acid) acts as a feed-back corepressor by combining with an intracellular aporepressor protein, so that this complex is able to block the function of an operator. As a result, the whole operation is prevented from being transcribed into mRNA, and the expression of all enzymes necessary for the synthesis of the end product enzyme is abolished.

Equatorial rain forests

An area located near the equator worldwide, covering seven percent of the earth's surface, characterized by high precipitation, absent or short dry season, high tree and vegetative growth rates, high humidity, high photosynthetic rates and extreme biodiversity. The equatorial rain forests produce much of the oxygen in the Earth's atmosphere and absorbs large quantities of carbon dioxide from the air.

Equilibria

Rapid transformations between two or more chemical forms, the rates of which determine the ratios of the concentrations.

Equilibrium

A dynamic or static state of balance between opposing forces or actions. A dynamic equilibrium exists between two different phases of a given pure compound (liquid-gas, gas-solid, solid-liquid) when there is no net change in the amount of either phase when the two remain in contact; this occurs at a given temperature when the vapour pressures of each of the two phases of the compound are equal.

Equilibrium constant

Value that expresses how far the reaction proceeds before reaching equilibrium. A small number means that the equilibrium is towards the reactants side while a large number means that the equilibrium is towards the products side.

Equilibrium expressions

The expression giving the ratio between the products and reactants. The equilibrium expression is equal to the concentration of each product raised to its coefficient in a balanced chemical equation and multiplied together, divided by the concentration of the product of reactants to the power of their coefficients.

Equinox

Twice during the year, September 23 and March 21, the length of day and night are equal because the tilt of the Earth's axis (in relationship to the sun) is nullified and both the Northern and Southern Hemispheres receive equal quantities of sunlight.

Equivalence point

Occurs when the moles of acid equal the moles of base in a solution.

Equivalent

The equivalent is the mass of a compound that could replace the atomic mass of an element. An example would be the amount of substance to replace one gram of hydrogen or fourteen grams of nitrogen.

Equivalent mass

The equivalent mass is molecular mass of a substance divided by the valence of that compound. Valence is determined by multiplying the valence of the positive ion in a compound by the number of atoms of that ion. NaCl has one positive sodium atom with a valence of one. 1 x 1 gives a positive valence of 1.

Erbium

Symbol: "Er" Atomic Number: "68" Atomic Mass: 167.26amu. Erbium is one of the elements in the lanthanide series of inner transition elements. It may also be classified as a rare earth element.

Error, random

The random fluctuations observed in the output from a measurement apparatus or method when the input to the instrument or method is held constant.

Error, systematic

Errors in a measurement which stay more or less constant and which may be attributed to the particular design of the measurement. Such errors may in principle be accounted for and eliminated, in contrast to random errors, which may not be eliminated.

Ester
An inorganic or organic acid in which at least one -OH (hydroxyl) group is replaced by an -O-alkyl (alkoxy) group.

Ethane
$C_6H_5CH_2CH_3$, a hydrocarbon found in the atmosphere whose primary fate is to react with free radicals such as chlorine and nitrous oxide. This reaction would prevent these radicals from reacting with ozone which is needed in the stratosphere to block ultraviolet light from reaching the surface of the earth.

Ethanol
Also known as ethyl alcohol or alcohol, (C_2H_5OH) is an oxygenated hydrocarbon that can be burned as a fuel, or blended into gasoline. Thought of as an alternative fuel and clean fuel, ethanol is a renewable energy source that is made from corn or other grains, for instance in Brazil from sugar cane. If blended into gasoline, ethanol helps with the combustion process and therefore less unburned hydrocarbons form.

Ethers
Ethers are organic compounds with a formula R-O-R, where R is not equal to H. They may be derived from alcohols by elimination of water, but the major method is catalytic hydration of olefins. They are volatile highly flammable compounds; when containing peroxides they can detonate on heating. The term ether is often used synonymously with ethyl ether. The following are not examples of ethers because the oxygen atom is not connected to two different carbon atoms via single bonds or because the attached group is not an alkyl.

Ethylbenzene
C_8H_{10}, Colourless, flammable liquid with an aromatic odor, it is found in coal tar, petroleum, as well as in manufactured products like inks, insecticides, and paints. Ethylbenzene is also used to make styrene. It is during the manufacturing process that ethylbenzene becomes an airborne hazard. It takes about 3 days for ethylbenzene to breakdown into other chemicals.

Eudismic ratio
Eudismic ratio is the potency of the eutomer relative to that of the distomer.

Europium
Symbol: "Eu" Atomic Number: "63" Atomic Mass: 151.96amu. Europium is one of the elements in the lanthanide series of inner transition elements. It may also be classified as a rare earth element.

Eustatic changes
A consistent change in the sea level that affect oceans, throughout the world.

Eutomer
The Eutomer is the enantiomer of a chiral compound that is the more potent for a particular action.

Evaporation
Evaporation is a molecular phase change of a liquid to gas or vapour. The overall temperature of the system is not near the boiling point. While the average temperature of a liquid may be low, some molecules have high temperatures and high energy. Those molecules with higher energies are able to escape the system and

become a gas. The molecules evaporate one by one.

Evapotranspiration

The total water loss due to the transpiration of vegetation plus the evaporation from the soil; higher climatic temperatures result in a higher evapotranspiration rate.

Excimer

An excited dimer, "non-bonding" in the ground state. For example, a complex formed by the interaction of an excited molecular entity with a ground state counterpart of this entity.

Exciplex

An electronically excited complex of definite stoichiometry, "non-bonding" in the ground state. For example, a complex formed by the interaction of an excited molecular entity with a ground state counterpart of a different structure.

Excitance, radiant, spectral

The derivative of the incident radiant power with respect to the projected area of a specified emitting surface (W cm^{-2}) With the adjective spectral, differentiation with respect to wavelength is also implied (W cm^{-2} nm^{-1}). Irradiance and excitance are similar but refer to energy arriving at versus leaving from a surface, respectively.

Excited state

State of a system with energy higher than that of the ground state. This term is most commonly used to characterize a molecule in one of its electronically excited states, but can also refer to vibrational and/or rotational excitation in the electronic ground state.

Exhaustion

The process of dye material coming out of solution and remaining on fiber surfaces.

Exothermic

A chemical reaction in which more energy is released than is required to break bonds in the initial reaction. Energy appears as a product in the chemical equation.

Explosivity limits (or explosion limits); flammable limits

The concentration limits, usually of a substance in air, between which combustion will be self-sustaining.

Exponentiation

Raising something to a power.

Exposure

Subjecting a person, animal, plant, or material to an environment containing a significant concentration of an air pollutant.

Exposure chamber

In environmental studies, this is a suitable room or chamber in which the atmosphere may be controlled (relative humidity, pollutant concentrations, temperature, light intensity, etc.) and in which exposure to animals, plants, or materials can be made.

Extended rosin size

A liquid sizing agent based on saponified rosin, to which urea has been added.

Extinction coefficient

A measure of the rate of the reduction of transmitted light through a substance.

Extraction

Extraction is the separation of a component from its mixture by selective solubility. When a solution of one substance in one solvent is brought in with another solvent dissolved substance will distribute between the two solutants because of different solubility. Extraction is an efficient and fast method used for separating and concentrating matters. Extraction is best done several times in a succession, with smaller amount of solvent in it the matter is better dissolved. For example, caffeine can be separated from coffee beans by washing the beans with supercritical fluid carbon dioxide; the caffeine dissolves in the carbon dioxide, but flavour compounds do not. Vanillin can be extracted from vanilla beans by shaking the beans with an organic solvent, like ethanol.

Extrusion transformation

A transformation in which an atom or group Y connected to two other atoms or groups X and Z is lost from a molecule, leading to a product in which X is bonded to Z, e.g.,

$$X - Y - Z \qquad X - Z + Y$$

or

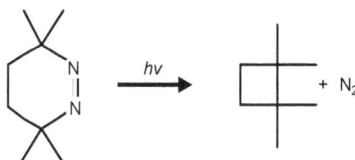

The reverse of an extrusion is called insertion.

Eye irritation

Experienced by many persons upon exposure to some compounds (often lachrymators) in polluted air SO_2, SO_3, HCl, formic acid, peroxyacetyl nitrate (PAN), formaldehyde, acrylaldehyde, etc.

F

Fallout

A measurement of air contamination consisting of the mass rate at which solid particles deposit from the atmosphere.

Fan pump

A very large centrifugal pump, usually in the basement below a paper machine, that may dilute thick stock with white water and/or send thin stock to the headbox.

Fanning

In blast furnace operation, the idling period between the blowing periods when the blast pressure is reduced to a minimum. This also applies to plume behaviour under inversion conditions.

Fastness

Resistance of a dyed material (e.g. paper) toward either light or fluids.

Fatty acid

A fatty acid has a carboxylic acid on a long chain of carbon atoms. The carboxylic acid may also be called the carboxyl functional group. Fatty acids are a major source of energy for the cell. Compounds called phospholipids are created from fatty acids.

Feathering

The tendency of ink to spread out in an irregular pattern due to wicking and/or an insufficient level of sizing agents in paper.

Felt filling

Undesirable accumulation of particulate matter within the void spaces of press felts.

Fermentation

A type of anaerobic respiration which uses atoms other than oxygen as the final electron acceptor. Fermentation occurs in bogs and marshes resulting in the production of CH_4 and CO_2 as well as other compounds such as ethanol, lactic acid, butyric acid, and acetone.

Fermium

Symbol: "Fm" Atomic Number: "100" Atomic Mass: (257)amu. Fermium is one of the elements in the actinide series of inner transition elements. It may also be classified as a rare earth element. It is a radioactive and unstable element and you will not find it in use anywhere. The element was named after the physicist Enrico Fermi.

Fibrils

Hair-like projections from a fiber surface, usually resulting from refining.

Field specimen

A field specimen is a sample taken from outside of the lab. This could refer to a piece of rock, plant life, or an organism.

Fillers

Inorganic solid particles, usually in the size range of 0.2 to 5 micrometres, and often comprised of CaCO3, clay, or titania.

Filter

A porous material on which solid particles present in air or other fluid which flows through it are largely caught and retained. Filters are made with a variety of materials: cellulose and derivatives, glass fibre, ceramic, synthetic plastics and fibres. Filters may be naturally porous or be made so by mechanical or other means. Membrane/ceramic filters are prepared with highly controlled pore size in a sheet of suitable material such as polyfluoroethylene, polycarbonate, or cellulose esters. Nylon mesh is sometimes used for reinforcement. The pores constitute 80-85% of the filter volume commonly, and several pore sizes are available for air sampling (0.45 to 0.8m are commonly employed).

Filtrate

Filtrate is the solid substance remaining after you remove the liquid of a solution. If you mix water and chalk, you can remove the chalk by filtering it out. The chalk left in the filter paper is called the filtrate.

Filtration

The process of segregation of phases; e.g., the separation of suspended solids from a liquid or gas, usually by forcing a carrier gas or liquid through a porous medium.

Fine paper

Paper formed from bleached, generally low-yield pulp, and usually containing filler.

Fines

Solid particles, often derived from wood, small enough to pass through either a forming fabric, a 200-mesh screen, or a 76 um hole.

Fingerprint

Numerical representation of a compound or library which describes in a computationally simple fashion a set of attributes (descriptors), such as atom connectives, 3-D structure or physical properties.

Firn

Granular snow that has endured a summer without melting and will transform into glacial ice.

First order reaction

A reaction whose rate is determined by the concentration of only one of its reactants leading to a reaction rate equation of Rate = k[X]

First-pass retention

The difference between headbox and traywater consistency, all divided by the headbox consistency.

Fixative

An additive having the tendency to help retain dye material on fiber surfaces, usually because of a strong positive charge.

Fixed gases

The gases in earth's atmosphere whose concentrations are considered stable or invariable. This includes gases such as O_2, N_2, and the noble gases, as opposed to variable gases such as CH_4 and CO_2 whose concentrations change because of reactivity or because there are large atmospheric sinks such as vegetation in the case of CO_2.

Flame photometry

The use of emission spectroscopy in the ultraviolet and visible regions to identify and estimate the amounts of various elements which are excited in a flame, an ore or high voltage spark.

Flare, solar

A bright eruption of energy from the sun's chromosphere.

Flash point

The lowest temperature at which a substance, e.g., fuel oil, will give off a vapour that will flash or burn momentarily when ignited.

Flash vacuum pyrolysis (FVP)

Thermal reaction of a molecule by exposing it to a short thermal shock at high temperature, usually in the gas phase.

Flocculation

A tendency for fibers to collect together in bunches in the presence of flow, and especially in the presence of retention aids; the same word also refers to the action of high-mass polymers in forming bridges between suspended colloidal particles, causing strong, relatively irreversible agglomeration.

Floccule

A small loosely aggregated mass of material suspended in or precipitated from a liquid; a cluster of particles.

Flora

A plant or plant life of a specific region or particular period.

Flow analysis

The determination of selected analytes by injection of discrete test portion plugs into a liquid now without or with segmentation by gas or nonmiscible liquids. Determination

is accomplished by suitable detectors (e.g., UV, visible; fluorescence, electrochemical) either directly or following on-line chemical reactions(s) and/or extraction.

Flow cytometry

Technique for characterizing or separating particles such as beads or cells, usually on the basis of their relative fluorescence.

Flow rate

The volume or mass flow per unit time.

Flow regulator

A device used in sampling to maintain constant airflow for a given period of time.

Flue

A passage for the conduction of combustion gases in an incinerator; synonymous with chimney. The term also applies to structures and openings of any kind used to transport gases in operations other than incineration.

Flue gar scrubber

Equipment for removing fly ash and other objectionable materials from the products of combustion by means of sprays or wet baffles.

Flue gas

Waste gas from the combustion process.

Fluid flow

The movement of air or other fluid in the open or in a duct, pipe, or passage. The flow can be of several types: a) Uniform flow is steady in time, or the same at all points in space; b) Steady flow is that for which the velocity at a point fixed with respect to a fixed system of coordinates is independent of time; c) Rotational flow has appreciable vorticity and cannot be described mathematically by a velocity potential function; d) Turbulent flow is that in which the fluid velocity at a fixed point fluctuates with time in a nearly random fashion; e) Laminar flow is that in which the mass of fluid may be considered separate laminae (sheets) with simple shear existing at the surface of contact of laminae if there is any difference in mean speed of the separate laminae; f) Streamline flow is that in which fluid particles move along the streamlines; this motion is characteristic of viscous flow at low Reynolds numbers.

Fluidic system

Device for synthesis or screening in which fluids such as reagents or assay buffers maybe directed to specified locations by the opening and closing of valves in a stationary network of tubes and wells.

Fluorescent

A property of some materials to absorb light of a lower wavelength, convert some of the energy to heat, and emit light of a longer wavelength.

Fluorescent whitening agent

A dye material that absorbs ultraviolet light and re-emits light in the blue region.

Fluorimetre

An instrument used to measure the intensity and the wavelength distribution of the light emitted as fluorescence from a molecule excited at a specific wavelength or wavelengths within the absorption band of a particular compound. Characteristic fluorescence bands may be used to identify specific pollutants such as the polynuclear aromatic hydrocarbons.

Fluorine

Symbol: "F" Atomic Number: "9" Atomic Mass: 19.00amu. Fluorine is member of the halogen group. Fluorine is a very reactive, poisonous gas. It is reactive because it combines with most other elements. You can also find it in rocket fuel, uranium refining, Freon, toothpaste, and etched glass.

Fluorous synthesis

Approach for solution phase synthesis which takes advantage of the ability of highly fluorinated groups to partition out of aqueous and most organic solutions into a third phase consisting of a fluorinated solvent.

Flux

The rate of continuous change, flow or movement of liquid, particles or energy. The rate of discharge of a liquid, removal of energy or particle depositing from one body to another. For example, flux emissions of sesqiterpines from vegetation was estimated to be 10-40 mg per square metre in a summer month of the western and southern US states.

Flux density, photon

At a given point in space, the number of photons incident in a time interval on a suitably small sphere centred at that point, divided by the cross-sectional area of that sphere and by the time interval.

Fluxional

A chemical species is said to be fluxional if it undergoes rapid degenerate rearrangements (generally detectable by methods which allow the observation of the behaviour of individual nuclei in a rearranged chemical species, e.g. NMR, X-ray). Example: Bullvalene (1 209 600 interconvertible arrangements of the ten CH groups).

The term is also used to designate positional change among ligands of complex compounds and organometallics.

Fly ash

A byproduct from the process of burning finely ground coal in an electric power generating plant. Fly ash composition is mainly spherical glassy silica particles released after the combustion cycle through exhaust gases. It's composed of additional elements that form mostly oxidized compounds that condense when they cool down from the combustion process.

Fly ash collector

Equipment to remove fly ash from the products of combustion.

Foehn

A warm, dry wind on the lee side of a mountain range that owes its relatively high temperatures largely to adiabatic heating during descent down mountain slopes, a descent that compresses and thereby heats the air.

Fog

A general term applied to a suspension of droplets in a gas. In meteorology, it refers to a suspension of water droplets resulting in a visibility of less than 1 km. An aerosol of liquid particles, in particular a low cloud.

Fog horizon

The top of a fog layer which is confined by a low-level temperature inversion and gives the appearance of the horizon (which it actually obscures) when viewed from above, against the sky.

Foil

An informal term for "hydrofoil," a stationary device upon which a forming fabric rests, causing vacuum and pressure pulses as the wet paper sheet passes over it, tending to enhance dewatering.

Force

An entity that when applied to a mass causes it to accelerate. Sir Isaac Newton's Second Law of Motion states: the magnitude of a force = mass * acceleration.

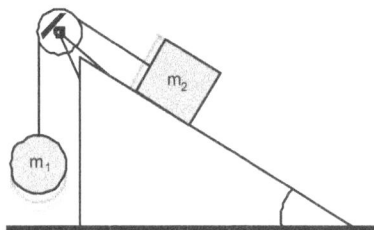

Formaldehyde

CH_2O, A colourless, pungent, carcinogenic, and toxic gas which can irritate membranes. It is used as formalin in its aqueous state (37 %). Formaldehyde is reactive due to its carbonyl functional group. In the oxidation of hydrocarbons in the atmosphere, formaldehyde is one of many aldehydes that is produced especially in urban environments.

Formation

In common speech, the word most often means "uniformity of paper" on a scale of 0.5 to 20 mm.

Formic acid

CHOOH, A weak acid that photolytically reacts in the atmosphere forming COOH radical and H radical. This compound often reacts with the hydroxyl radisal and atomic oxygen to form formic acid and a hydroperoxy radical. This is a sink for the hydroxyl radical and it also helps drive other reactions with the addition of hydroperoxy radicals to the atmosphere.

Forming fabric
The endless, moving screen upon which a sheet of paper is formed and dewatered.

Formula
This notation tells you the number of atoms in one molecule of a compound. A formula is written with element symbols and numbers in subscript (like the "2" in CO_2). The formula for salt is NaCl. The formula for water is CO_2.

Formula mass
The formula mass is the total atomic mass of a compound. You can determine the formula mass by adding the individual masses of each atom in the compound. The formula mass of NaCl is 58.44.

Fortified rosin size
A major component of most rosin size products, produced by reacting the levopimeric acid component of rosin with maleic anhydride.

Fossil fuels
There are coal, crude oils, oil shales, tar sands and natural gases such as butane, ethane, methane which occur naturally from the decomposition of plant and sea and land organisms over millions of years. These natural resources contain stored energy from the sun which is released upon combustion. These fuels also release various types of pollutants such as sulphur dioxide, carbon dioxide and nitrogen dioxide when burned.

Fractional distillation
A type of distillation that separates two substances with boiling points that are very close to each other. You increase the temperature in very small amounts.

Fragment ion in mass spectrometry
An ion obtained when a molecule in the gaseous mixture under analysis is split into fragments during the ionization process (impact with the ionizing electron beam). An ion produced by the loss of one or more fragments from a parent molecular ion.

Francium
Symbol: "Fr" Atomic Number: "87" Atomic Mass: (223)amu. One of the alkali metal family. Francium is the heaviest of the alkali metals and is extremely rare in nature. It can be created in a lab and acts like cesium.

Free electron
Electron which is not attached to a nucleus.

Free energy
A measure of the tendency of a chemical change to occur spontaneously.

Free radicals
Highly reactive atoms or molecules with incomplete (electronic) octets and therefore uneven numbers of electrons. Free radicals species are very electrophilic, will abstract atoms from other molecules to complete their octets, and will, in the process, generate new radicals. In the atmosphere, most free radical species have short life times; however, they can promote the conversion of oxygen to ozone and also take part in the catalytic cycle of ozone destruction.

Free state
Atoms that have a valence number of zero. Look to the noble gases for a valence number of zero.

Freeness

The ease with which paper stock releases water during a standard test by gravity.

Freezing out

Term used in combustion for the analysis of incinerator flue gas components (largely the organic fraction) in which a series of traps at progressively lower temperatures are employed. In more general use, the term implies the removal of a condensable gas or liquid by condensation in a trap at low temperatures.

Freezing point

A temperature point when a liquid becomes a solid. The word congeal is also used to describe the process of a liquid becoming a solid.

Freons

Stable liquids or gases usually produced for solvents, aerosol propellants, refrigeration, air conditioner or styrofoam purposes. These high vapour pressure liquids/ gases are chemically stable and have long atmospheric lifetimes; therefore, they can eventually become well-mixed in the troposphere and ultimately diffuse into the stratosphere. Upon encountering high energy UV light in the upper stratosphere these species are photodissociated and ultimately release all of their atoms there.

Frequency

Number of events in a given unit of time. When describing a moving wave, means the number of peaks which would pass a stationary point in a given amount of time.

Frequency distribution

If the range of observed measurement values is subdivided into a regular sequence of smaller intervals, this distribution is a plot of the frequency of occurrence of values falling into each interval.

Front

The marked boundaries of two air masses of differing densities. The difference in densities can be related to temperature, pressure or humidity. Frontal affinity chromatography (fac) FAC is a quantitative method that enables sensitive and reproducible measurements of interactions between lectins and oligosaccharides. The method is suitable even for the measurement of low-affinity interactions and is based on a simple procedure and a clear principle.

Frontal wedging

The lifting of air resulting when cool air acts as a barrier over which warmer, lighter air will rise.

Ftir

Fourier-transform infrared spectroscopy, an excellent way to determine what materials are present in a deposit sample (qualitative).

Fugitive dusts

A term used to describe indirect air pollution caused primarily from dust and dirt loosened from dirt roads. This dust can cover large areas and is predominantly found in rural areas and construction sites.

Fugitive sizing

A tendency of certain paper samples to temporarily loose their water-resistant properties.

Fully combinatorial

Containing, or designed to contain, all possible combinations of building blocks. Pool/split libraries are generally fully combinatorial while parallel synthesis libraries may not be.

Fume

Fine solid panicles (aerosol), predominantly less than 1m in diameter, which results from the condensation of vapour from some types of chemical reaction. Usually this is formed from the gaseous state generally after volatilization from melted substances and often accompanied by chemical reactions such as oxidation.

Fumigation

An atmospheric phenomenon in which pollution, retained by an inversion layer near its level of emission, is brought rapidly to ground level as the inversion breaks up. This term also applies to the exposure of material (e.g., grain) to chemicals to kill insects, etc.

Functional group

This is a specific group of atoms within a molecule that is responsible for the characteristic chemical reactions of that molecule. The same functional group will undergo the same or similar chemical reaction(s) regardless of the size of the molecule it is a part of.

Furnish

A mixture of cellulosic fibers, optional fillers, and water from which paper is made.

Fusion or melting

The change from a solid to a liquid. The solid particles overcome the attractive forces holding them in fixed positions and start to move over one another.

G

Gadolinium

Symbol: "Gd" Atomic Number: "64" Atomic Mass: 157.25amu. Gadolinium is one of the elements in the lanthanide series of inner transition elements. It may classified as a rare earth element. This silvery metal is used in many alloys. One of its best uses is in nuclear reactors because it can stop neutrons and contain radioactivity of dangerous reactions.

Gaia hypothesis

An hypothesis proposed during the early 1970s by James Lovelock which states that all living organisms have the ability to affect their surroundings such as the atmosphere, lithosphere, and climate to maximize its biological success. The hypothesis connects the evolution and survival of a species to the evolution and conditions of its environment.

Gallium

Symbol: "Ga" Atomic Number: "31" Atomic Mass: 69.72amu. It is classified as a basic metal. Gallium is a very brittle, silvery metal. You will find it in electronics, alloys, and thermometers.

Galvanic cell

A Galvanic cell consists of two half-cells. In its simplest form, each half-cell consists of a metal and a solution of a salt of the metal. The salt solution contains a cation of the metal and an anion to balance the charge on the cation. In essence, the half-cell contains the metal in two oxidation states and the chemical reaction in the half-cell is an oxidation-reduction (redox) reaction.

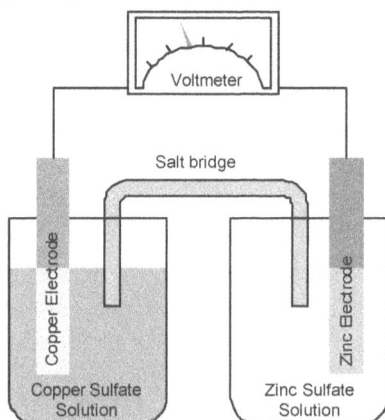

Gas

A state of matter in which the particles are far apart and are rapidly moving past one another. In this state matter has a variable shape and a variable volume. ie. the shape and volume are determined by the container it fills.

Gas analysis installation

Assembly for the purpose of determining one or more components in a gaseous mixture. It generally comprises the following elements: sample probe, region of primary treatment of the gases, region of secondary treatment of gases, points for venting to the atmosphere and for calibration sample injection, transfer line, and the analytical unit.

Gas black

(also carbon black, channel black, furnace black) Finely divided carbon (graphite) produced by incomplete combustion or thermal decomposition of natural gas.

Gas chromatography

A method of separating the components of a gas mixture. The sample is passed, in a stream of carrier gas, through a column which has different retention properties relative to the components of interest. Different components pass through the column at different rates and are detected as they elute from the column. Comprises all chromatographic methods in which the moving phase is a gas.

Gas chromatography, detector in

Generally a device which provides an analogue output proportional to the instantaneous concentration of the substance or its instantaneous eluting rate in the carrier gas.

Gas chromatography, electrochemical detector

An electrochemical cell which responds to certain substances in the carrier gas eluting from the column. The electrochemical process may be an oxidation, reduction or a change in conductivity.

Gas chromatography, electron capture detector

A small radioactive source containing ^3H or ^{63}Ni ionizes the molecules of the carrier gas (nitrogen or argon-methane), and a potential difference creates a small current. This current is reduced when an electronegative substance (such as a halocarbon) is introduced. The reduction in current is a measure of the concentration of the electronegative substance. The detection limit (threshold) varies greatly according to the substances to be analysed and can reach a mixing ratio of 10^{-12}. The linear dynamic range may be 10^4 but the maximum measuring value generally lies below 1 ppmv.

Gas chromatography, flame ionization detector

The gases emerging from the column are fed into a hydrogen flame across which an electrical potential is placed. Certain molecules ionize easily in the flame and the current produced is proportional to the instantaneous flow rate of the eluted component. The detector is relatively insensitive to inorganic molecules and is most used for organic compounds. Concentrations below 1 ppmv are easily detected. The linear dynamic range is between 10^3 and 10^5.

Gas chromatography, flame photometric detector

The eluent from the column is fed into a hydrogen-rich flame and produces light emission. Optical filters are used to select the wavelength range of the emission which is characteristic of specific atoms (usually sulphur or phosphorous). The detector is very specific. depending on the choice of optical filters. It can detect the S- and P-containing compounds down to 10 ppmv, but the detector is nonlinear.

Gas chromatography, helium ionization detector

A weak beta source and a high potential raise the helium atom of the carrier gas to a metastable state. All other substances having an ionization potential lower than 18 eV are ionized, and the current that results is used to measure the components. The detector is usually employed to measure inorganic compounds at concentrations between 0.1 and 10 ppmv. It has a linear range of about Id but is somewhat unstable and requires great care to ensure the helium purity and to eliminate all leaks in the system.

Gas chromatography, mass spectrometric detector

A mass spectrometer can be used as a detector and gives qualitative and quantitative data on the various eluted substances. The mass spectrum of the eluted compounds provide evidence beyond the elution time as to the chemical nature of the species.

Gas chromatography, photoionization detector

Radiation from an ultraviolet lamp ionizes certain species in the carrier gas. A potential difference is applied and the resulting ionization current is detected. The detector is only useful for substances with ionization potentials below about 11 eV. This makes it quite useful for detecting one component of a combined eluent when the other component, for instance nitrogen, has a high ionization potential. The detector has a small linear dynamic range and is capable of detecting substances below 1 ppmv.

Gas chromatography, thermal conductivity detector

In general, two cells arranged in a bridge configuration detect the change in thermal conductivity of the gas at the output of the column. This detector is sensitive to any substance with

thermal conductivity different from that of the carrier gas. The lowest detectable limit is between 0.5 and 100 ppmv. The linear dynamic range is of the order of Id. This type of detector is often used for measuring components at relatively high concentrations.

Gas chromatography, ultrasonic detector

Sound is generated in a reference cell and a measuring cell. An eluted component passing through the measuring cell changes the velocity of sound in the cell. This change is detected by a phase shift of acoustic signals between the two cells. This detector is usually employed for inorganic gases in the region where thermal conductivity detectors are not sufficiently sensitive. The detection threshold is of the order of 0.1 ppmv. The linear dynamic range is of the order of 10^3.

Gas constant

A physical constant used in the simplified ideal gas law equation (PV=nRT). In chemistry, the gas constant is most often represented by the letter R.

Gaseous diffusion separator

Instrumentation to separate a gas mixture into its components by means of differences in the diffusion rates of the component molecules. This method has been used in separation of various isotopes of uranium (by means of UF_6) and hydrogen (H_2O, HDO, D_2O, HTO, etc.)

Gas-liquid chromatography; partition chromatography

Comprises all gas-chromatographic methods in which the stationary phase is a liquid distributed on a solid support. Separation is achieved by partition of the components of a sample between the phases. In this and in gas-solid chromatography the first word specifies the mobile phase and the second word the stationary phase. Liquid stationary phases are supported on solids, but the solid support affects the chromatographic process. For classification, the term relating to the predominant effect is chosen.

Gasoline
An oil derived hydrocarbon mixture used as fuel in internal combustion engines. In the US more than 40% of carbon dioxide emissions come from transportation engines burning gasoline.

Geiger counter
Instrument that measures radiation output.

Gel phase
Description applied to certain solid supports which display properties intermediate between solid and liquid phases, e.g. in the apparent mobility of the support as determined by nuclear magnetic resonance (NMR) spectroscopy.

Geminate pair
Pair of molecular entities in close proximity in solution within a solvent cage and resulting from reaction (e.g. bond scission, electron transfer, group transfer) of a precursor that constitutes a single kinetic entity.

Geminate recombination
The reaction with each other of two transient molecular entities produced from a common precursor in solution. If reaction occurs before any separation by diffusion has occurred, this is termed "primary geminate recombination". If the mutually reactive entities have been separated, and

come together by diffusion, this is termed "secondary geminate recombination".

General acid catalysis
The catalysis of a chemical reaction by a series of Brønsted acids (which may include the solvated hydrogen ion) so that the rate of the catalysed part of the reaction is given by"k_{HA}[HA] multiplied by some function of substrate concentrations. (The acids HA are unchanged by the overall reaction.) General catalysis by acids can be experimentally distinguished from specific catalysis by hydrogen cations (hydrons) by observation of the rate of reaction as a function of buffer concentration.

General base catalysis
The catalysis of a chemical reaction by a series of Brønsted bases (which may include the lyate ion) so that the rate of the catalysed part of the reaction is given by "k_B[B] multiplied by some function of substrate concentration.

General circulation models
Three dimensional computer simulations of climate and weather which, through calculations, are used to investigate gravity wave fields. The models may help to predict atmospheric chemistry distribution and meteorological trends for the future.

Generic structure
The general structural formula of a library, consisting of the scaffold plus an indication of the position of attachment of the various residues.

Genetic algorithm
Method for library design by evaluating the fit of a parent library to some desired property (e.g. the level of activity in a biological assay or the computationally determined diversity

of the compound set) as measured by a fitness function. The design of more optimal daughter libraries is then carried out by a heuristic process with similarities to genetic selection in that it employs replication, mutation, deletions, etc. over a number of generations.

Genome

A genome is the complete set of chromosomal and extrachromosomal genes of an organism, a cell, an organelle or a virus; the complete DNA (deoxyribonucleic acid) component of an organism.

Geologic time scale

A time scale in which the earth and its atmosphere are dated. It is broken into two division; Relative Time: Determines the age relative to other surrounding objects; Absolute Time: Obtained with radiometric dating of the object.

Geostrophic wind

A wind forming from the apparent Coriolis and pressure gradient forces along straight isobars above the boundary layer.

Geothermal energy

An alternative energy source that uses the earth's interior heat as the primary energy source for the generation of electricity. Alternative here refers to different from historical sources of energy, that is, hydrocarbons.

Germanium

Symbol: "Ge" Atomic Number: "32" Atomic Mass: 72.59amu. Germanium is classified as a semi-metallic element. Germanium is a grayish crystalline metal that is very brittle. You will find it in glass lenses, fluorescent lights, electronics, and many alloys.

Gibbs energy diagram

A diagram showing the relative standard Gibbs energies of reactants, transition states, reaction intermediates, and products, in the same sequence as they occur in a chemical reaction. These points are often connected by a smooth curve (a "Gibbs energy profile", commonly still referred to as a "free energy profile") but experimental observation can provide information on relative standard Gibbs energies only at the maxima and minima and not at the configurations between them. The abscissa expresses the sequence of reactants, products, reaction intermediates and transition states and is usually undefined or only vaguely defined by the reaction coordinate (extent of bond breaking or bond making). In some adaptations the abscissas are however explicitly defined as bond orders, Brønsted exponents, etc.

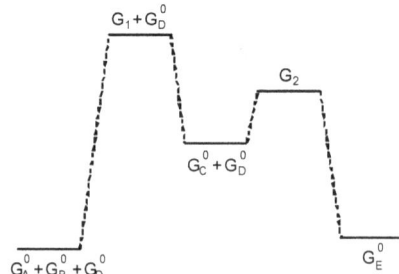

$G_1 + G_D^0$; G_2 ; $G_C^0 + G_D^0$; $G_A^0 + G_B^0 + G_D^0$; G_E^0

Gibbs free energy

A measure of the tendency of a chemical change to occur spontaneously. Gibbs equation is given as G = H – T S where H equals the change in enthalpy, T equals the Kelvin temperature, and ÄS equals the change in entropy.

Gigayears

Time measured in billions of years; a common measure of geologic time.

Glaciation

The process of forming glaciers.

Glacier

A slow-moving mass of ice formed in higher latitudes and elevations. When snowfall is greater than melting and the increasing amounts of snow become compacted and pressurized it forms firn (see above) and ultimately a glacier. As the glacier moves, it carries rocks and soil, and can form u-shaped valleys over geologic time.

Global climate change

Change in the average global surface temperature, precipitation level, seal level, arctic sea ice, etc. Global climate change can be affected directly or indirectly by anthropogenic processes such as fossil fuel combustion and can also be influenced by natural occurrences. Most significant are changes in the atmospheric concentrations of atmospheric water vapour, CO_2, CH_4, N_2O, and CFCs.

Global climate model

A computer programme that is used by atmospheric scientists to study and predict world-wide trends in weather patterns and the forces and physical laws that affect climate. The formulae are complicated and require skilled mathematicians, atmospheric scientists, and powerful computers for execution. Five regimes that influence climate are often taken into consideration: atmosphere, hydrosphere, biosphere, cryosphere, and pedosphere.

Global warming

The overall increase of the Earth's atmospheric temperature due to a buildup of greenhouse gases. In spring 2007 research predicted that the earth's Arctic Ocean might be completely ice-free at the end of the summer by the year 2020; however, ice would return in the winter. In 2010 research posed that September Arctic ice thickness was changing by >10% per decade.

Gloss

The ability of paper to reflect some portion of the incident light at the mirror angle.

Glycerol

Glycerol is a biological compound that has three carbons with three alcohol functional groups. It is the backbone molecule of many fats when combined with fatty acids.

Glycol

CH_2OHCH_2OH: A chemical compound containing two hydroxyl groups (-OH groups). Also known as a Ethane, 1,2-Diol.

Glycolic aldehyde

($C_2H_4O_2$), also called hydroxyacetaldehyde, is formed during the oxidation of ethane and isoprene, and also by the emission of biomass fires. It is the simplest form of sugar. Glycol aldehydes have also been found in trace amounts in dust clouds near the Milky Way of outer space.

Glycolysis

The metabolic pathway that converts glucose, $C_6H_{12}O_6$, into pyruvate, $C_3H_5O_3$

Gold

Symbol: "Au" Atomic Number: "79" Atomic Mass: 196.97amu. Gold is one of the transition elements. Gold is one of the Earth's precious metals. You will find the yellow coloured metal used in jewelry, electronics, coins, satellites, and even medicines. Gold is very non-reactive and will not oxidize in air.

Gondwanaland

A hypothetical supercontinent comprising approximately the present continents of the southern hemisphere.

Gpcr

G-protein coupled receptors form a large super-family of proteins composed of three major classes and more than 30 subfamilies. They are integral membrane proteins characterized by seven membrane-spanning (transmembrane; TM) regions. They are involved with signal transduction across cell membranes. Many medically and pharmacologically important proteins are included in this super-family: e.g., Acetylcholine receptors, Dopamine receptors, and Opioid receptors.

Gradient

A differential ratio; the change in a quantity such as the mixing ratio of an impurity in air, the temperature of the air, etc., with height or distance.

Graham's law

The rate of diffusion of a gas is inversely proportional to the square root of its molar mass.

Gram

A gram is metric unit of measure for mass. It is the weight of one milliliter of water at a temperature of 39.2 degrees Fahrenheit.

Gram-mole

This is a specific measure of mass. The mass of a substance when there is one mole of the substance. For sodium chloride, the formula mass is 58.44. One gram-mole of sodium chloride is 58.44 grams.

Graniting

Uneven staining of fibers in pulp, usually due to a very high affinity of dye for fibre, together with insufficient dilution and/or poor mixing.

Gratzel solar cell

Grätzel solar cell is photoelectrochemical cell, developed by Michael Grätzel and collaborators, simulates some characteristics of the natural solar cell, which enables photosynthesis take place. In natural solar cell the chlorophyll molecules absorb light (most strongly in the red and blue parts of the spectrum, leaving the green light to be reflected). The absorbed energy is sufficient to knock an electron from the excited chlorophyll. In the further transport of electron, other molecules are involved, which take the electron away from chlorophyll. In Grätzel cell, the tasks of charge-carrier generation and transport are also assigned to different species. His device consists of an array of nanometer-sized crystallites of the semiconductor titanium dioxide, welded together and coated with light-sensitive molecules that can transfer electrons to the semiconductor particles when they absorb photons. So, light-sensitive molecules play a role equivalent to chlorophyll in photosynthesis. In Grätzel cell, the light-sensitive molecule is a ruthenium ion bound to organic bipyridine molecules, which absorb light strongly in the visible range; titanium dioxide nanocrystals carry the received photoexcited electrons away from electron donors. On the other hand, a donor molecule must get back an electron, so that it can absorb another photon. So, this assembly is immersed in a liquid electrolyte containing molecular species (dissolved iodine molecules) that can pick up an electron from an electrode immersed in the solution and ferry it to the donor molecule. These cells can convert sunlight with efficiency of 10 % in direct sunlight and they are even more efficient in diffuse daylight.

Gravimetric methods

A determination by weight; e.g., in the older method of Cl^- ion determination, a weighed amount of sample is dissolved in water, $AgNO_3$ solution added, AgCl is precipitated, dried and weighed. From the known mass fraction of silver in AgCl, the weights of the initial sample and that of the AgCl precipitated, the percentage of chlorine in the sample can be calculated readily.

Gravitation

A process used to separate compounds that have different densities. When river water is thoroughly mixed, sand will settle on the bottom of a glass before the silt. Sand settles first because it has a greater density.

Gravity

A natural force exerted on a body toward the earth's surface or between two bodies. Gravity has a strong effect on how matter interacts. Gravitational attraction depends on the masses of the bodies involved and the distance between them. Centrifugal force caused by the earth's rotation on its axis tends to lessen the force of gravity.

Greenhouse effect

The phenomenon in which outgoing infrared radiation that would normally exit from a planet's atmosphere but instead, is trapped or reflected because of the presence of the atmosphere and its components is called the greenhouse effect. It has been calculated that this effect is necessary to maintain the earth's climate and surface temperature and, more importantly, the liquid state of water in the majority of the earth's biosphere; however, the best scientific estimates to date suggest that increasing amounts of greenhouse gases are resulting in higher temperatures worldwide. This could result in melting of icecaps that would raise the sea level and cause devastating floods in coastal areas, more extremes in rainfall and intensity, and the distribution of species in the biosphere.

Greenhouse gases

Those atmospheric components that absorb strongly in the infrared region of the spectrum. Infrared radiation is reflected and emitted by the earth's surface as heat and causes a fairly large warming effect when trapped by these gases in the atmosphere. In order of abundance and importance as greenhouse gases are water vapour, carbon dioxide, ozone, nitrous oxide, methane, and chlorofluoro-carbons (CFCs). Absorption by water vapour, the most common greenhouse gas, explains why many humid or cloudy days feel much hotter than dry, clear days of the same air temperature.

Grit

Airborne solid particles in the atmosphere which are of natural or manmade origin and which remain in suspension for some time; in the United Kingdom the size of the grit particles is defined as greater than 75m in diameter.

Ground level inversion

The inversion of the normal temperature gradient in the atmosphere; the temperature of the air increases with increasing height of the air above the ground. This leads to poor mixing of gases released below the inversion.

Group

On the periodic table, the columns are called groups. Elements are arranged in groups by the number of electrons that are in the outside shell. The elements of each group have the same number of electrons in their outer shells.

Guar gum

A natural polymer that has been used as a dry-strength additive, often as a cationic derivative.

Gulf stream

The Gulf Stream is a powerful current in the Atlantic Ocean. Its movement is related to density redistribution, differences in temperature, the Earth's rotation, and wind currents. The relatively temperate weather in Great Britain is, to a large degree, controlled by the Gulf Stream redistributing energy from equatorial solar radiation to the North Atlantic.

Gustiness

Intensity of turbulence; the ratio of the root mean square of wind velocity fluctuations to the mean wind velocity.

H

Haber process

An industrial process for manufacturing ammonia from hydrogen and nitrogen.

Hafnium

Symbol: "Hf" Atomic Number: "72" Atomic Mass: 178.49amu. Hafnium is one of the transition elements. Hafnium is often found with zirconium. This silvery metal has been put to use in nuclear reactor control rods and in many alloys.

Half life

The amount of time it takes for half an initial amount to disintegrate.

Half-cell

The anode or cathode and the chemicals that react there.

Half-reaction

The reduction or oxidation portion of a redox reaction.

Halide mineral

This is a mineral that is made of compounds with one or more halogen atoms. Salt (Halite) is considered a halide because it has sodium and chloride in the formula.

Halogen

Halogen is the name of the seventh group of elements. They all have seven electrons in their outer shell. They are also very reactive.

Hammond principle (or Hammond postulate)

The hypothesis that, when a transition state leading to an unstable reaction intermediate (or product) has nearly the same energy as that intermediate, the two are interconverted with only a small reorganization of molecular structure. Essentially the same idea is sometimes referred to as "Leffler's assumption", namely, that the transition state bears the greater resemblance to the less stable species (reactant or reaction intermediate/product). Many text books and physical organic chemists, however, express the idea in Leffler's form, but attribute it to Hammond. As a corollary, it follows that a factor stabilising a reaction intermediate will also stabilize the transition state leading to that intermediate.

Hansch analysis

Hansch analysis is the investigation of the quantitative relationship between the biological activity of a series of compounds and their physicochemical substituent or global parameters representing hydrophobic, electronic, steric and other effects using multiple regression correlation methodology.

Hapten

A hapten is a low molecular weight molecule that contains an antigenic determinant but which is not itself antigenic unless combined with an antigenic carrier.

Hard acid

A Lewis acid with an acceptor centre of low polarizability. Other things being approximately equal, complexes of hard acids and bases or soft acids and bases have an added stabilization (sometimes called "HSAB" rule). For example the hard O- (or N-) bases are preferred to their S- (or P-) analogues by hard acids. Conversely a "soft acid" possesses an acceptor centre of high polarizability and exhibits the reverse preference for coordination of a soft base. These preferences are not defined in a quantitative sense.

Hard base

A Lewis base with a donor centre (e.g. an oxygen atom) of low polarizability; the converse applies to "soft bases".

Hard drug

A nonmetabolizable compound, characterized either by high lipid solubility and accumulation in adipose tissues and organelles, or by high water solubility. In the lay press the term refers to a powerful drug of abuse such as cocaine or heroin.

Hard sizing

Strong resistance of paper to penetration by water or other fluid, over a long time.

Hardness

Hardness is a measure of difficulty you can scratch a substance. Diamonds have a greater hardness than copper sulfate crystals. Copper sulfate is softer than a diamond.

Hardness points

Steel rods used by geologists to test the hardness of minerals and rocks.

Hassium

Symbol: "Hs" Atomic Number: "108" Atomic Mass: (265)amu. Hassium is one of the postactinide elements. Scientists have created these in labs and may have found only a few atoms of the element.

Haze

A state of reduced visibility (1-2 km) resulting from the increased light scatter due to the presence of fine dust or aerosol particles (H_2SO_4, NH_4HSO_4, products of the ozone-terpene reactions, etc.).

Haze horizon

The top of a haze layer which is confined by a low-level temperature inversion so that it gives the appearance of the horizon which it may obscure.

Heat

The total amount of kinetic energy of the particles in a sample of matter; the form of energy produced by molecular motion. Heat energy always flows from a warmer object to a cooler object.

Heat capacity

A measure of how much heat is needed to raise the temperature of one gram of anything one degree Celsius.

Heat of formation

The amount of energy required or released when one mole of a compound is formed from its elements. Values are generally given for measurements made under standard conditions of 101.3 kPa and 25°C

Heat of Fusion

The amount of energy required to transform a substance from a liquid state to a solid state. The amount of energy is measured in calories and is a measure of how many calories must be removed from the system since solids hold less energy overall than liquids.

Heisenberg uncertainty principle
This principle states that it is not possible to know a particle's location and momentum precisely at any time.

Helium
Symbol: "He" Atomic Number: "2" Atomic Mass: 4.00amu. Helium is a very non-reactive element. It is the first in the group of noble or inert gases. You can find it in balloons, scuba tanks, lasers, nuclear reactors, and blimps.

Hemicellulose
Component of wood comprised of relatively short, slightly branched or irregular chains of sugar units, yielding increased swelling ability.

Henderson-Hasselbach equation
An equation of the form pH = pK_a - lg([HA]/[A]) for the calculation of the pH of solutions where the ratio [HA]/[A] is known.

Henry's law
An expression describing the equilibrium partitioning of a gas or vapour between two volumes of a gas and liquid in contact with each other. For dilute solutions of gases which do not react to form dissociated (or ionized) species in solution, the equilibrium concentration of a gas X, [X], dissolved in a liquid is proportional to the partial pressure of this gas, p_x: [X] = $H_x p_x$. Common practice in atmospheric chemistry is the use of concentration in mol L^{-1} and pressure

of gas in atm with resulting units of mol L^{-1} atm^{-1} of the Henry's law constant, H_x. The simple form of this law is suitable to describe the solubility in water of many gaseous species which are of atmospheric interest (O_3, O_2, H_2O_2, etc.), but a modified form of Henry's law must be used to describe the solubility of gases which react with water (e.g., SO_2).

Hess's law
The overall enthalpy change in a reaction is equal to the sum of the enthalpy changes of the individual steps of the process.

Heterobimetallic complex
A metal complex having two different metal atoms.

Heteroconjugation
(1) Association between a base and the conjugate acid of a different base through a hydrogen bond (B'···HB$^+$ or A'H···A). The term has its origin in the conjugate acid-base pair and is in no way related to conjugation of orbitals. Heteroassociation is a more appropriate term.
(2) Some authors refer to conjugated systems containing a heteroatom, e.g. pyridine, as "heteroconju-gated systems". This usage is discouraged since it inappropriately suggests an analogy to homoconjugation (2), and conflicts with the currently accepted definition of that term.

Heterocycle
A cyclic molecule with more than 2 types of atoms as part of the ring. (e.g. Furan, a 5-membered ring with four carbons and one oxygen, or a Pyran, a 6-membered ring with five carbons and one oxygen)

Heterogeneous

Describes a sample of matter that has parts with different compositions.

Heterogeneous mixture

A mixture in which the ingredients are not uniformly dispersed.

Heterogeneous reaction

A reaction that involves reactants in more than one phase.

Heteroleptic

Transition metal or Main Group compounds having more than one type of ligand.

Heterolytic bond-dissociation energy

The energy required to break a given bond of some specific compound by heterolysis. For the dissociation of a neutral molecule AB in the gas phase into A^+ and B^- the heterolytic bond-dissociation energy $D(A^+B^-)$ is the sum of the bond dissociation energy, $D(A-B)$, and the adiabatic ionization energy of the radical A minus the electron affinity of the radical B^-.

Heteroreceptor

A heteroreceptor is a receptor regulating the synthesis and/or the release of mediators other than its own ligand.

Hexagonal crystal

This crystal shape has six sides and no specific length. It looks like an elongated hexagon.

High-throughput screening

Process for rapid assessment of the activity of samples from a combinatorial library or other compound collection, often by running parallel assays in plates of 96 or more wells. A screening rate of 100 000 assays per day has been termed "Ultra High-Throughput Screening" (UHTS).

Hildebrand parametre

A parameter measuring the cohesion of a solvent (energy required to create a cavity in the solvent).

Hit

Library component whose activity exceeds a predefined, statistically relevant threshold.

Hit explosion

Process of establishing structure-activity relationships around a hit by preparing new libraries or series of analogues using related building blocks and/or scaffolds to those employed in the preparation of that hit.

HO_2-radical

The hydroperoxyl radical. A reactive radical which, together with the HO-radical, constitute the elements of a radical chain reaction which results in the oxidation of NO to NO_2 and ultimately O_3 formation in the troposphere; see HO-radical. The HO_2-radical is also a major source of H_2O_2 in the troposphere through the reaction, $2HO_2 \longrightarrow H_2O_2 + O_2$.

Hofmann rule

"The principal alkene formed in the decomposition of quaternary ammonium hydroxides that contain different primary alkyl groups is always ethylene, if an ethyl group is present." Originally given in this limited form by A.W. Hofmann, the rule has since been extended and modified as follows: "When two or more alkenes can be produced in a b-elimination reaction, the alkene having the smallest number of alkyl groups attached to the double bond carbon atoms will be the predominant product." This orientation described by the Hofmann rule is observed in elimination reactions of quaternary ammonium salts and tertiary sulfonium salts, and in certain other cases.

Holmium
Symbol: "Ho" Atomic Number: "67" Atomic Mass: 164.93amu. Holmium is one of the elements in the lanthanide series of inner transition elements. It may also be classified as a rare earth element.

Homo
Acronym for Highest Occupied Molecular Orbital.

Homoaromatic
Whereas in an aromatic molecule there is continuous overlap of p-orbitals over a cyclic array of atoms, in a homoaromatic molecule there is a formal discontinuity in this overlap resulting from the presence of a single sp^3 hybridized atom at one or several positions within the ring; p-orbital overlap apparently bridges these sp^3 centres, and features associated with aromaticity are manifest in the properties of the compound. Pronounced homoaromaticity is not normally associated with neutral molecules, but mainly with species bearing an electrical charge, e.g., the "homotropylium" cation, $C_8H_9^+$, In bis, tris, (etc.) homoaromatic species, two, three, (etc.) single sp^3 centres separately interrupt the pi-electron system.

Homogeneous
Describes a sample of matter that has uniform characteristics throughout.

Homogeneous mixture
a uniform intermixture of particles. Samples from different parts of this mixture have the same composition.

Homogeneous reaction
a reaction in which all the reactants are in the same phase.

Homoleptic
Transition metal or Main Group compounds having only one type of *ligand* are said to be homoleptic, e.g. $TaMe_5$.

Homologue
The term homologue is used to describe a compound belonging to a series of compounds differing from each other by a repeating unit, such as a methylene group, a peptide residue, etc.

Homolytic cleavage
Where bond breaks leaving each atom with one of the bonding electrons, producing two radicals.

Hormone
A hormone is a substance produced by endocrine glands, released in very low concentration into the bloodstream, and which exerts regulatory effects on specific organs or tissues distant from the site of secretion.

Hst
A widely used test of resistance to penetration of an acidic water solution through paper. Results are given as the seconds required for reflectance of the un-exposed side of the sheet to decrease to 80% of its initial value.

Humidity
A general term referring to the water content of a gas.

Hybrid orbitals
Orbitals created by mixing other orbitals.

Hybridization
The process wherein orbitals of similar energies are combined to form a set of equivlent 'hybrid' orbital.

Hydrated ions

Ions surrounded by water molecules.

Hydration

A chemical reaction in which a hydroxyl group (OH-) and a hydrogen cation (an acidic proton) are added to the two carbon atoms bonded together in the carbon-carbon double bond which makes up an alkene functional group.

Hydroboration

A reaction adding BH_3 or B_2H_6 or an alkylborane to an alkene to produce intermediate products consisting of 3 alkyl groups attached to a boron atom. This molecule is then used in other reactions, for example, to create an alcohol by reacting it with H_2O_2 in a basic solution.

Hydrocarbons

When the only elements involved in organic compounds are Carbon and Hydrogen the resulting class of compounds is called Hydrocarbons. The simplest Hydrocarbon is methane (CH_4). Other common well known hydrocarbons are propane (C_3H_8) and octane (C_8H_{18}).

Hydrocracking unit

Used in the thermal decomposition of heavy (high molecular weight) hydrocarbons to smaller (low molecular weight) hydrocarbons; high pressures of hydrogen and a special catalyst are employed. Sulphur compounds in the fuel are reduced to H_2S, and the final hydrocarbon product can be obtained relatively sulphur-free.

Hydrogen

Symbol: "H" Atomic Number: "1" Atomic Mass: 1.01amu. Hydrogen is the first element in the periodic table. It is very light and the smallest atom. There is more hydrogen in the universe than any other element. On Earth, it is usually found with oxygen in water.

Hydrogen bond

The hydrogen bond is a form of *association* between an electronegative atom and a hydrogen atom attached to a second, relatively electronegative atom. It is best considered as an electrostatic interaction, heightened by the small size of hydrogen, which permits proximity of the interacting dipoles or charges. Both electronegative atoms are usually (but not necessarily) from the first row of the Periodic Table, i.e., N, O, or F. Hydrogen bonds may be intermolecular or intramolecular. With a few exceptions, usually involving fluorine, the associated energies are less than 20-25 kJ mol^{-1} (5-6 kcal mol^{-1}).

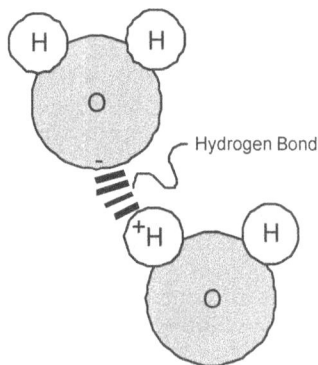

Hydrogen bonding

Strong type of intermolecular dipole-dipole attraction. Occurs between hydrogen and F, O or N.

Hydrogenation

Addition of a hydrogen atoms to an alkene or alkane to produce a saturated product.

Hydrolysis

Reaction with water molecules (sometimes accelerated by acid or base) resulting in breakage of a chemical bond.

Hydrolysis reaction

A reaction that occurs when water is added to a compound. In the case of a disaccharide, the molecule is broken up into monosaccharides with the addition of water.

Hydrolyzate

The breakdown product of a reactive sizing agent, leading to a net decrease in efficiency and possible deposit problems.

Hydrometeor

Any condensed water particle in the atmosphere of sufficient size to be potentially capable of undergoing precipitation (in fogs, clouds, some hazes, rain-drops, snow-flakes, etc.).

Hydron

General name for the ion H^+ either in natural abundance, or where it is not desired to distinguish between the isotopes, as opposed to proton for $^1H^+$, deuteron for $^2H^+$ and triton for $^3H^+$.

Hydronium ion

the H_3O^+ ion, which is formed by the combination of a proton with a water molecule. Its presence accounts for the properties of acids.

Hydrophile

Something that loves the water phase, often due to the presence of oxygen atoms or charged chemical groups.

Hydrophilic

Something that is attracted to water. The term is also used to describe portions of molecules that dissolve well in polar water molecules. "Hydro" means water. "Philic" means to "like or love."

Hydrophilic interactions

Interactions between molecules where nonpolar portions of the molecule are attracted to any interaction with polar water molecules. The molecule will align itself so that the hydrophobic portions have the best chance of coming into contact with the other polar molecules.

Hydrophilicity

Hydrophilicity is the tendency of a molecule to be solvated by water.

Hydrophobic

Something that is afraid or repulsed by water. The term is also used to describe portions of molecules that do not dissolve well in polar water molecules. "Hydro" means water. "Phobic" means to be afraid of or dislike.

Hydrophobic interaction

The tendency of hydrocarbons (or of *lipophilic* hydrocarbon-like groups in solutes) to form *intermolecular* aggregates in an aqueous *medium*, and analogous intramolecular interactions. The name arises from the attribution of the phenomenon to the apparent repulsion between water and hydrocarbons. However, the phenomenon ought to be attributed to the effect of the hydrocarbon-like groups on the water-water interaction. The misleading alternative term "hydrophobic bond" is discouraged.

Hydrophobicity

Hydrophobicity is the association of non-polar groups or molecules in an aqueous environment which arises from the tendency of water to exclude non polar molecules.

Hydrosphere

The gaseous, liquid, and solid water of the earth (oceans, icecaps, lakes, rivers, etc.) as distinguished from the lithosphere and the atmosphere.

Hydroxide mineral

A mineral that is made up of compounds with a hydroxide group bonded to a metal. Bauxite is a good example of a hydroxide mineral.

Hydroxyl group

This is a side group which is one hydrogen atom bonded to one oxygen atom. The result is a negatively charged ion (OH^-).

Hydroxylation

A chemical process that introduces one or more hydroxyl groups (-OH) into a compound (or radical) thereby oxidizing it.

Hygrometer, capacitance

Hygrometer using the capacitance variations of a capacitor whose dielectric medium consists of the gas or of a material in contact with this gas.

Hygrometer, dew point (cooled surface condensation)

Instrument in which the sample is passed over a cooled surface. The temperature at which dew forms on the cooled surface is a function of the water content of the gas passing over the surface.

Hygrometer, electrical

A hygrometer whose sensitive element has electrical properties which vary with the humidity of the gas which traverses the hygrometer.

Hygrometer, electrolytic

Hygrometer using a hygroscopic substance (for example, diphosphorus pentoxide, P_2O_5) which is transformed into an electrolyte (phosphoric acid, H_3PO_4) in contact with the moisture in the gas. The electrolyte (phosphoric acid) is electrolysed continuously and the electrolysis current is measured. At a constant flow of the gas to be analysed, the electrolysis current is a linear function of the water concentration.

Hygrometer, frost point

Instrument in which the sample is passed over a cooled surface. The temperature at which frost forms on it is a function of the water content of the gas passing over the surface.

Hygrometer, mechanical

An apparatus containing an element (hair, goldbeater's skin, carbon-film) whose dimension or mass varies as a function of its water content.

Hygrometer, psychrometric

Instrument by which the relative humidity of the atmosphere may be determined. It is generally composed of two temperature sensors, one of which measures the temperature of the air; the other sensor is moistened with water and senses the cooling due to evaporation of water. The temperature difference between the two sensors is a function of relative humidity; sometimes referred to as a "wet- and dry-bulb" hygrometer.

Hygrometry and moisture analysis

The measurement or indication of the water content of the ambient air or of a sample of gas.

Hysteresis

Regarding a material quantity or instrument's reading. Dependence of a value on the direction of change from a previous characteristic value. It may be quantified by the difference between the upscale and downscale variation starting from fixed lower and upper measurement points (inversion).

I

Ideal gas

A gas is considered ideal when its pressure, temperature, and volume follow the relationship:

$$pV = nRT$$

where p is the pressure, V is the volume, n is the number of moles of gas present, R is the molar gas constant (SI units, $J\ K^1\ mol^{-1}$), and T is the thermodynamic temperature (K). When the pressure is measured in Pa and the volume in m^3, then R equals 8.3144 $J\ mol^{-1}\ K^{-1}$. With pressure in atm and volume in cm^3, R = 82.057 $cm^3\ atm^{-1}\ mol^{-1}\ K^{-1}$. For non-ideal gases, the equation of state is a more complex function of p, V, and T. For most common gases encountered in atmospheric chemistry, the ideal gas law is followed well at low pressures and up to pressures somewhat above one atm. With compounds such as NO_2 and formic acid (HCO_2H) which dimerize easily [forming N_2O_4 and $(HCO_2H)_2$, respectively , measured pressures must be corrected using the equilibrium constants for these dimerizations to estimate the amount of the monomer and dimer species present. GB: A pure gaseous substance B is treated as an ideal gas when the approximation $f_B^* = p$ is used (where f_B^* is the fugacity of B and p its pressure.)

Identity

A math property which states:

A + 0 = A and A * 1 = A.

Igneous rock

A rock type that has been created from super-heated magma. The three main types of rock are igneous, sedimentary, and metamorphic.

Illuminance

Photometric counterpart of irradiance (not of radiance or intensity). Common units are footcandle, lumens cm^{-2}, lumens m^{-2}. Not a radiometric quantity, but a photometric quantity.

Immiscible

liquids that are insoluble in one another. Oil and water are an example.

Immission

A German term, pronounced in English, "eye-mission"; the transfer of pollutants from the atmosphere to a "receptor"; for example, pollutants retained by the lungs. It does not have the same meaning as ground level concentration, but is the opposite in meaning to emission. This term has not been used commonly in the English language.

Immission dose

The integral of the immission flow into the receptor over the exposure period.

Immission flux

The immission rate divided by the unit surface area of the receptor.

Immission rate

The mass (or other physical quantity) of pollutant transferring per unit time into a receptor.

Impaction

A forcible contact of particles of matter with a surface.

Impactor, cascade

An instrument used for the classification of aerosols according to size and for possible subsequent chemical analysis. Air is drawn through a series of orifices of decreasing size; the air flow is normal to collecting surfaces on which aerosols are collected by inertial impaction. The particles, separated stepwise by their momentum differences into a number of size ranges, are collected simultaneously.

Impingement

Equivalent to impaction; often refers to impaction on a liquid surface.

Impinger

A sampling instrument employing impingement for the collection of particulate matter. Common types are:
a) the midget impinger employing impingement in 1-10 cm^3 water,
b) the standard impinger employing impingement in 75 cm^3 water, and
c) dry impingers. Impingers are also suitable for sampling certain gases and vapours.

Impure substance or mixture

A substance consisting of two or more particles that can be separated by physical means. eg. evaporation. Its properties are dependent upon the composition of the mixture. eg. The concentration of a copper sulfate solution determines it colour.

In situ scaffold formation

Process whereby a scaffold is formed during library production which contains residues of at least two building blocks.

Incinerator

Equipment in which solid, liquid, or gaseous combustible wastes are ignited and burned. Types include flue-fed and multiple-chamber incinerators with several stages of combustion.

Inclusion compound (or inclusion complex)

A complex in which one component (the host) forms a cavity or, in the case of a crystal, a crystal lattice containing spaces in the shape of long tunnels or channels in which molecular entities of a second chemical species (the guest) are located. There is no covalent bonding between guest and host, the attraction being generally due to van der Waals forces. If the spaces in the host lattice are enclosed on all sides so that the guest species is "trapped" as in a cage, such compounds are known as "clathrates" or "cage" compounds".

Indicators

chemical substances that change colour at certain pH values. The colours and pH values vary with the indicator.

Indium

Symbol: "In" Atomic Number: "49" Atomic Mass: 114.82amu. It is classified as a basic metal. This metal is a lot like zinc. It is a soft, silvery metal used in electronics and mirrors. One interesting note is that there are more isotopes of indium than any other element.

Individual perception threshold (IPT)
A term used in odor testing which signifies the lowest concentration of a particular species at which a subject indicates both an initial positive and repeated response.

Induction period

The initial slow phase of a chemical reaction which later accelerates. Induction periods are often observed with radical reactions, but they may also occur in other systems (for example before steady-state concentration of the reactants is reached).

Inductive effect

In strict definition, an experimentally observable effect (on rates of reaction, etc.) of the transmission of charge through a chain of atoms by electrostatic induction. A theoretical distinction may be made between the field effect, and the inductive effect as models for the Coulomb interaction between a given site within a molecular entity and a remote unipole or dipole within the same entity. The experimental distinction between the two effects has proved difficult, except for molecules of peculiar geometry, which may exhibit "reversed field effects". Ordinarily the inductive effect and the field effect are influenced in the same direction by structural changes in the molecule and the distinction between them is not clear. This situation has led many authors to include the field effect in the term "inductive effect". Thus the separation of values into inductive and *resonance* components does not imply the exclusive operation of a through-bonds route for the transmission of the non-conjugative part of the substituent effect.

Inductomeric effect

A molecular polarizability effect occurring by the inductive mechanism of electron displacement. The consideration of such an effect and the descriptive term have been regarded as obsolescent or even obsolete, but in recent years theoretical approaches have reintroduced substituent polarizability as a factor governing reactivity, etc. and its parametrization has been proposed.

Inert

The word inert is used to describe the elements in group eight. They all have enough electrons to fill their outer shell. It is the column where Helium is at the top. Inert gases are very non-reactive.

Inert gas

A non-reactive gas under particular conditions. For example nitrogen at ordinary temperatures, and the noble gases (helium, argon, krypton, xenon and radon) are unreactive toward most species.

Inertial separator

Any dry type collector which utilizes the relatively greater inertia of particles to effect their removal from a gas stream; e.g., cyclonic and impingement separators, gravity settling chambers, and high-velocity gas reversal chambers.

Infrared gas analyser

Instruments with various degrees of sophistication are employed to monitor certain species with characteristic infrared absorption bands. E.g., relatively simple systems are employed to detect carbon monoxide (CO) in air; these are built with matching cells, one containing a reference CO sample with the air to be tested in the other. Filtered infrared light which lies largely within the CO absorption region is passed through both cells. In one use of the instrument, the pressure difference which results from the preferential heating of the cell with the higher CO concentration is measured. The signal can be calibrated to yield the CO concentration. Sophisticated infrared systems involving Fourier transform spectrometers or infrared laser diodes are employed to detect particular molecular species of interest in atmospheric chemistry (NO_2, H_2O_2, CH_2O, CO, HNO_3, etc.) and to study their reactions in the real atmosphere or in simulated atmospheres in the laboratory. Long path lengths for the infrared beam are required to detect the small concentrations of most species.

Inhibitor

An inhibitor is a compound that slows down the process of a reaction. You may also hear the term negative catalyst.

Inner transition elements

Elements in the periodic table that have three shells that are not filled with electrons. The shells are usually the outer three shells. Uranium and holmium are examples of inner transition elements. The actinide and lanthanide series are all inner transition elements.

Inorganic

Not mainly comprised of carbon, hydrogen, and oxygen.

Insoluble

An insoluble substance is one that is not able to dissolve in another substance. Some solutes are not able to dissolve in some solvents. Carbonates are often insoluble compounds. They just sink to the bottom of solutions.

Instability (with reference to instrumentation)

Change which takes place in instrument reading over a stated period of unattended operation for a given value of the air quality characteristic. It can be characterized by the variation with time of its mean, specifying the drift, and by the dispersion. Span instability is the change which takes place in instrument span over a stated period of unattended operation. Zero instability is the change in instrument reading in response to a zero sample over a stated period of unattended operation.

Instantaneous (spot) sampling

Obtaining a sample of the atmosphere in a period which is short compared with the duration of the sampling exercise. Such samples are often called "grab" samples, a term nor recommended. These are useful for the analysis of hydrocarbons and other complicated mixtures of trace gases which are relatively stable in a stainless steel canister or tank and can be transported back to the laboratory for chromatographic or other analysis which cannot be done satisfactorily in the field. The use of plastic bags (constructed of Mylar, FEP Teflon, Tedlar (PVC) or other films) to collect instantaneous samples and to store them for analysis is not recommended. It is very difficult to eliminate pinholes, the reproducibility of heat seals used in constructing the bags is not easy to achieve, gases can permeate through the bag walls, and impurities can be introduced through off-gassing of the bag walls.

Instrument reading (with reference to air quality measurements)

Output signal of a measuring system obtained as a response related to the concentration or the value of the air quality characteristic.

Intensive property

A property that does not depend on the size of the sample. Melting points, boiling points, colour, conductivity, and density are examples.

Interfering substance

Something in the aqueous mixture that interferes with the function of papermaking additives such as retention aids, sizing agents, strength agents, etc.

Intermediate

Molecules that exist only during a chemical reaction; not before or after the reaction.

Intermolecular forces

Intermolecular forces are forces of attraction or repulsion which act between neighboring particles: atoms, molecules or ions. They are weak compared to the intramolecular forces, the forces which keep a molecule together.

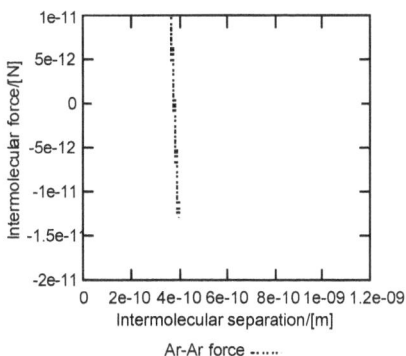

Ar-Ar force ·······

Internal bond

A measure of the energy required to delaminate paper (failure in plane of the sheet).

Internal sizing

Addition of hydrophobizing materials (sizing agents) at the wet end of a paper machine.

Intramolecular bonding

the attractive forces within a molecule that holds the atoms together. Covalent bonding and ionic bonding, for example.

Intramolecular catalysis

The acceleration of a chemical transformation at one site of a molecular entity through the involvement of another functional ("catalytic") group in the same molecular entity, without that group appearing to have undergone change in the reaction product. The use of the term should be restricted to cases for which analogous intermolecular catalysis by chemical species bearing that catalytic group is observable. Intramolecular catalysis can be detected and expressed in quantitative form by a comparison of the reaction rate with that of a comparable model compound in which the catalytic group is absent, or by measurement of the effective molarity of the catalytic group.

Intramolecular forces

Forces within molecules. Forces caused by the attraction and repulsion of charged particles.

Intrinsic activity

Intrinsic activity is the maximal stimulatory response induced by a compound in relation to that of a given reference compound. This term has evolved with common usage. It was introduced by Ariëns as a proportionality factor between tissue response and receptor occupancy. The numerical value of intrinsic activity (alpha) could range from unity (for full agonists, i.e., agonist inducing the tissue maximal response) to zero (for antagonists), the fractional values within this range denoting partial agonists. Ariëns' original definition equates the molecular nature of alpha to maximal response only when response is a linear function of receptor occupancy.

Inverse
A math property which states:
A + (-A) = 0 and A * (1/A) = 1.

Inverse agonist
An inverse agonist is a drug which acts at the same receptor as that of an agonist, yet produces an opposite effect. Also called negative antagonists.

Inversion height
The height above ground level at which there is change in sign of the normal temperature "lapse rate", dT/dz (the rate of change of the temperature with height). Several temperature inversions may be present in the air over a given site at different altitudes as result of various meteorological factors.

Inversion of an emulsion
Dilution and agitation of a water-in-oil emulsion under conditions that change it to an oil-in-water emulsion, as in makedown of certain retention aid emulsion products.

Inversion, temperature
A departure from the normal decrease of temperature with increasing altitude. A temperature inversion may be produced, for example, by the movement of a warm air mass over a cool one. Intense surface inversions may form over the land during nights with clear skies and low winds due to

the radiative loss of heat from the surface of the earth. The temperature increases as a function of height in this case.

Iodine
Symbol: "I" Atomic Number: "53" Atomic Mass: 126.90amu. Iodine is member of the halogen family. Iodine is a bluish black solid but can quickly become a bluish gas. It is less reactive than other halogens. The element is used as an ingredient in medicine, as a dye, and as an essential element in your diet. Without iodine, you could get a goitre (swelling of your thyroid).

Ion
An atom or group of atoms that has an electrical charge due to the gain or loss of electrons. Gaining electrons results in the particle having a negative charge (these are called anions). Losing electrons produces a positive charge (cations).

Ion channel
An integral membrane protein that provides for the regulated transport of a specific ions across a membrane.

Ion-dipole forces
Intermolecular force that exists between charged particles and partially charged molecules.

Ionic agglomerate
An ionic agglomerate is a group or atoms which are held together by electrovalent bonds.

Ionic bonds
When atoms combine by forming bonds through transferring electrons from one atom to another, the type of bond formed is called an Ionic Bond. This type of bond is referred to as Ionic because when an atom accepts electrons from an atom of a different

element the accepting atom becomes a negatively charged Ion and the donating atom becomes a positively charged Ion. These two charged ions are held together, bonded, by electrostatic attraction between the charges and the bond thus formed is referred to as an Ionic Bond. This bond is the primary type of bond occurring in the salts of Inorganic Chemistry with common table salt, Sodium Chloride - Na^+Cl^- being a prime example.

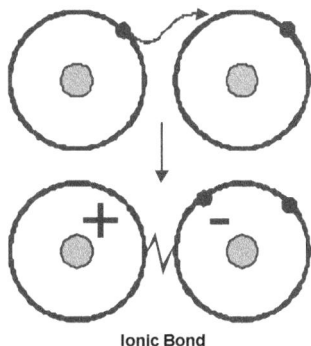

Ionic Bond

Ionic compound
A compound, usually between a metal and a nonmetal, that is the result of ionic bonding.

Ionization energy
The energy required to remove the most loosely held electron from an atom.

Ionization potential in mass spectrometry
The minimum electron energy necessary for the production of the molecule ion. The term ionization energy is preferred.

Ionizes
When a substance breaks into its ionic components.

Ir thermography
Infrared thermography Screening technique where the heat of reaction of a multitude of samples is simultaneously measured. Has been applied in particular to the screening of libraries of potential catalysts.

Iridium
Symbol: "Ir" Atomic Number: "77" Atomic Mass: 192.22amu. Iridium is one of the transition elements. Iridium is another member of the platinum family of metals. You might find it in alloys and in materials that need to withstand very high temperatures.

Iron
Symbol: "Fe" Atomic Number: "26" Atomic Mass: 55.85amu. Iron is on of the transition metals. You can find it in steel, meteorites, and the core of the Earth. Iron is everywhere in the universe.

Irreversible reaction
A chemical reaction after which the resulting agents cannot be changed back into the reactions ingredients.

Isobar
Lines on a plot joining points of equal barometric pressure in the atmosphere.

Isoelectronic
atoms or ions that have the same electron configuration.

Isokinetic line
A line in a given surface connecting points with equal wind speed; also called isotach or isovel.

Isokinetic sampling
A technique for collecting airborne particulate in which the sampling device has a collection efficiency of unity for all sizes of particles in sampled air, regardless of wind

velocity and direction of the instrument. The air stream entering the collector has a velocity (speed and direction) equal to that of the air in the gas stream just ahead of the sampling port of the collector.

Isomer

An isomer is a molecule or compound that has the same number of atoms as another but a different structure. Two molecules with the same chemical structure but have different structures are structural isomers. When atoms are arranged, bonds can be created in different directions. Glucose and fructose are good examples of structural isomers.

Isosteres

Isosteres are molecules or ions of similar size containing the same number of atoms and valence electrons, e.g., O^{2-}, F^-, Ne.

Isotherm

Lines joining points of equal temperature in the atmosphere.

Isotope

Isotopes are atoms of the same element that have different atomic masses. The change in mass occurs because the atoms have different numbers of neutrons. Their charges are all the same but their masses are different. Atomic masses are not even numbers because they represent the average mass of the atoms. The atomic mass includes the mass of isotopes and normal atoms.

Isotope exchange

A chemical reaction in which the reactant and product chemical species

are chemically identical but have different isotopic composition. In such a reaction the isotope distribution tends towards equilibrium (as expressed by fractionation factors) as a result of transfers of isotopically different atoms or groups. For example,

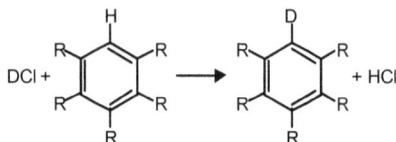

Isotope pattern in mass spectrometry Set of peaks related to ions with the same chemical formula but containing different isotopes; e.g., the 16 and 17 mass/charge peaks in a CH_4 sample arising from $^{12}CH_4^+$ and $^{13}CH_4^+$ ions.

Isotopic scrambling

The achievement, or the process of achieving, an equilibrium distribution of isotopes within a specified set of atoms in a chemical species or group of chemical species.

Isotropic

A quantity which is independent of direction. Anisotropic and nonisotropic refer to quantities which are direction dependent.

Iterative deconvolution

Multistep application of deconvolution where successively smaller sublibraries are prepared and tested to identify individual active members of a combinatorial library.

Iupac nomenclature

The international standard set of rules for naming molecules. International Union of Pure and Applied Chemistry.

J

J-chain

A polypeptide found in the dimeric immunoglobulin A and the pentameric immunoglobulin M, involved in joining together the subunits of each multimer.

Jet cooking

Exposing a suspension (usually of starch granules) to high temperature under elevated pressure.

Joule

The SI unit of energy, equal to the work required to move a 1 kg mass against an opposing force of 1 newton. $1 \text{ J} = 1 \text{ kg m}^2 \text{ s}^{-2} = 4.184$ calories.

Jumping library

A tool for the mapping and sequencing of large stretches of a chromosome. Starting at one point in the polynucleotide sequence, a distal point is located without having to first sequence the intervening bases. The double-stranded DNA is divided into large fragments with a rare cutter and one end of each piece is ligated to a selective marker and cyclized, then cut with a frequent cutter.

Jumping PCR

A technique for reconstruction and replication of randomly damaged double-stranded DNA, e.g. That found in mummified tissues or museum samples. In the first PCR cycle each primer is extended until a break in the template is encountered, but in the second cycle the newly synthesized strands find other templates that are intact in the region where the first templates were damaged.

K

Kaiser test

Analytical method for the determination of primary amines. Particularly useful for resin-bound analysis as the chromophoric product is released into solution allowing quantitation by colourimetry.

Kaolin

Another word for clay, a platey aluminium silicate mineral that is used as a white filler.

Kekulé structure (for aromatic compounds)

A representation of an aromatic molecular entity (such as benzene), with fixed alternating single and double bonds, in which interactions between multiple bonds are assumed to be absent. For benzene, are the Kekulé structures.

and

Kelvin

The SI Unit of temperature. It is the temperature in degrees Celsius plus 273.15.

Kelvin temperature scale

A temperature scale in which zero (0 K) is the lowest theoretical temperature. It is called absolute zero. All atomic motion stops at absolute zero. A change in temperature of 1 K is equal to a change in temperature of 1°C. 0 K = -273.15°C.

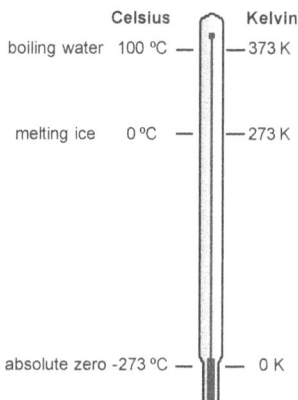

	Celsius		Kelvin
boiling water	100 ºC		373 K
melting ice	0 ºC		273 K
absolute zero	-273 ºC		0 K

Ketone

The functional group characterized by a carbonyl group (O=C) linked to two other carbon atoms, or a chemical compound that contains a carbonyl group

Keytones

When the elements making up the organic compound are once again Carbon, Hydrogen and Oxygen and when there is an internal (within the molecule) carbon-oxygen double bond, the Functional Group becomes C_2-C=O and the compounds are called Keytones. The most commonly known Keytone is Acetone (CH_3-C=0 -CH_3) the main ingredient in fingernail polish remover.

Kinetic control (of product composition)

The term characterizes conditions (including reaction times) that lead to reaction products in a proportion governed by the relative rates of the parallel (forward) reactions in which the products are formed, rather than by the respective overall equilibrium constants.

Kinetic electrolyte effect (kinetic ionic-strength effect)

The general effect of an added electrolyte (i.e. an effect other than, or in addition to, that due to its possible involvement as a reactant or catalyst) on the observed rate constant of a reaction in solution. At low concentrations (when only long-range coulombic forces need to be considered) the effect on a given reaction is determined only by the *ionic strength* of the solution and not by the chemical identity of the ions.

Kinetic energy

Energy an object has because of its mass and velocity. Objects that not moving have no kinetic energy. (Kinetic Energy = 0.5* mass*velocity^2.

Kinetics

The study of reaction rates in chemical reactions.

Kinetics, chemical reaction

The study of the rates at which reactions occur, the influence of conditions (such as temperature, concentration of reactants, surface/ volume ratio, etc.) on these rates, and the determination of rate coefficients.

Kjeldhal's method

Kjeldhal's method is an analytical method for determination of nitrogen in certain organic compounds. The method was developed by the Danish chemist Johan Kjeldahl (1849-1900). It involves addition of a small amount of anhydrous potassium sulphate to the test compound, followed by heating the mixture with concentrated sulphuric acid, often with a catalyst such as copper sulphate. As a result ammonia is formed. After alkalyzing the mixture with sodium hydroxyde, the ammonia is separated by distillation, collected in standard acid, and the nitrogen determined by back-titration.

Knorr resin

Amide-releasing, acid-cleavable solid support.

Koppel-Palm solvent parameters

Parameters to measure separately the ability of a solvent to enter into non-specific solvent-solute interactions (permittivity and refractive index n_D) and specific solvent-solute interaction (solvent basicity or nucleophilicity *B* and solvent acidity or electrophilicity *E*) as contributing to overall solvent polarity.

Krypton

Symbol: "Kr" Atomic Number: "36" Atomic Mass: 83.80amu. It is one of the noble or inert gases. A non-reactive element, krypton actually makes some compounds. It has been used in flash photography and lasers.

L

Labile

The term has loosely been used to describe a relatively unstable and transient chemical species or (less commonly) a relatively stable but reactive species. It must therefore not be used without explanation of the intended meaning.

Lachrymator

A substance which produces a flow of tears in a person or animal (e.g., acetyl chloride, acrylaldehyde, etc.).

Ladder synthesis

Strategy for library assembly where a portion of compound is capped following incorporation of each building block, such that the final sample comprises a mixture of all possible truncated products. This may be designed such that approximately equimolar quantities of each truncated form are present as an approach to gain maximal diversity, or such that each truncate is present in a small amount relative to the fully elaborated product. In the latter case, analysis of the pattern of products serves to identify the parent and is termed ladder encoding.

Lanthanide series

The lanthanide series is one of two sets of inner transition elements. Elements 57 through 71 are a part of this series. The elements include cerium, europium, and holmium.

Lanthanum

Symbol: "La" Atomic Number: "57" Atomic Mass: 138.91amu. Lanthanum is one of the elements in the lanthanide series of inner transition elements. It may also be classified as a rare earth element. It is the first element in the lanthanide series. It is a metallic element found in many minerals of the Earth's crust.

Lapse rate

The variation of an atmospheric variable with height; unless otherwise stated the variable is temperature.

Lapse rate, temperature

The rate of change of temperature with altitude (dT/dz). The rate of temperature decrease with increase in altitude which is expected to occur in an unperturbed dry air mass is $9.8 \times 10^{-3} °C\ m^{-1}$. This is called the dry adiabatic lapse rate. The lapse rate is taken as positive when temperature decreases with increasing height. For air saturated with H_2O, the lapse rate is less because of the release of the latent heat of water as it condenses.

Lattice

An ordered geometrical arrangement consisting of fixed points in which particles (atoms, ions or molecules) vibrate.

Lattice substitution

A mechanism whereby crystalline substances can have a charged character, when an occasional atom having a different valence takes the place of the atom that usually occupies a certain position in the crystal.

Law of conservation of energy
In any physical and chemical change, energy may change from one form to another but it cannot be created or destroyed. Also known as the First Law of Thermodynamics.

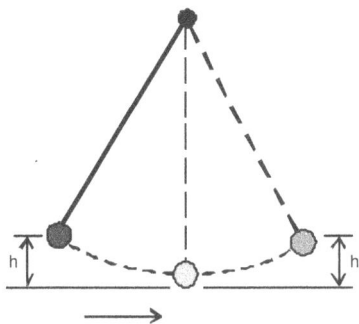

Law of conservation of mass
the total mass of the reacting substances (the reactants) is equal to the total mass of the products of a chemical reaction. Matter cannot be created or destroyed during chemical reactions.

Law of partition
A situation that enables a solute to dissolve in solvents based on the solubility of those solvents. If you mix oil in water and add sugar, the sugar will dissolve more readily in the water because there is a higher solubility.

Lawrencium
Symbol: "Lr" Atomic Number: "103" Atomic Mass: (260)amu. Lawrencium is one of the elements in the actinide series of inner transition elements. It may also be classified as a rare earth element. It is a radioactive and unstable element and you will not find it in use anywhere.

Le Chatlier's principle
States that a system at equilibrium will oppose any change in the equilibrium conditions.

Lead
Symbol: "Pb" Atomic Number: "82" Atomic Mass: 207.20amu. It is classified as a basic metal. Lead is a bluish metal found as an element and in many minerals. It has been used in several alloys, radiation shielding, and even insecticides. Lead is toxic to living organisms.

Lead compound
A compound that exhibits pharmacological properties which suggest its value as a starting point for drug development.

Lead discovery
Lead discovery is the process of identifying active new chemical entities, which by subsequent modification may be transformed into a clinically useful drug.

Lead generation
Lead generation is the term applied to strategies developed to identify compounds which possess a desired but non-optimized biological activity.

Lead optimization
The synthetic modification of a biologically active compound, to fulfill stereo electronic, physicochemical, pharmacokinetic and toxicological clinical usefulness.

Least nuclear motion, principle of
The hypothesis that, for given reactants, the reactions involving the smallest change in nuclear positions will have the lowest energy of activation. (It is also often simply

referred to as principle of least motion).

Left-to-right convention

Arrangement of the structural formulae of the reactants so that the bonds to be made or broken form a linear array in which the electrons move from left to right.

Levelling effect

The tendency of a solvent to make all Brønsted acids whose acidity exceeds a certain value appear equally acidic. It is due to the complete transfer to a protophilic solvent of a hydron from a dissolved acid stronger than the conjugate acid of the solvent. The only acid present to any significant extent in all such solutions is the lyonium ion . For example, the solvent water has a levelling effect on the acidities of $HClO_4$, HCl, and HI: aqueous solutions of these acids at the same (moderately low) concentrations have the same acidities. A corresponding levelling effect applies to strong bases in protogenic solvents.

Lewis acid

A molecular entity (and the corresponding chemical species) that is an electron-pair acceptor and therefore able to react with a Lewis base to form a Lewis adduct , by sharing the electron pair furnished by the Lewis base. For example:
Me_3B (Lewis acid) + $:NH_3$ (Lewis base) $Me_3B^--N^+H_3$ (Lewis adduct)

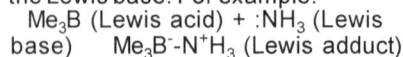

Lewis acidity

The thermodynamic tendency of a substrate to act as a Lewis acid . Comparative measures of this property are provided by the equilibrium constants for Lewis adduct formation of a series of Lewis acids with a common reference Lewis base.

Lewis base

A reagent that forms covalent bonds by donating a pair of electrons.

Lewis basicity

The thermodynamic tendency of a substance to act as a Lewis base . Comparative measures of this property are provided by the equilibrium constants for Lewis adduct formation for a series of Lewis bases with a common reference Lewis acid.

Lewis structures

A way of representing molecular structures based on valence electrons.

Libraries from Libraries

Strategy for accelerating library production, whereby an existing library is subjected to a relatively minor modification in order to generate a new library, thus avoiding the majority of chemical development and rehearsal required for a new library.

Library equivalent

The number of samples which equals the number of compounds in the library. Particularly applied to libraries in which individual beads are encoded, where one library equivalent is the number of beads which equals the number of compounds in the library.

Lifetime (mean lifetime), τ

The lifetime of a chemical species which decays in a first-order process is the time needed for a concentration of this species to decrease to 1/e of its original value. Statistically, it represents the mean life expectancy of an excited species. In a reacting system in which the decrease in concentration of a particular chemical species is governed by a first-order rate law , it is equal to the reciprocal of the sum of the (pseudo) unimolecular rate constants of all processes which cause the decay. When the term is used for processes which are not first order, the lifetime depends on the initial concentration of the species, or of a quencher, and should be called apparent lifetime instead.

Ligand

If it is possible to indicate a "central atom" in a polyatomic molecular entity, the atoms or groups bound to that atom are called ligands. The term is generally used in connection with metallic "central atoms". In biochemistry a part of a polyatomic molecular entity may be considered central, and atoms, groups or molecules bound to that part are considered ligands.

Ligand design

The design of ligands using structural information about the target to which they should bind, often by attempting to maximize the energy of the interaction.

Light absorption

An ability of many substances to convert light energy into heat, resulting in less reflected light and often producing a colour effect.

Light scattering

The redirection of a light beam due to interactions with molecules (Rayleigh and Raman scattering) and aerosols (Mie scattering). Scattered light received at any point in the atmosphere (sometimes called sky radiation) is a very important component of the total radiation received from the sun; it is dependent on the solar zenith angle, elevation, aerosol concentration, etc. The deflection of a light beam by discrete variation in refractive index due to the presence of particles or by spatial refractive index fluctuations.

Lignin

Three-dimensional, natural phenolic resin that binds fibers together in wood.

Limestone

Limestone is a sedimentary rock composed primarily of calcium carbonate in the form of the mineral calcite. Some 10 % to 15 % of all sedimentary rocks are limestones. Limestone is usually organic, but it may also be inorganic. Calcium carbonate may have been directly precipitated from the sea-water or by the lithification of coral reefs, marine organism shells, or marine organism skeletons.

Limiting condition of operation

Range of physical and operational parameters in which the method meets given values of performance characteristics with 95% probability.

Limiting reactant

A limiting reactant is the limiting factor or element in a chemical reaction. If you have eight million hydrogen atoms and only one oxygen atom, you can only make one molecule of water. Oxygen would be your limiting reactant.

Limiting reagent

A chemical in a reaction that is used up before other ingredients in the reaction, thus limiting how much of the resulting substance can be produced.

Line formula

A two-dimensional representation of molecular entities in which atoms are shown joined by lines representing single or multiple bonds, without any indication or implication concerning the spatial direction of bonds. For example, methanol is represented as

$$H - C - O - H$$

with H atoms above and below the central C, and the central C bonded to O which is bonded to H.

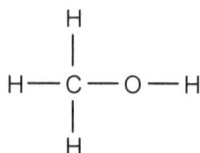

(The term should not be confused with the representation of chemical formulae by the "Wiswesser line notation", a method of string notation. Formulae in this notation are also known as "Wiswesser line formulae".)

Line spectra

Spectra generated by excited substances. Consists of radiation with only specific wavelengths.

Linear free-energy relation

A linear correlation between the logarithm of a rate constant or equilibrium constant for one series of reactions and the logarithm of the rate constant or equilibrium constant for a related series of reactions. Typical examples of such relations (also known as linear Gibbs energy relations) are the Brønsted relation , and the Hammett equation. The name arises because the logarithm of an equilibrium constant (at constant temperature and pressure) is proportional to a standard free energy (Gibbs energy) change, and the logarithm of a rate constant is a linear function of the free energy (Gibbs energy) of activation.

Linear range

Concentration range over which the intensity of the signal obtained is directly proportional to the concentration of the species producing the signal.

Linear solvation energy relationships

Equations involving the application of solvent parameters in linear or multiple (linear) regression expressing the solvent effect on the rate or equilibrium constant of a reaction.

Line-shape analysis

Determination of rate constants for a chemical exchange from the shapes of spectroscopic lines of dynamic processes. The method is most often used in nuclear magnetic resonance spectroscopy.

Linker

Bifunctional chemical moiety attaching a compound to a solid support or soluble support which can be cleaved to release compounds from the support. A careful choice of linker allows cleavage to be performed under appropriate conditions compatible with the stability of the compound and assay method.

Lipid

Water-insoluble molecule which is soluble in nonpolar solvents such as ether. Divided into two classes: Saponifiable and nonsaponifiable.

Lipinski's Rule of 5

Set of criteria for predicting the oral bioavailability of a compound on the basis of simple molecular features (MolWt <= 500, clogp <= 5.0, Hbond donors <= 5, Hbond acceptors <=5, Free-rotation bonds <= 10). Often used to profile a library or virtual library with respect to the proportion of drug -like members which it contains. An algorithm, developed by Christopher A. Lipinski (of Pfizer) and colleagues, in which many of the cutoff numbers are five or multiples of five. There are actually four rules, and Pfizer has developed a additional number of criteria for adoption of lead candidates.

Lipophile

Something that loves oil, usually due to a predominance of alkyl or aromatic groups.

Lipophilic

Literally "fat-loving". Applied to molecular entities (or parts of molecular entities) having a tendency to dissolve in fat-like (e.g. hydrocarbon) solvents.

Lipophilicity

Lipophilicity represents the affinity of a molecule or a moiety for a lipophilic environment. It is commonly measured by its distribution behaviour in a biphasic system, either liquid-liquid (e.g., partition coefficient in octan-1-ol/water) or solid/liquid (retention on reversed-phase high performance liquid chromatography (RP-HPLC) or thin-layer chromatography (TLC) system).

Liquefaction

A process that increases the pressure on a gas until it becomes a liquid. This process happens at room temperature.

Liquid

Liquids are an in-between phase of matter, between solids and gases. One characteristic of a liquid is that it fills the shape of any container. Liquids usually have a flat surface because of gravity pulling down on the molecules.

Liquid phase chemistry

Synthetic process employing a macromolecular soluble support.

Liter

A liter is a metric unit of measure for volume. One liter is equal to one thousand milliliters.

Lithium

Symbol: "Li" Atomic Number: "3" Atomic Mass: 6.94amu. It is one member of the alkali metal family. Lithium is a very light metal, so light that it can float on water. Lithium can be found in batteries, medicine, mineral water, nuclear reactors, and air conditioning.

Lithometeor

A particle of dry substance in the atmosphere, as contrasted to a hydrometeor.

Lithosphere

The crust of the earth, usually thought of as discrete from and in contact with the hydrosphere and the atmosphere.

Litmus

A chemical indicator which is red in acidic solution and blue in basic solution.

Loading

Characteristic property of a solid support which describes the amount of a specific chemical species per unit mass of the support.

Log-normal distribution

A distribution function F(y), in which the logarithm of a quantity is normally distributed, i.e.,
$$F(y) = f_{gauss}(\ln y)$$
where $f_{gauss}(x)$ is a Gaussian distribution. The size distribution of atmospheric aerosols are often described using this distribution function, although the term also applies to gaseous pollutants.

London forces

Attractive forces between apolar molecules, due to their mutual polarizability. They are also components of the forces between polar molecules. Also called "dispersion forces".

Lone (electron) pair

Two paired electrons localized in the valence shell on a single atom. Lone pairs should be designated with two dots. The term "nonbonding electron pair" is more appropriate, and is found in many modern text books.

Lone pair/unshared pair

Two electrons that are not shared between atoms within a molecule.

Lumen

Central space within a wood fiber that may collapse during refining and drying of paper.

Luminance

Photometric counterpart of radiance, producing the visual sensation called brightness. Typical units are: candela m^{-2} (nit), candela cm^{-2} (stilb), foot lambert (2.426 nit). As with all photometric quantities, luminance does not refer to a specific wavelength, but applies to light emitted by a standard source (formerly a "standard international candle", now a blackbody radiator emitting at the temperature of solidifying platinum, 2042 K). Conversion from photometric units to radiometric units (e.g., $J\ s^{-1}$) requires convolution over wavelength of the relative spectral response of the human eye (photopic response tables).

Luminescence

The emission of light by a molecule or ion which is at temperatures below those required for incandescence. Luminescence can originate from electronically excited states of molecules or ions. If the excited state is short lived, as is the case for excited singlet to ground state singlet electronic transitions, the emission follows excitation within a short time period (about 10^{-9} to 10^{-6} s commonly) and is called fluorescence. The fluorescence from the polycyclic aromatic compounds provides a useful means of identification and quantification of these species.

Lustre

The shine produced by metals reflecting light.

Lutetium

Symbol: "Lu" Atomic Number: "71" Atomic Mass: 174.97amu. Lutetium is one of the elements in the lanthanide series of inner transition elements. It may also be classified as a rare earth element.

Lyate ion

The anion produced by hydron removal from a solvent molecule. For example, the hydroxide ion is the lyate ion of water.

Lyonium ion

The cation produced by hydronation of a solvent molecule. For example, $CH_3OH_2^+$ is the lyonium ion of methanol.

M

Machine chest
Usually the last large tank that contains thick-stock pulp before it is made into paper.

Macrometeorology
Study of the largest-scale aspects of the atmosphere, e.g., general global circulation.

Macromolecule
A molecule having a molecular weight in the range of a few thousand to many millions: proteins, nucleic acids and polysaccharides.

Macroporous resin
Polymer which contains a permanent network of pores independent of the state of swelling of the resin. This class of resin thus displays much better solvent tolerance than gel-type resins.

Magnesium
Symbol: "Mg" Atomic Number: "12" Atomic Mass: 24.31amu. Magnesium is a member of the alkaline metals family. Magnesium is a very light metallic element. It is also a trace element, needed by both plants and animals. You will also find magnesium in medicines and flash bulbs.

Makedown
Diluting and agitating a concentrated additive or powder so that it is ready to pump to the paper machine.

Malleable
Able to be hammered into thin sheets.

Manganese
Symbol: "Mn" Atomic Number: "25" Atomic Mass: 54.94amu. This element is one of the transition elements. Manganese can be found in many minerals and small round nodules at the bottom of the ocean. It is also used in many alloys and the creation of some types of glass.

Mannich reaction
Mannich reaction is a process in which hydrogen atoms in organic compounds are replaced with a methyl group.

Manometer, U-tube
An instrument for measuring pressure differences. Usually a liquid such as mercury, water, or some low vapour pressure liquid of the desired density is placed in a U-tube.

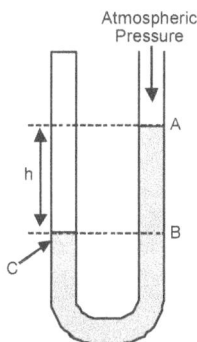

One end of the tube is evacuated and the other is open to the system in which the pressure is to be measured. Differences between the lengths of the liquid columns in the arms (coupled with a knowledge of the density of the liquid) are used to monitor the pressure changes.

Marangoni effect

A tendency of foam bubbles to be flexible and to repair themselves after they are squeezed.

Markovnikov's rule

States that "when an unsymmetrical alkene reacts with a hydrogen halide to give an alkyl halide, the hydrogen adds to the carbon of the alkene that has the greater number of hydrogen substituents, and the halogen to the carbon of the alkene with the fewer number of hydrogen substituents."

Mask

Device which acts as a barrier to the passage of a reagent (often light). A pattern of holes in the mask allows selective passage of reagent and results in a corresponding pattern of reagent deposition or photode-protection on a surface placed behind the mask. This allows the generation of spatially addressable libraries.

Mass

A measure of the amount of material in a substance.

Mass action expression

A mathematical relationship that compares the concentration of reactants and products in an equilibrium system. The concentration of each substance is raised to the power indicated by its coefficient in a balanced equation. Also referred to as the equilibrium constant expression, K_{eq}.

Mass balance

Summation of the masses of a given element in its various compounds before and after reaction (changes) in the atmosphere; provides a test of the completeness of the accounting of the various reaction paths for this element which can be had through the compounds which have been analysed.

Mass number

The total number of protons and neutrons (together known as nucleons) in an atomic nucleus

Mass spectrometer

An instrument used in gas analysis which operates by ionising gaseous atoms or molecules, generally, with electrons of relatively low energy. The parent ions and ion fragments produced are accelerated electrically into a mass separator (involving electric and magnetic fields) which separates ions of specific mass to charge ratio. In a quadrupole mass spectrometer the mass separator involves four parallel rods between which a fixed direct current voltage is applied together with a superimposed radiofrequency voltage.

Mass spectrometer, focusing system; deflection system

Assembly permitting the separation of ions according to their mass to charge ratio.

Mass spectrometer, ion collector

Device for the capture of selected ions such as a Faraday cup collector (with a d.c. amplifier) or an electron multiplier.

Mass spectrometer, ion source

Generally an assembly composed of:
a) an ionization chamber in which a

stream of electrons flows from a hot filament across a stream of gas to collector. The potential between filament and collector is usually between 50 and 70 v; b) a device for the acceleration of these ions.

Mass spectrometry, mass peak in
Record of the ion current, at a specific mass to charge ratio, received by the collector.

Mass spectrometry, mass range in
Range of mass numbers which can be characterized by a mass spectrometer with sufficient resolution to differentiate adjacent peaks.

Mass spectrometry, mass spectrum in
The series of signals at mass numbers corresponding to the ions produced by the sample; each compound has a characteristic mass spectrum. This is sometimes referred to as the cracking pattern.

Massive habit
This is a large crystal with no definite shape. Sulphur is often found in this form.

Matrix isolation
In physical chemistry and spectroscopy a term which refers to the isolation of a reactive or unstable species by dilution in an inert matrix (argon, nitrogen, etc.), usually condensed on a window or in an optical cell at a low temperature, to preserve its form for identification by spectroscopic or other means.

Matter
Anything that has mass and takes up space. (ie. has volume)

Maximum allowable concentration
The maximum concentration of a pollutant which is considered harmless to healthy adults during their working hours, assuming they breathe uncontaminated air at all other times.

Maximum emission concentration
Standards for maximum concentration of air pollutant emission from stationary or mobile sources.

Maximum storage life
Period during which there is no change in concentration in excess of the value of the uncertainty of the concentration.

Measured value (of air quality characteristic)
Estimated value of the air quality characteristic derived from instrument readings; this usually involves calculations related to the calibration process and conversion to required quantities.

Measurement resolution (in atmospheric trace component analysis)
The minimum value above which the difference of two values of air quality characteristic can be distinguished with 95% probability.

Measurement, upper limit of (in atmospheric trace component analysis)
Highest value of the air quality characteristic which can be measured by an instrument; its variations, caused for example by instability, are expected to lie within specified limits. The difference between the lower detection limit and the upper limit of

measurement constitutes the dynamic range of the instrument.

Mechanism

A detailed description of the process leading from the reactants to the products of a reaction, including a characterization as complete as possible of the composition, structure, energy and other properties of reaction intermediates, products, and transition states. An acceptable mechanism of a specified reaction (and there may be a number of such alternative mechanisms not excluded by the evidence) must be consistent with the reaction stoichiometry, the rate law, and with all other available experimental data, such as the stereochemical course of the reaction. Inferences concerning the electronic motions which dynamically interconvert successive species along the reaction path (as represented by curved arrows, for example) are often included in the description of a mechanism.

Mechanism-based inhibition

Irreversible *inhibition* of an enzyme due to its catalysis of the reaction of an artificial substrate. Also called "suicide inhibition".

Medicinal chemistry

Medicinal chemistry is a chemistry-based discipline, also involving aspects of biological, medical and pharmaceutical sciences. It is concerned with the invention, discovery, design, identification and preparation of biologically active compounds, the study of their metabolism, the interpretation of their mode of action at the molecular level and the construction of structure-activity relationships.

Medium

The phase (and composition of the phase) in which chemical species and their reactions are studied in a particular investigation.

Meisenheimer adduct

A cyclohexadienyl derivative formed as Lewis adduct from a nucleophile (Lewis base) and an aromatic or heteroaromatic compound, also called Jackson-Meisenheimer adduct. In earlier usage the term "Meisenheimer complex" was restricted to the typical Meisenheimer alkoxide adducts of nitro-substituted aromatic ethers, e.g.,

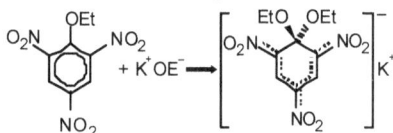

Analogous cationic adducts, such as

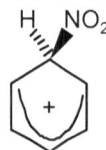

considered to be reaction intermediates in electrophilic aromatic substitution reactions, are called "Wheland intermediates", and sometimes, inappropriately, s-complexes.

Meitnerium

Symbol: "Mt" Atomic Number: "109" Atomic Mass: (266)amu. Meitnerium is one of the postactinide elements. Scientists have created these in labs and may have found only a few atoms of the element.

Melting point

The melting point is the temperature at which a substance changes state from solid to liquid. Ice has its melting point at zero degrees Celsius. The solid melts.

Member

a) Specific compound which is included in a library;
b) The uncharacterized physical product of a library synthesis.

Memory effect (in instruments used for atmospheric trace component analysis)

Dependence of an instrument reading on one or several previous sample(s).

Mendelevium

Symbol: "Md" Atomic Number: "101" Atomic Mass: (258)amu. This is one of the elements in the actinide series of inner transition elements. It may also be classified as a rare earth element.

Mercury

Symbol: "Hg" Atomic Number: "80" Atomic Mass: 200.59amu. Mercury is one of many transition elements. Mercury is one of the few elements that exist as a liquid at room temperature. This silvery metal is very toxic but still has many uses in alloys (amalgams). You will find it used in pesticides, lamps, electronics, explosives, and even dentistry.

Mesolytic cleavage

Cleavage of a bond in a radical ion whereby a radical and an ion are formed. The term reflects the mechanistic duality of the process, which can be viewed as homolytic or heterolytic depending on how the electrons are attributed to the fragments.

Mesomeric effect

The effect (on reaction rates, ionization equilibria, etc.) attributed to a substituent due to overlap of its p or pi orbitals with the p or pi orbitals of the rest of the molecular entity. Delocalization is thereby introduced or extended, and electronic charge may flow to or from the substituent. The effect is symbolized by M. Strictly understood, the mesomeric effect operates in the ground electronic state of the molecule. When the molecule undergoes electronic excitation or its energy is increased on the way to the transition state of a chemical reaction, the mesomeric effect may be enhanced by the electromeric effect, but this term is not much used, and the mesomeric and electromeric effects tend to be subsumed in the term resonance effect of a substituent.

Mesomerism

Essentially synonymous with resonance. The term is particularly associated with the picture of pi electrons as less localized in an actual molecule than in a Lewis formula. The term is intended to imply that the correct representation of a structure is intermediate between two or more Lewis formulae. See also aromatic (2), delocalization.

Mesopause

That region of the atmosphere between the mesosphere and the thermosphere at which the temperature is a minimum.

Mesophase

The phase of a liquid crystalline compound between the crystalline and the isotropic liquid phase.

Mesoscale

In meteorology, the size or scale of phenomena smaller than ordinary cyclones or weather systems but larger than such microscale phenomena as the thickness of the boundary layer, the wakes of objects, etc. Thunderstorms involve mesoscale processes, and other meteorological events the size of cities are usually mesoscale processes.

Mesosphere

That region of the atmosphere which lies above the stratopause (about 47-52 km) and below the mesopause (about 80-90 km) and in which temperature decreases with increasing height; this is region in which the lowest temperatures of the atmosphere occur.

Meta position

Meta position in organic chemistry is the one in which there are two same functional groups tied to a ring of benzene in position 1 and 3. The abbreviation m- is used, for example, m-Hydroquinone is 1,3-dihydroxybenzene.

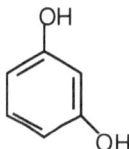

Metabolism

The term metabolism comprises the entire physical and chemical processes involved in the maintenance and reproduction of life in which nutrients are broken down to generate energy and to give simpler molecules (catabolism) which by themselves may be used to form more complex molecules.

Metabolite

A metabolite is any intermediate or product resulting from metabolism.

Metal

A metal is a special type of element. Scientists say something is a metal because of the way it acts in nature. Metals conduct electricity well. That's why they are used in wires. They also

conduct heat well. That's why your pans are made of metal.

Metallic bond

A chemical bond joining metal atoms. eg. magnesium. Valence electrons are mobile and move between the atoms creating positive metallic ions. The attraction is between the positive metallic ions and the negatively charged mobile electrons.

Metamorphic rock

This is a rock type that has been reheated and crystallized. Metamorphic rocks can be created from both sedimentary and igneous rocks. The three main types of rock are igneous, sedimentary, and metamorphic.

Metathesis

A bimolecular process formally involving the exchange of a bond (or bonds) between similar interacting chemical species so that the bonding affiliations in the products are identical (or closely similar) to those in the reactants.

$$RCH\!\!=\!\!CHR + R'CH\!\!=\!\!CHR' \longrightarrow \begin{array}{cc} RCH & CHR \\ \| & + \| \\ R'CH & R'CH \end{array}$$

(The term has its origin in inorganic chemistry with a different meaning, but this older usage is not applicable in physical organic chemistry.)

Meteorological range

The distance L_v = 3.9/b_{scat}; this is the distance over which an average observer could just see a large black object against the horizon sky during daytime, under isotropic conditions of b_{scat} and illumination.

Methane

Methane is a simple hydrocarbon with one carbon and four hydrogen atoms. It is very flammable. It is a compound found in the atmosphere of many planets.

Method (as employed in atmospheric trace component analysis)

Procedure for sampling and analysing one or more air quality characteristics. The accuracy may be established using either a reference material or reference procedures. Two or more methods are considered equivalent methods if the values for their statistical and functional performance characteristics (for example bias, precision, sensitivity, etc.) and tolerances in the presence of specified interferant(s) and under specified operating conditions, fall within minimum specified limits.

Me-too drug

A me-too drug is a compound that is structurally very similar to already known drugs, with only minor pharmacological differences.

Metric system

The system of measurement used in almost all of science. It is a system based on measures of tens. Measures from the metric system include meters, liters, and grams.

Mho

Units of conductivity that are used in the study of electricity.

Micellar catalysis

The acceleration of a chemical reaction in solution by the addition of a surfactant at a concentration higher than its critical micelle concentration so that the reaction can proceed in the environment of surfactant aggregates (micelles). (Rate enhancements may be due, for example, to higher concentration of the reactants in that environment, more

favourable orientation and solvation of the species, or enhanced rate constants in the micellar pseudophase of the surfactant aggregate.) Micelle formation can also lead to a decreased reaction rate.

Micelle

Micelle is an electrically charged colloidal particle, usually organic in nature, composed of aggregates of large molecules, e.g., in soaps and surfactants. For aqueous solutions, the hydrophilic end of the molecule is on the surface of the micelle, while the hydrophobic end (often a hydrocarbon chain) points toward the centre.

Microclimatology

The science that deals with the climate of restricted areas and investigates their phenomena and causes.

Micrometeorology

The study of the meteorological processes on scales from a millimetre or less up to tens or hundreds of metres; e.g., meteorology of a local site that is usually small and often is confined to a shallow layer of air next to the ground.

Micro-particles

Particulate additives used for retention and drainage promotion, characterized by having very high surface area and negative charge.

Microscopic diffusion control (encounter control)

The observable consequence of the limitation that the rate of a bimolecular chemical reaction in a homogeneous medium cannot exceed the rate of encounter of the reacting molecular entities. If (hypothetically) a bimolecular reaction in a homogeneous medium occurred instantaneously when two reactant molecular entities made an encounter, the rate of reaction would be an encounter-controlled rate, determined solely by rates of diffusion of reactants. Such a hypothetical "fully diffusion controlled rate" is also said to correspond to "total microscopic diffusion control", and represents the asymptotic limit of the rate of reaction as the rate constant for the chemical conversion of the encounter pair into product (or products) becomes large relative to the rate constant for separation (or dissociation) of the encounter pair.

Microscopic reversibility, principle of

In a reversible reaction, the mechanism in one direction is exactly the reverse of the mechanism in the other direction. This does not apply to reactions that begin with a photochemical excitation.

Middle atmosphere

The combined stratosphere and mesosphere in the atmosphere.

Middle lamella

Area between fibers in wood that is filled with lignin, a natural, phenolic "glue".

Migratory aptitude

The term is applied to characterize the relative tendency of a group to participate in a rearrangement. In nucleophilic rearrangements (migration to an electron-deficient centre), the migratory aptitude of a group is loosely related to its capacity to stabilize a partial positive charge, but exceptions are known, and the position of hydrogen in the series is often unpredictable.

Mineral

Inorganic compounds usually found in crystalline form. They are made up of pure compounds or elements. Amethyst and quartz are good examples of minerals. These substances are not carbon-based or biologically active materials. A plant is not a mineral. A protein is not a mineral. Calcium Carbonate is a mineral. Granite is made up of minerals.

Mineral colour

All minerals have colours that are unique to their chemical properties. Many minerals of the same compound have different colours because of small impurities in the mineral structure. Colour is always measured in natural light (not fluorescent).

Mineral hardness

Hardness is measure of mineral properties. Some minerals are harder than others are. Diamonds are the hardest and something like talc or calcium carbonate is not hard at all. The harder a mineral, the less it will scratch. Friedrich Mohs designed the hardness scale.

Mineral luster

When light is reflected from a mineral, it is called luster. All minerals reflect light in a unique way. Something like talc will not reflect much light while a diamond will reflect large amounts of light (vitreous). Other elements have a metallic shine.

Mineral streak

Minerals are often ground down into a power. That powder can then be wiped across a white surface and leave a colour streak. It is a more accurate alternative to measuring the colour of the solid crystal.

Mineral transparency

Transparency is a quality of how much light you can see through a substance. A window made of glass is very transparent while a piece of coal is not transparent at all. The several measures of transparency include transparent (clear), translucent (cloudy), and opaque (no light passes).

Mineral vein

A strip of pure mineral found in a rock. Gold is often found in veins deep inside mountains.

Minimum detection limit

See detection limit, lower and detection threshold.

Minimum pressure of utilization

Lower limiting value of the pressure which still permits the use of the calibration gas mixture. The concentration of the components are no longer guaranteed below this limit for one of the following reasons: desorption of the component of interest occurs as the cylinder pressure drops; desorption of other species such as water vapour occurs as the cylinder pressure drops.

Miscible

Two or more liquids that are soluble in one another.

Mist

A qualitative term applied to a suspension of droplets in a gas. In the atmosphere a mist produces a generally thin, grayish veil over the landscape. It reduces visibility to a lesser extent than fog but somewhat more than haze (visibility of less than 2 km but greater than 1 km).

Mixing control

The experimental limitation of the rate of reaction in solution by the rate of mixing of solutions of the two reactants. It can occur even when the reaction rate constant is several powers of 10 less than that for an encounter-controlled rate. Analogous (and even more important) effects of the limitation of reaction rates by the speed of mixing are encountered in heterogeneous (solid/liquid, solid/gas, liquid/gas) systems.

Mixing height

The height to which significant mixing of added pollutants occurs within the atmosphere. In reference to stack gases, it is considered the height at which stack effluent begins mixing with the atmosphere as it leaves the stack.

Mixing ratio

In meteorology, the dimensionless ratio of the mass of a substance (such as water vapour) in an air parcel to the mass of the remaining substances in the air parcel. For trace substances, this is approximated by the ratio of the mass of the substance to the mass of air.

Mixture

Mixtures are substances held together by physical, not chemical, forces. Most things you find things in nature are mixtures. Rocks, the ocean, and just about everything is a mixture.

Mobile phase in chromatography

The carrier fluid with the chemical to be analysed passing through the chromatographic column.

Mobility

In aerosol physics, the velocity of a particle per unit applied force.

Möbius aromaticity

A monocyclic array of orbitals in which there is a single out-of-phase overlap (or, more generally, an odd number of out-of-phase overlaps) reveals the opposite pattern of aromatic character to Hückel systems; with 4n electrons it is stabilized (aromatic), whereas with 4n + 2 it is destabilized (antiaromatic). In the excited state 4n + 2 Möbius pi-electron systems are stabilized, and 4n systems are destabilized. No examples of ground-state Möbius pi systems are known, but the concept has been applied to transition states of pericyclic reactions.

Mode

In a plot of the frequency of occurrence of a variable versus the variable, a maximum point is a mode. A bimodal distribution is one which contains two maxima.

Mohs scale

This is a scale that measures the hardness of rocks and minerals. Friedrich Mohs devised the scale in 1812. The scale goes from one to ten with ten being the hardest substance. A diamond would have a value of 10 while a quartz crystal would only have a value of 7.

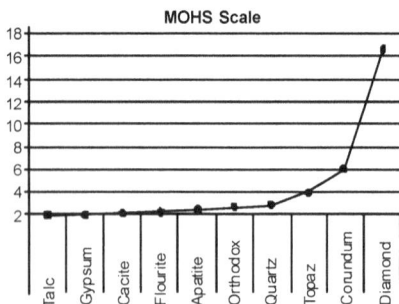

MOHS Scale

Moieties

Chemical compounds or functional groups or portions of those compounds.

Moiety

In physical organic chemistry moiety is generally used to signify part of a molecule, e.g. in an ester R^1COOR^2 the alcohol moiety is R^2O. The term

should not be used for a small fragment of a molecule.

Molality

A measure of the number of moles of a solute compared to one thousand grams of the solvent. Scientists use 'm' when they describe the molality of a system. It is a measure of mass as opposed to volume. Volume is used in measuring molarity.

Molar

An term expressing molarity, the number of moles of solute per liters of solution.

Molar heat capacity

the heat energy required to raise the temperature of one mole of a substance by 1 Celsius (or 1 kelvin).

Molar mass

the mass, in grams, of one mole of a substance. Molar mass is numerically equivalent to atomic (or molecular or formula) mass, except the unit is $g \cdot mol^{-1}$, not amu

Molarity

A measure of the number of moles of a solute that are dissolved in a liter of solution. As concentration increases, the molarity of the solution also increases. Scientists use the letter 'M' to describe the molarity of a solution.

Mole (abbreviated mol)

The S.I. unit of amount of substance. 1 mol of a substance contains 6.022×10^{23} specified entities. The amount of substance of a system which contains as many elementary entities as there are atoms in 0.012 kg of carbon-12. When the mole is used, the elementary entities must be specified and may be atoms, molecules, ions, electrons, other particles, or specified groups of such particles.

Mole fraction
The number of moles of a particular substance expressed as a fraction of the total number of moles.

Molecular entity
Any constitutionally or isotopically disti nct atom, molecule, ion, ion pair, radical, radical ion, complex, conformer etc., identifiable as a separately distinguishable entity. Molecular entity is used in this glossary as a general term for singular entities, irrespective of their nature, while chemical species stands for sets or ensembles of molecular entities. Note that the name of a compound may refer to the respective molecular entity or to the chemical species, e.g. methane, may mean a single molecule of CH_4 (molecular entity) or a molar amount, specified or not (chemical species), participating in a reaction. The degree of precision necessary to describe a molecular entity depends on the context. For example "hydrogen molecule" is an adequate definition of a certain molecular entity for some purposes, whereas for others it is necessary to distinguish the electronic state and/or vibrational state and/or nuclear spin, etc. of the hydrogen molecule.

Molecular formula
Shows the number of atoms of each element present in a molecule.

Molecular geometry
Shape of a molecule, based on the relative positions of the atoms.

Molecular graphics
Molecular graphics is the visualization and manipulation of three-dimensional representations of molecules on a graphical display device.

Molecular mass
Molecular mass is another term for formula mass. You can determine the formula mass by adding the individual masses of each atom in the compound. The formula mass of NaCl is 58.44.

Molecular mechanics calculation
An empirical calculational method intended to give estimates of structures and energies for conformations of molecules. The method is based on the assumption of "natural" bond lengths and angles, deviation from which leads to strain, and the existence of torsional interactions and attractive and/or repulsive van der Waals and dipolar forces between non-bonded atoms. The method is also called "(empirical) force-field calculations".

Molecular metal
A non-metallic material whose properties resemble those of metals, usually following oxidative doping; e.g. polyacetylene following oxidative doping with iodine.

Molecular modeling
Molecular modeling is a technique for the investigation of molecular structures and properties using computational chemistry and graphical visualization techniques in order to provide a plausible three-dimensional representation under a given set of circumstances.

Molecularity
The number of reactant molecular entities that are involved in the "microscopic chemical event" constituting an elementary reaction. (For reactions in solution this number is always taken to exclude molecular entities that form part of the medium and which are involved solely by virtue of their solvation of solutes.) A reaction with a molecularity of one is called "unimolecular", one with a molecularity

of two "bimolecular" and of three "termolecular".

Molecules

We the elements of matter as being made up of individual atoms with a specific atomic structure that was unique for each element. Atoms of different elements can bind together to form multi-atom structures which are referred to as molecules. Molecules of a given substance such as carbon dioxide have a defined composition and ratio of elements. For Instance carbon dioxide (CO_2) contains one atom of carbon and two atoms of oxygen. This unit of three atoms is referred to as one molecule of carbon dioxide.

Molybdenum

Symbol: "Mo" Atomic Number: "42" Atomic Mass: 95.94amu. Molybdenum is one of the transition elements. This element has been confused with lead in the past. When pure, it is a silvery white metal and can be found in many alloys, aircraft parts, and even as a trace mineral in some plants.

Monitoring (in atmospheric trace component analysis)

In a broad sense of the term, repeated measurements to follow changes over a period of time. In a restricted sense of the term, regular measurement of pollutant levels in relation to some standard or in order to assess the effectiveness of a system of regulation and control.

Monitoring systems (in atmospheric trace component analysis)

Automatic systems placed in a smokestack, a work place, or in the ambient atmosphere which measure

and record the amounts of specified air pollutants which are present.

Monoclinic crystal

A crystal that has a shape like a cube but is flattened in one dimension.

Monomer

Member of a building block set which can be repeatedly incorporated into a library to give a set of compounds of repeating structure, e.g. amino acids in a peptide library.

Monosaccharide

A monosaccharide is one sugar molecule. They usually have six carbon, twelve hydrogen, and six oxygen atoms in one molecule with the formula $(CH_2O)x$. They may also be in a six-carbon ring or a five carbon ring.

Monthly averages (with reference to atmospheric component analysis)

For reporting integrated analyses of ambient air on a monthly rate, an average value is calculated; i.e., it is given on the basis of a 30-day month.

Multi-valent

Having two or more electrical charges per molecule (ion); for example, soluble aluminium forms the trivalent $Al3+$ ion at low pH.

Mutagen

A mutagen is an agent that causes a permanent heritable change (i.e., a mutation) into the DNA (deoxyribonucleic acid) of an organism.

Mutual prodrug

A mutual prodrug is the association in a unique molecule of two, usually synergistic, drugs attached to each other, one drug being the carrier for the other and vice versa.

N

Native element mineral

A mineral that is made up of a pure element. Gold is often found alone and as a native element.

Negative catalyst

A negative catalyst is another term for an inhibitor. A negative catalyst has an opposite reaction from a catalyst.

Neodymium

Symbol: "Nd" Atomic Number: "60" Atomic Mass: 144.24amu. Neodymium is one of the elements in the lanthanide series of inner transition elements. It may also be classified as a rare earth element. This reactive metal tarnishes easily and can be found in lasers, alloys, and even lenses for specialized types of eyewear.

Neon

Symbol: "Ne" Atomic Number: "10" Atomic Mass: 20.18amu. Neon is a non-reactive gas. It has no colour and no smell, but when you send electricity through neon, it glows red. It is one of the noble or inert gases.

Nephelometry

Analytical methods which depend on the measurement of the intensity of scattered light emanating from an illuminated volume of an aerosol. The ratio of scattered intensity to illuminating intensity is compared with a standard of known properties.

Neptunium

Symbol: "Np" Atomic Number: "93" Atomic Mass: 237.05amu. Neptunium is one of the elements in the actinide series of inner transition elements. It may also be classified as a rare earth element. A silvery, radioactive element that can be used in nuclear reactors because its atomic structure is so close to plutonium.

Net ionic equation

An equation that shows only ions that undergo change during a chemical reaction; spectator ions are omitted.

Network, air sampling

A number of air sampling stations which are established in a given geographical region at which periodic measurements of both pollutant concentrations and meteorological quantities (wind speed, direction, rain fall, humidity, etc.) are made to determine the extent and the nature of the air pollution and to establish trends in the concentrations of the air pollutants with time.

Neutral

An object that does not have a positive or negative charge.

Neutralization

The addition of just the right amount of material having an opposite charge to achieve a zero surface (or "colloidal") charge on suspended matter in an aqueous sample.

Neutralization reaction

A reaction between an acid and a base that results in salt and water.

Neutron

One of the particles found in the nucleus of an atom. Whereas an electron has a negative (-) charge and a proton has a positive (+) charge, a neutron has a neutral charge (0).

New chemical entity

A new chemical entity (NCE) is a compound not previously described in the literature.

Nickel

Symbol: "Ni" Atomic Number: "28" Atomic Mass: 58.70amu. This element is one of the transition elements in period four. You can find nickel used in coins, many minerals, desalinization plants, and in batteries with cadmium.

NIH shift

The intramolecular hydrogen migration which can be observed in enzymatic and chemical hydroxylations of aromatic rings. It is evidenced by appropriate deuterium labelling, i.e.

In enzymatic reactions the NIH shift is generally thought to derive from the rearrangement of arene oxide intermediates, but other pathways have been suggested.

Niobium

Symbol: "Nb" Atomic Number: "41" Atomic Mass: 92.91amu. Niobium is one of the transition elements. This ductile metal (when pure) is found in many minerals. It actually turns blue when in the air and is used in spacecraft and superconducting magnets.

Nitrene

Generic name for HN: and substitution derivatives thereof, containing an electrically neutral univalent nitrogen atom with four non-bonding electrons. Two of these are paired; the other two may have parallel spins (triplet state) or antiparallel spins (singlet state). The name is the strict analogue of carbene and, as a generic name, it is preferred to a number of alternatives proposed ("imene", "imine radical", "azene", "azylene", "azacarbene", "imin", "imidogen").

Nitrenium ion

The cation H_2N^+ and its N-hydrocarbyl derivatives R_2N^+, in which the nitrogen has a positive charge, and two unshared electrons. A synonymous term is aminylium ion.

Nitric acid (HNO_3)

A major acid formed in the atmosphere from the reaction of HO-radicals with NO_2 (HO + NO_2 + M(N_2/O_2) HNO_3 + M), also through the reaction of N_2O_5 with water droplets (N_2O_5 + H_2O(liquid)· 2HNO_3), and by reaction of NO_3 with CH_2O or certain other organic species (NO_3 + CH_2O HNO_3 + HCO). This is a strong acid and one of the two major acidic components of acid deposition; H_2SO_4 is the other.

Nitric oxide (NO)

The major oxide of nitrogen emitted from combustion sources such as power plants, the exhaust of mobile sources, incinerators, etc. It is an important source of NO_2 through its oxidation by hydroperoxyl (HO_2) and alkylperoxyl, acylperoxyl, and arylperoxyl radicals (RO_2) and ozone in the atmosphere.

Nitrile

Any organic compound which has a -Ca"N functional group.

Nitrogen

Symbol: "N" Atomic Number: "7" Atomic Mass: 14.00amu. Nitrogen is found as a gas in nature and it is classified as a non-metal. It makes up over 75 percent of the air surrounding the Earth. It is also found in the soil and used by plants. You will also find nitrogen in ammonia, steel making, freezing liquids, and oil refineries.

Nitrogen pentoxide (dinitrogen pentoxide, N_2O_3)

An oxide of nitrogen which forms in the atmosphere through the oxidation of NO_2 by O_3 : $NO_2 + O_3$ $NO_3 + O_2$; $NO_3 + NO_2$ N_2O_5. Its formation is favored in polluted air masses of high O_3 and NO_2 content and during the night. It is a precursor to nitric acid through its reaction with water (liquid) or aqueous aerosols.

Nitrous acid

Nitrous acid (molecular formula HNO_2) is a weak and monobasic acid known only in solution and in the form of nitrite salts. Nitrous acid is used to make diazides from amines; this occurs by nucleophilic attack of the amine onto the nitrite, reprotonation by the surrounding solvent, and double-elimination of water. The diazide can then be liberated to give a carbene or carbenoid.

Nitrous oxide (N_2O)

This oxide of nitrogen is released into the atmosphere through biological activity and from other sources. It does not absorb light which is present within the troposphere, and it is unreactive toward transient species including the HO-radical. Its major loss mechanism involves transport to the stratosphere where it undergoes photodecomposition and reaction with $O(^1D)$ to form NO in part. It is present in air at about 0.3 ppmv.

Nm

An abbreviation for nanometers. A nanometer is equal to 10^{-9} metres.

Nobelium

Symbol: "No" Atomic Number: "102" Atomic Mass: (259)amu. Nobelium is one of the elements in the actinide series of inner transition elements. It may also be classified as a rare earth element.

Noble gas

The Noble Gases are the all of the elements in the furthest right column of the periodic table. They all have filled outer shells and are very non-reactive.

Noble gas elements

Elements in the periodic table whose outermost shells are filled with electrons (8). Helium, neon, and argon are examples of noble gas elements. They are very non-reactive.

Node

Part of the orbital area in an atom where it is impossible to find an electron.

Nonclassical carbocation

A carbocation the ground state of which has delocalized (bridged) bonding pi- or sigma-electrons. (N.B.: Allylic and benzylic carbocations are not considered nonclassical.)

Nonelectrolyte

This is a solute that cannot conduct electricity when dissolved in the solvent (water). Water alone cannot conduct electricity well. Sugar is a good example of a nonelectrolyte substance that, when added to water, does not change the solution's ability to conduct electricity. Salt is a good electrolyte.

Non-metal

An element that is dull, is a poor electrical and thermal conductor and that is brittle.

Nonpolar covalent bond

A bond where elections are equally shared between two atoms.

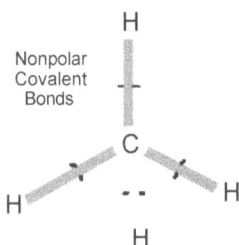

Non-process elements

Materials dissolved in process water that tend to circulate around the system and not become part of the paper product.

Non-reactive

This is the opposite of reactive. Non-reactive elements do not easily combine with the other elements. Helium, neon, and argon are examples of very non-reactive elements.

Normal conditions

A qualitative term, dependent on the preference of the investigator; it often implies ambient pressure and "room temperature". Preferably the variables of temperature and pressure should be quoted as values representative of the actual conditions (or range of conditions) employed in the study.

Normality

A measure of substance equivalents that are dissolved in a volume of solution. Equivalents are a measure of the actual mass of material divided by the equivalent mass. That equivalent mass is the atomic mass of the compound divided by the valence of the compound. Scientists use the letter 'N' to describe the normality of a solution. Normality can also be determined by multiplying the molarity of a solution by the net positive valence for the compound.

Nuclear fusion

When parts of the nucleus of atoms are forced together to create a new one.

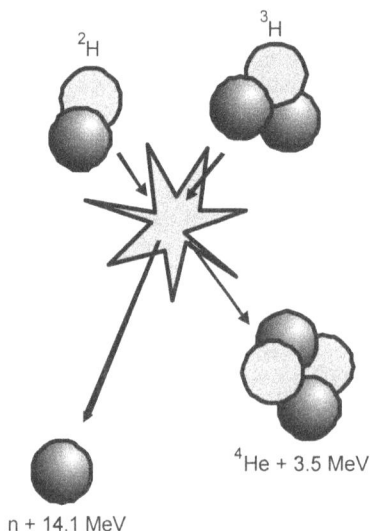

^{4}He + 3.5 MeV

n + 14.1 MeV

Nuclear magnetic resonance (NMR)

NMR spectroscopy makes it possible to discriminate nuclei, typically protons, in different chemical environments. The electron distribution gives rise to a chemical shift of the resonance frequency. The chemical shift of a nucleus is expressed in parts per million (ppm) by its frequency, n, relative to a standard, ref, and defined as = 106 (n-ref)/o, where o is the operating frequency of the spectrometer. It is an indication of the chemical state of the group containing the nucleus. More information is derived from the spin-spin couplings between nuclei, which give rise to multiplet patterns.

Nuclear model

The atom is composed of a positively charged nucleus containing most of the atoms mass and is surrounded by a large amount of empty space which is orbited by negatively charged electrons.

Nuclear reaction

When a reaction affects the nucleus of an atom.

Nucleic acid

A nucleic acid is a macromolecule composed of linear sequences of nucleotides that perform several functions in living cells, e.g., the storage of genetic information and its transfer from one generation to the next DNA (deoxyribonucleic acid), the expression of this information in protein synthesis (mRNA, tRNA) and may act as functional components of subcellular units such as ribosomes (rRNA).

Nucleofuge

A *leaving group* that carries away the bonding electron pair. For example, in the *hydrolysis* of an alkyl chloride, Cl⁻ is the nucleofuge. The tendency of atoms or groups to depart with the bonding electron pair is called nucleofugality.

Nucleophile

Literally, nucleus lover. A negatively or neutrally charged reagent that forms a bond with an electrophile by dontating both bonding electrons. Nucleophiles are Lewis Bases.

Nucleophilic substitution reaction

A reaction in which a halide is removed from a molecule and replaced with a nucleophile.

Nucleoside

A nucleoside is a compound in which a purine or pyrimidine base is bound via a N-atom to C-1 replacing the hydroxy group of either 2-deoxy-D-ribose or of D-ribose, but without any phosphate groups. The common nucleosides in biological systems are adenosine, guanosine, cytidine, and uridine (which contain ribose) and deoxyadenosine, deoxyguanosine, deoxycytidine and thymidine (which contain deoxyribose).

Nucleotide

A nucleotide is a nucleoside in which the primary hydroxy group of either 2-deoxy-D-ribose or of D-ribose is esterified by orthophosphoric acid.

Nucleus

The nucleus of an atom is the center of the atom. The electrons orbit around the center and are arranged in shells. Protons and neutrons live in the nucleus.

Nuisance threshold

That concentration of an air pollutant that is considered undesirable. In the case of a substance with an objectionable odor, it is the smallest concentration of the substance which can be detected by a human being (nose).

O

Octahedral crystal

This is a crystal that has eight sides. Think of a shape with two pyramids attached at their bases.

Octet

In Lewis structures the goal is to make almost all atoms have an octet. This means that they will have access to 8 electrons regularly, even if they do have to share some of them.

Odor threshold

The concentration of a compound which produces an odor which is detectable by a human being (nose). For certain compounds this threshold is very low (e.g., 1 part in 10^9 for certain suphides).

Olation

Formation of bonds between aluminium atoms in aqueous solution, involving OH groups as the bridges (a step in polymerization).

Oligonucleotide

An oligonucleotide is an oligomer resulting from a linear sequences of nucleotides.

Omission library

Strategy for identifying active library members by the systematic omission of building blocks from mixtures. Observation of reduced activity in a certain pool suggests that the building block which was omitted in that pool contributes to activity.

Oncogene

An oncogene is a normal cellular gene which, when inappropriately expressed or mutated, can transform eukaryotic cells into tumour cells.

Onium ion

(1) A cation (with its counterion) derived by addition of a hydron to a mononuclear parent hydride of the nitrogen, chalcogen and halogen family, e.g. H_4N^+ ammonium ion.
(2) Derivatives formed by substitution of the above parent ions by univalent groups, e.g. $(CH_3)_2S^+H$ dimethylsulfonium, $(CH_3CH_2)_4N^+$ tetraethylammonium.
(3) Derivatives formed by substitution of the above parent ions by groups having two or three free valencies on the same atom. Such derivatives are, whenever possible, designated by a specific class name. E.g. $R_2C = NH_2^+$ iminium ion.

Online

An operation or measurement that occurs automatically and continuously during an industrial process.

Opacity

Ability of paper to hide things such as print images on subsequent sheets or printed on the back.

Opaque

The inability of light to pass through a substance. Light is scattered.

Open burning
The occasional burning of outdoor stores of lumber, sawdust, scrapped cars, tires, textiles, open dumps, etc.

Open hearth furnace
Reverberatory furnace, containing a basin-shaped hearth, for melting and refining suitable types of pig iron, iron ore, and scrap for steel production. A large amount of dust from ore and other materials and splashings from slag are carried away by the waste gases; a supplementary chamber is commonly used for collecting slag and dust.

Open system
A system in which products are removed as they form and/or additional reactants are added.

Optical brightener
An informal term for "fluorescent whitening agent," a dye material that absorbs ultraviolet light and re-emits light in the blue region.

Optical yield
In a *chemical reaction* involving chiral reactants and products, the ratio of the optical purity of the product to that of the precursor, reactant or catalyst. This should not be confused with "enantiomeric excess". The optical yield is in no way related to the chemical yield of the reaction.

Optimization
The process of synthesizing chemical variations, or analogs, of a lead compound, with the goal of creating those compounds with improved pharmacological properties.

Orbit
An orbit is the path one object takes when it spins around another object. An electron has a path in a circle around the center of the atom. The Earth has an orbit around the sun. Since electrons can move in any direction around the center of the atom, their space is called a shell.

Orbital
The orbital is where an atom keeps its electrons. An atom can have up to seven orbitals. We also call it a shell.

Orbital steering
A concept expressing that the stereochemistry of approach of two reacting species is governed by the most favourable overlap of their appropriate orbitals.

Orbital symmetry
The behaviour of an atomic or localized molecular orbital under molecular symmetry operations characterizes its orbital symmetry. For example, under a reflection in an appropriate symmetry plane, the phase of the orbital may be unchanged (symmetric), or it may change sign (antisymmetric), i.e. the positive and negative lobes are interchanged. A principal context for the use of orbital symmetry is the discussion of chemical changes that involve "conservation of orbital symmetry". If a certain symmetry element (e.g. the reflection plane) is retained along a reaction pathway, that pathway is "allowed" by orbital symmetry conservation if each of the occupied orbitals of the reactant(s) is of the same symmetry type as a similarly (e.g. singly or doubly) occupied orbital of the product(s).

Organic acids
When the elements making up the organic compound are Carbon, Hydrogen and Oxygen and when there is a terminal combination of a carbon-oxygen double bond linked to an "O H" group, the Functional Group becomes

O=C-OH and the compounds are called Organic Acids. The most commonly known organic acid is Acetic Acid ($CH_3C=O$ -OH) also known as Vinegar.

Organic chemistry

Chemistry is the science concerned with the composition, structure and properties of matter. Organic chemistry is the science of the composition, structure and properties of the element Carbon along with Hydrogen, Oxygen and Nitrogen. These four elements, dominated by Carbon, make up over 50% of all living (Organic) matter.

Organic compounds

A given Organic Compound is made up of molecules of various unique combinations of Carbon, Hydrogen, Oxygen and Nitrogen. These molecules are made up of atoms of these elements linked by Covalent bonds. Two examples of Organic Compounds are carbon dioxide (CO_2) and methane (CH_4).

Organic functional groups

Organic Compounds can be grouped according to their Functional Groups. Functional Groups are unique combinations of atoms that impart to the Organic Compound specific and consistent properties. One example of an Organic Functional Group is the -OH group. When this group is present in an Organic Compound the compound is referred to as an Alcohol.

Orphan drug

An orphan drug is a drug for the treatment of a rare disease for which reasonable recovery of the sponsoring firm's research and development expenditure is not expected within a reasonable time. The term is also used to describe substances intended for such uses.

Ortho position

Ortho position in organic chemistry is the one in which there are two same functional groups, tied to a ring of benzene in the positions 1 and 2. The abbreviation o- is used, for example, o-Hydroquinone is 1,2-dihydroxybenzene.

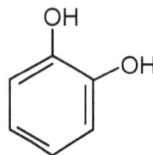

Orthogonality

a) Property of protecting groups or linkers allowing removal, modification or cleavage of one such without affecting others;

b) Pooling strategy whereby library members are incorporated in more than one pool, and are mixed with a different set of other members in each pool. Thus a hit results in two or more active pools with only one member in common.

Orthorhombic crystal

This crystal forms a prism that has three edges at ninety-degree angles.

Osmium

Symbol: "Os" Atomic Number: "76" Atomic Mass: 190.20amu. This element is one of the transition elements. Osmium is found in nature with platinum and nickel. It actually has the highest melting point of the group and is used in alloys that require a lot of strength.

Osmosis

This process happens when water molecules move from an area of high concentration to low concentration. They need to pass through a semi-permeable membrane. It often happens when larger molecules are not able to cross the membrane and concentrations need to be evened out.

Osmotic pressure

A tendency for soluble materials to flow across a barrier in whatever direction will achieve more nearly equal ionic strength on each side.

Outer-sphere (electron transfer)

An outer-sphere electron transfer is a reaction in which the electron transfer takes place with no or very weak (4 - 16 kJ mol^{-1}) electronic interaction between the reactants in the transition state. If instead the donor and the acceptor exhibit a strong electronic coupling, the reaction is described as inner-sphere electron transfer. The two terms derive from studies concerning metal complexes and it has been suggested that for organic reactions the term "nonbonded" and "bonded" electron transfer should be used. See also *inner-sphere electron transfer*.

Over-cationized

A papermaking system to which so much cationic material has been added that the zeta potential is reversed to strongly positive.

Overfire

High-velocity air jets issuing from nozzles in a furnace enclosure to provide turbulence and oxygen to aid combustion, or to provide cooling air; overfire air is also known as secondary air.

Oxidant (with reference to atmospheric chemistry)

A very qualitative term which includes any and all trace gases which have a greater oxidation potential than oxygen

(for example, ozone, peroxyacetyl nitrate, hydrogen peroxide, organic peroxides, NO_3, etc.). It is recommended that alternative, more definitive terms be used which define the specific oxidant of interest whenever possible.

Oxidants

Chemicals that tend to convert alcohol groups to carboxylic acid groups. Oxidants are used for bleaching and as part of biocide treatments.

Oxidation

(1) The complete, net removal of one or more electrons from a *molecular entity* (also called "de-electronation").

(2) An increase in the *oxidation number* of any atom within any *substrate*.

(3) Gain of oxygen and/or loss of hydrogen of an organic substrate. All oxidations meet criteria (1) and (2), and many meet criterion (3), but this is not always easy to demonstrate. Alternatively, an oxidation can be described as a transformation of an organic substrate that can be rationally dissected into steps or primitive changes. The latter consist in removal of one or several electrons from the substrate followed or preceded by gain or loss of water and/or hydrons or hydroxide ions, or by nucleophilic substitution by water or its reverse and/or by an intramolecular molecular rearrangement. This formal definition allows the original idea of oxidation (combination with oxygen), together with its extension to removal of hydrogen, as well as processes closely akin to this type of transformation (and generally regarded in current usage of the term in organic chemistry to be oxidations and to be effected by

"oxidizing agents") to be descriptively related to definition (1). For example the oxidation of methane to chloromethane may be considered as follows: $CH_4 - 2e^- - H^+ + OH^- = CH_3OH$ (oxidation) CH_3Cl (reversal of hydrolysis)

Oxidation number
An integer assigned to an atom in a compound that helps track electrons during redox reactions. Sometimes called "apparent charge." During a redox reaction, an increase in oxidation number of an atom indicates a loss of electrons, or oxidation; a decrease in oxidation number indicates a gain of electrons, or reduction.

Oxidation reaction
A reaction where a substance loses electrons.

Oxidation-reduction-reaction
A reaction involving the transfer of electrons.

Oxidative addition
The insertion of a metal of a metal complex into a covalent bond involving formally an overall two-electron loss on one metal or a one-electron loss on each of two metals, i.e.,
$L_nM^m + XY \quad L_nM^{m+2}(X)(Y)$, or 2 $L_nM^m + XY \quad L_nM^{m+1}(X) + L_nM^{m+1}(Y)$
In free-radical chemistry, the term is used to indicate a free radical addition to a carbon-carbon double bond, under oxidative conditions.

Oxide mineral
A mineral that is made up of compounds with an oxygen atom bonded to a metal. A ruby is a good example of an oxide mineral.

Oxidized species
In chemistry, a term used to characterize the degree of oxidation (or reduction) in atoms, molecules, and ions. An atom in a molecule or an ion which has a high oxidation state. An element or atom in a compound can be oxidized by reaction with oxygen, while it can be reduced by reaction with hydrogen. An oxidized species may be formed also through the loss of electrons (either to the positive electrode in a cell, or through transfer to another atom or group of atoms).

Oxidizer
An oxidizer can also be called an oxidizing agent. It is something that can oxidize another substance. Some major oxidizing elements are chlorine and oxygen.

Oxidizing agent
A substance that accepts/gains electrons and undergoes reduction. It "allows" the other substance to undergo oxidation.

Oxoacid
When one or more hydroxide (OH) groups are bonded to a central atom.

Oxolation
Conversion of the olated form of aluminium polymers to Al-O-Al bonds, usually involving the application of heat during drying of paper.

Oxygen
Symbol: "O" Atomic Number: "8" Atomic Mass: 16.00amu. Oxygen is a gas and is classified as a non-metal. It is found in the crust of the Earth and in the air. Animals need oxygen to survive. It is also very reactive.

Oxygen, molecular (O$_2$)
A reactive species which comprises about 21% by volume of the gases present in the earth's atmosphere. It is a necessary species for the existence of most forms of life on earth. It is a highly reactive gas which

is capable of combining with most of the other elements.

Ozone (O_3)

Ozone (O_3) or trioxygen, is a triatomic molecule, consisting of three oxygen atoms. It is an allotrope of oxygen that is much less stable than the diatomic allotrope (O_2). Ozone in the lower atmosphere is an air pollutant with harmful effects on the respiratory systems of animals and will burn sensitive plants; however, the ozone layer in the upper atmosphere is beneficial, preventing potentially damaging electromagnetic radiation from reaching the Earth's surface. Ozone

is present in low concentrations throughout the Earth's atmosphere.

Ozone hole

A region of the stratosphere over Antarctica in which a marked decrease in the concentration of ozone has been observed in the Antarctic spring in recent years. The origin of this phenomenon is not yet established, but several theories based on both physical (transport related) and chemical processes (involvement of the halocarbons and their products of oxidation) have been suggested. The latter explanation appears to be in better accord with recent findings.

P

PAC, poly-aluminium chloride

A cationic flocculant solution formed by partial neutralization of aluminium chloride's acidity.

Palladium

Symbol: "Pd" Atomic Number: "46" Atomic Mass: 106.40amu. Palladium is one of the transition elements. Palladium is another member of the platinum group. It is a white colour and will not tarnish (oxidize) in air. You will find it used in jewelry, surgical instruments, and watches.

PAM, poly-acrylamide

Very-high mass copolymers or acrylamide and other monomers, used as retention aids.

Paper chromatography

A method of separating substances as they are carried by a solvent as it moves through paper.

Para position

Para position in organic chemistry is the one in which there are two same functional groups tied to a ring of benzene in the position 1 and 4. The abbreviation p- is used, for example, p-Hydroquinone is 1,4-dihydroxybenzene.

OH

OH

Parallel synthesis

Strategy whereby sets of discrete compounds are prepared simultaneously in arrays of physically separate reaction vessels or microcompartments without interchange of intermediates during the assembly process. Contrast Pool/Split.

Parenchyma

Cells within a tree that are two small to be considered fibers, often used to store food.

Parent isotope

An element that undergoes nuclear decay.

Partial agonist

A partial agonist is an agonist which is unable to induce maximal activation of a receptor population, regardless of the amount of drug applied.

Partial library

Partly assembled library, or portion thereof, which is reserved to be completed once initial property relationships have been identified. For instance, part of an intermediate pool may not be treated with the final building block until the optimal residue at the final position is known, thus avoiding the need to prepare that pool from the starting materials.

Partial pressure

Partial pressure is the pressure of one gas in a system of two or more nonreacting gases.

Partial pressure
The pressure exerted by a certain gas in a mixture.

Partial release
Cleavage process designed to release a compound from a solid support in discrete portions, e.g. by using orthogonal linkers or by controlled application of cleavage reagent or condition.

Particle (atmospheric)
A small discrete mass of solid or liquid matter.

Particle counter
A device for measuring the number of suspended particles (in a certain size range) per volume unit of a gaseous or liquid medium.

Particle size
To describe the size of liquid or solid particles (aerosol) the average or equivalent diameter is used. For nonspherical particles collected in an impactor, for example, the aerodynamic diameter of a particle of arbitrary shape and density refers to the size of a spherical particle of unit density that would deposit on a given impactor surface.

Particle size distribution
The size of the liquid or solid particles in the atmosphere usually extends from >0.01 to <100m in diameter. In the earth's atmosphere the distribution function which describes the number of particles as a function of diameter, mass, or surface area of the aerosol can be determined reasonably well with modern instrumentation.

Particle theory of matter
All matter is composed of individual particles (atoms, ions, molecules) which are attracted to one another and are constantly moving in all physical states (solids, liquids, gases)

Particulate matter
A general term used to describe airborne solid or liquid particles of all sizes. The term aerosol is recommended for general use in describing airborne particulate matter.

Passivation
Continuously spraying a barrier chemical onto a forming fabric or other equipment to prevent deposits of tacky materials.

Passive sampler
A device for preconcentration of trace substances from gaseous media based on molecular diffusion without controlled conveyance of the gas to be investigated (e.g., work place air).

Paste rosin size
A sizing agent mixture of rosin free acid and saponified rosin, no longer in common use.

Pattern recognition
Pattern recognition is the identification of patterns in large data sets using appropriate mathematical methodologies.

Pcb
Polychlorinated biphenyls; toxic compounds which have been employed as insulating fluids in some electrical transformers.

Pcc
Precipitated calcium carbonate, a bright filler having a variety of possible shapes and sizes.

Peak concentration (trace atmospheric component)
The highest concentration of a given trace component which was measured

with a continuous analyser during a specified sampling period.

Peak, chromatographic

The portion of a differential chromatogram recording the detector response or eluate concentration while a single compound emerges from the column. If separation is incomplete, two or more components may appear as one unresolved peak.

PEI, poly-ethylenimine

A class of very highly charged cationic polymers, usually highly branched, useful for charge control and drainage promotion, especially under acidic to neutral conditions.

PEO, poly-ethylene oxide

A very-high-mass, non-ionic retention aid that usually requires sequential addition of a phenolic cofactor (or lignin).

Peptide

A molecule composed of two or more amino acids. Larger peptides are generally referred to as polypeptides or proteins.

Peptide bond Peptide

A planar, amide linkage between the amino group of one amino acid and the carboxyl group of another, with the elimination of a molecule of water.

Peptidomimetic

A peptidomimetic is a compound containing non-peptidic structural elements that is capable of mimicking or antagonizing the biological action(s) of a natural parent peptide. A peptidomimetic does no longer have classical peptide characteristics such as enzymatically scissille peptidic bonds.

Peptoid

A peptoid is a peptidomimetic that results from the oligomeric assembly of N-substituted glycines.

Percent composition

Expresses the mass ratio between different elements in a compound.

Percent yield

The percentage of yield that occurred versus the theoretical yield.

Percentage composition

This composition measurement reflects the percentage of total mass for a specific element. The percentage composition of sodium in sodium chloride (NaCl) is about 39%. Just take the total mass of one element of the compound and divide it by the total mass of the compound. Then multiply by 100.

Pericyclic reaction

A chemical reaction in which concerted reorganization of bonding takes place throughout a cyclic array of continuously bonded atoms. It may be viewed as a reaction proceeding through a fully conjugated cyclic transition state. The number of atoms in the cyclic array is usually six, but other numbers are also possible. The term embraces a variety of processes, including cycloadditions, cheletropic reactions, electrocyclic reactions and sigmatropic rearrangements, etc. (provided they are concerted).

Period

Periods are the rows of the periodic table. All elements in a period have the same number of atomic shells, or orbitals.

Period of unattended operation

Period for which given values of performance characteristics of an instrument can be guaranteed to remain within 95% probability without servicing or adjustment.

Periodic table

This famous table organizes all of the known chemical elements by their atomic number. The periodic table usually shows the atomic number, atomic symbol, and, atomic mass of the element.

Periselectivity

The differentiation between two symmetry-allowed processes, for example the [2+4] vs. [4+6] cycloaddition of cyclopentadiene to tropone.

Permanent wet strength

Wet strength that does not depend on the time duration of immersion, once wetting is complete.

Permeation tube

A device used for dynamic preparation of test gas mixtures by means of controlled permeation of a gaseous analyte out of a container through polymer material into a carrier gas stream. These devices containing certain condensable gases (e.g., NO_2, SO_2, etc.) when operated at closely controlled temperatures can be used as primary standards calibrated in terms of the weight loss per unit time.

Permeation Tube

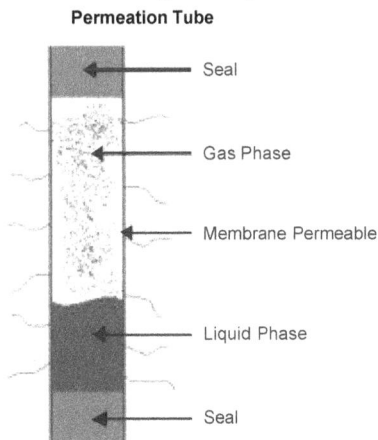

- Seal
- Gas Phase
- Membrane Permeable
- Liquid Phase
- Seal

Peroxide

Peroxides are compounds of structure ROOR in which R may be any organic group. In inorganic chemistry, salts of the anion O_2^{-2}. They are strong oxidising agents.

Persistent

The term persistent is used to characterize radicals which have lifetimes of several minutes or greater in dilute solution in inert solvents. Persistence is a kinetic or reactivity property. In contrast, radical stability, which is a thermodynamic property, is expressed in terms of the C-H bond strength of the appropriate hydrocarbon. The lifetime of a radical is profoundly influenced by steric shielding of the radical centre by bulky substituents.

Petrochemicals

Petrochemicals are the industrially important organic chemicals which are derived from oil or natural gas.

Pfeiffer's rule

Pfeiffer's rule states that in a series of chiral compounds the eudismic ratio increases with increasing potency of the eutomer.

Ph

pH is a measure of acidity. In logarithmic value, the pH is equal to the logarithm of one over the concentration of hydrogen ions. A pH less than seven indicates an acid. Seven is a neutral solution. A value above seven indicates a base.

Ph scale

A scale which measures the acidic or basic strength of a solution. pH < 7 is acidic (6 is a weak acid and 1 is a strong acid), pH = 7 is neutral, pH > 7 is basic (8 is a weak base and 14 is a strong base).

Phage display

Use of genetically engineered phage to present peptides as segments of their native surface proteins. Peptide libraries may be produced by populations of phage with different gene sequences.

Pharmacokinetics

Pharmacokinetics refers to the study of absorption, distribution, metabolism and excretion (ADME) of bioactive compounds in a higher organism.

Pharmacology

The science of studying both the mechanisms and the actions of drugs, usually in animal models of disease, to evaluate their potential therapeutic value.

Pharmacophore

A pharmacophore is the ensemble of steric and electronic features that is necessary to ensure the optimal supramolecular interactions with a specific biological target structure and to trigger (or to block) its biological response. A pharmacophore does not represent a real molecule or a real association of functional groups, but a purely abstract concept that accounts for the common molecular interaction capacities of a group of compounds towards their target structure.

Pharmacophore (pharmacophoric pattern)

A pharmacophore is the ensemble of steric and electronic features that is necessary to ensure the optimal supramolecular interactions with a specific biological target structure and to trigger (or to block) its biological response.

Pharmacophoric descriptors

Pharmacophoric descriptors are used to define a pharmacophore, including H-bonding, hydrophobic and electrostatic interaction sites, defined by atoms, ring centers and virtual points.

Phase

In chemistry, a physically distinct, homogeneous portion of a heterogeneous mixture.

Phase switch

Strategy for compound isolation, whereby the desired material is rendered sufficiently different from reagents, side-products and other impurities that it may be separated from them by simple physical processes such as filtration or extraction.

Phases of Matter

A phase is another name for a physical state of matter. Some scientists talk about what phase a piece of matter exists in. That's another way of saying what state that piece of matter is currently in. Examples of phases and states are solids, gases, and liquids.

Phase-transfer catalysis

The phenomenon of rate enhancement of a reaction between chemical species located in different phases (immiscible liquids or solid and liquid) by addition of a small quantity of an agent (called the "phase-transfer catalyst") that extracts one of the reactants, most commonly an anion, across the interface into the other phase so that reaction can proceed. These catalysts are salts of "onium ions" (e.g. tetraalkyl-ammonium salts) or agents that complex inorganic cations (e.g. crown ethers). The catalyst cation is not consumed in the reaction although an anion exchange does occur.

Phenol

A toxic, colourless crystalline solid with the chemical formula C_6H_5OH and whose structure is that of a hydroxyl group (-OH) bonded to a phenyl ring. It is also known as carbolic acid.

Phenolic

Having to do with aromatic (benzene) rings connected to an OH group, as in lignins.

Phenyl

A functional group with the formula -C_6H_5

Phosphate mineral

A mineral that is made up of compounds with a phosphate group bonded to a metal. Turquoise is a good example of a phosphate mineral.

Phosphorus

Symbol: "P" Atomic Number: "15" Atomic Mass: 30.97amu. Phosphorus is a very reactive element and is classified as a non-metal. Plants and animals need phosphorus to survive. When you go looking for it, you can find it in the soil. You will also find it in baking soda, making china, fireworks, fertilizers, and glass making.

Photochemical reaction

A reaction involving an electronically excited state of a molecule or atom which can occur following light absorption of sufficient energy per quantum (usually ultraviolet or visible radiation). In electronically excited molecules one of several types of photochemical reaction may occur: photodecomposition into molecular fragments or radicals, photodecomposition into stable, smaller products, photoisomerization, intersystem crossing (a singlet to triplet state, etc.), internal energy conversion (e.g., excited singlet to vibrationally excited, singlet ground state), fluorescence, phosphorescence, electronic or vibrational energy quenching, etc.

Photochemistry

The chemistry of excited electronic states of atoms and molecules formed by the absorption of light by an atom or molecule. The primary processes in photochemistry of a given compound are the various reaction channels of the electronically excited species. These can be molecular decomposition into stable molecules or radicals, molecular isomerization, fluorescence, phosphorescence, electronic quenching by collision, etc. The reactions of the molecular fragments which are formed photochemically, are correctly referred to as thermal reactions, in that they are analogous to the reactions induced following thermal decomposition at high temperatures.

Photolithography

Process by which selective masking generates light patterns which direct chemical transformations to certain areas of a photosensitive surface. Coupling of different building blocks to discrete sites may give rise to spatially addressable arrays of compounds.

Photolysis

The cleavage of one or more covalent bonds in a molecular entity resulting from absorption of light, or a photochemical process in which such cleavage is an essential part. For example: Cl_2 2 Cl. The term is used incorrectly to describe irradiation of a sample, although in the combination flash photolysis this usage is accepted.

Photon

Massless packet of energy, which behaves like both a wave and a particle.

Photophoresis

In aerosol physics, the motion of particles due to the influence of light. In many cases, this amounts to a special form of thermophoresis due to the heating of the particles by the light.

Photosynthesis

A metobolic process involving plants and some types of bacteria (e.g., Chromataceae, Rhodospirillaceae, Chlorobiaceae) in which light energy absorbed by chlorophyll and other photosynthetic pigments results in the reduction of CO_2 followed by the formation of organic compounds. In plants the overall process involves the conversion of CO_2 and H_2O to carbohydrates (and other plant material) and the release of O_2.

Ph-rate profile

A plot of observed rate coefficient, or more usually its decadic logarithm, against pH of solution, other variables being kept constant.

Physical change

A change in appearance from one form to another which does not result in the production of a new substance. eg. a change in physical state (solid, liquid or gas) or a substance being dissolved. Physical changes are easy to reverse.

Physical property

A property that can be observed or measured without altering the substance. ie. no new substance is formed. eg. colour, physical state, density, crystal shape as a solid, melting and boiling point.

Physical separation

A means of separating impure substances into pure substances based upon the physical properties of the mixture. No new substances are formed. eg. filtration, evaporation, dissolving

Phytotoxicant

An agent which produces a toxic effect in vegetation.

Pi bonds

A type of covalent bond in which the electron density is concentrated around the line bonding the atoms.

Pi-adduct (π-adduct)

An *adduct* formed by electron-pair donation from a pi orbital into a sigma orbital, or from a sigma orbital into a pi orbital, or from a pi orbital into a pi orbital. For example:

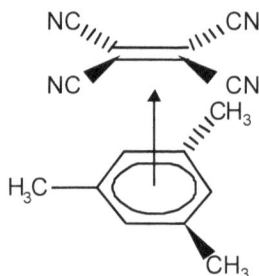

Pigment

Pigments are the substances that give paint colour. Pigments are derived from natural or synthetic materials that have been ground into fine powders. A pigment is different from a dye in that a pigment is insoluble in the media in which it is used.

Pin

An elongated device in which the tip acts as a solid support. An array of pins may typically be held such that sets of pins may be simultaneously inserted or retracted from solvents or reagents allowing library preparation by parallel synthesis.

Pinholes

Small holes in paper, often caused by entrained air bubbles, where it is possible to see light through the sheet.

Pitch

Wood extractives, in the context of tacky deposits onto papermaking equipment or spots in the product.

Placebo

A placebo is an inert substance or dosage form which is identical in appearance, flavour and odour to the active substance or dosage form. It is used as a negative control in a bioassay or in a clinical study.

Planck

Planck contributed to the understanding of the electromagnetic spectrum by realizing that the relationship between the change in energy and frequency is quantized according to the equation & Del; E=hv where h is Planck's constant.

Plant damage

Damage to living plants by certain air pollutants (SO_2, certain metal fluorides, O_3, peroxyacetyl nitrate, nitrogen oxides, etc.) often is evident as leaf tissue collapse, chlorosis, and growth alteration.

Plate counts

A common test to estimate the concentration of free-floating biological cells, by greatly diluting the sample and spreading the diluted sample on top of some growth medium, and later counting the colonies of cells.

Platinum

Symbol: "Pt" Atomic Number: "78" Atomic Mass: 195.08amu. This is one of the many transition elements. Platinum is one of the Earth's precious metals. This shiny, silvery element has uses in jewelry, electronics, magnets, and airplane parts. Platinum is very non-reactive and does not oxidize in air.

Plume

The gaseous and aerosol effluents which are emitted from a chimney and the volume of space which they occupy (often visible). The shape of the plume and the concentrations of pollutants in it at various points along the path of the plume are sensitive functions of the meteorology, local topography, and the chemistry which occurs in the plume. Urban plumes are observed over many urban areas and downwind of these areas in which a combination of man sources of pollution are concentrated.

Plutonium

Symbol: "Pu" Atomic Number: "94" Atomic Mass: (244)amu. Plutonium is one of the elements in the actinide series of inner transition elements. It may be classified as a rare earth element. It is a radioactive and unstable element and you will find it in nuclear devices and reactors.

pOH

pOH is the measure of hydroxide ion concentration. The scale is the reverse of the pH scale. Seven is still neutral but values below seven are basic and values above seven are acidic.

Point of Diversity

Portion of a molecule, or step in a synthetic scheme, where different building blocks may be introduced.

Polar effect

For a reactant molecule RY, the polar effect of the group R comprises all the processes whereby a substituent may modify the electrostatic forces operating at the reaction centre Y, relative to the standard $R^{o}Y$. These forces may be governed by charge separations arising from differences in the *electronegativity* of atoms (leading to the presence of dipoles), the presence of unipoles, or electron *delocalization*. It is synonymous with *electronic effect* or "electrical effect" of a substituent as distinguished from other substituent effects, e.g. *steric effects*.

Polar molecules

Molecule with a partial charge.

Polarization

A method of light microscopy that uses light waves that are oriented in the same plane.

Polonium

Symbol: "Po" Atomic Number: "84" Atomic Mass: (209)amu. Polonium is a rare element often found in nature with uranium. It is radioactive and very dangerous. You may find it as a byproduct of reactions in a nuclear reactor.

Polyethylene glycol (PEG)

Polymer which has been applied both as a soluble support and (as a graft copolymer with a polystyrene matrix) as a linker for combinatorial synthesis. The soluble support may have hydroxyls at both termini, or one or both may be capped or modified with additional functionality.

Polyamine

A highly charged cationic polymer, often used for charge control or as a pretreatment before certain retention aid treatments.

Polyatomic ion

An ion made up of two or more elements covalently-bonded.

Polycyclic compounds

Compounds of a structure containing more than one ring (cyclic series of covalent bonds). Atoms of elements other than carbon and hydrogen may be present in these ring structures (nitrogen, sulphur, oxygen, etc.).

Poly-DADMAC

Poly-diallyldimethylammonium chloride, a fully-charged, cationic polymer often used as the standard for cationic demand titrations.

Polymer

A large molecule (macromolecule) composed of repeating structural units (monomers) typically connected by covalent chemical bonds.

Polyprotic acid

An acid that can give up more than one hyrogoen atom. H_2SO_4 for example.

Polysaccharide

These are very complicated carbohydrates made of simple sugars (glucose, fructose) in long chains. The chains include many monosaccharides. They are found in the cell wall and other areas of organisms. Cellulose is a good example of a polysaccharide.

Pool/split

Strategy for assembly of a combinatorial library. The solid support is divided into portions, each of which is subjected to reaction with a single building block. Pooling of these portions results in a single batch of solid support bearing a mixture of components. Repetition of the divide, couple, recombine processes results in a library where each discrete particle of solid support carries a single library member, and the number of members is equal to the product of the number of building blocks incorporated at each step (i.e. fully combinatorial).

Position of Equilibrium

This measurement is the point in a chemical reaction where the forward reaction rate equals the reverse reaction rate.

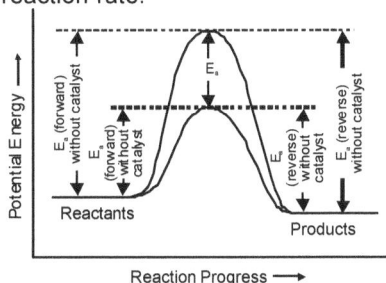

Positional scan

Strategy for identifying individual compounds of interest from a library, whereby a collection of sub-libraries is prepared, equal in number to the total number of building blocks used in the entire library. In each pool, one point of diversity is held constant by incorporating a single building block, while the other positions use all possible building blocks.

Positive valence

This term describes the trait of elements that tend to give up electrons in electrovalent compounds. These are the positive ions of salts. Think about sodium, magnesium, and boron.

Post-consumer waste

Paper that has been printed or converted, distributed to end-users, and collected from consumers as waste paper.

Potassium

Symbol: "K" Atomic Number: "19" Atomic Mass: 39.10amu. One of the alkali metal family. Potassium is a metallic element and one of the essential elements for organisms to survive. You can also find potassium in potash, many minerals, and fertilizers.

Potency

Potency is the dose of drug required to produce a specific effect of given intensity as compared to a standard reference. Potency is a comparative rather than an absolute expression of drug activity. Drug potency depends on both affinity and efficacy. Thus, two agonists can be equipotent, but have different intrinsic efficacies with compensating differences in affinity.

Potential energy

Energy which something has but which is not being used, such as a motionless rock at the top of a cliff. Potential energy (reaction) surface A geometric hypersurface on which the potential energy of a set of reactants is plotted as a function of the coordinates representing the molecular geometries of the system. For simple systems two such coordinates (characterizing two variables that change during the progress from reactants to products) can be selected, and the potential energy plotted as a contour map. For simple *elementary reactions*, e.g. A-B + C   A + B-C, the surface can show the potential energy for all values of the A, B, C geometry, providing that the ABC angle is fixed.

Potential energy profile

A curve describing the variation of the potential energy of the system of atoms that make up the reactants and products of a reaction as a function of one geometric coordinate, and corresponding to the "energetically easiest passage" from reactants to products (i.e. along the line produced by joining the paths of steepest descent from the transition state to the reactants and to the products). For an elementary reaction the relevant geometric coordinate is the reaction coordinate; for a stepwise reaction it is the succession of reaction coordinates for the successive individual reaction steps. (The reaction coordinate is sometimes approximated by a quasi-chemical index of reaction progress, such as "degree of atom transfer" or bond order of some specified bond.).

Potential temperature

The temperature that a dry air parcel would have if lowered or raised adiabatically to level of 1000 mbar pressure (or other arbitrary standard pressure).

Potentiometer

a) In electronics, a potentiometer is a sensitive voltage measuring device based on a null technique which provides infinite impedance at null;

b) In chemistry, potentiometric methods involve the measurement with a potentiometer of voltage generated in a cell. A high impedance digital voltmeter is often used today as a convenient alternative to a potentiometer.

Praseodymium

Symbol: "Pr" Atomic Number: "59" Atomic Mass: 140.91amu. Praseodymium is one of the elements in the lanthanide series of inner transition elements. It may also be classified as a rare earth element. This soft, silvery metal can be found in many minerals and even some cigarette lighter sparking mechanisms.

Precipitate

Insoluble materials in a mixture formed as a result of interaction between soluble components, often resulting in turbidity or settling of the solid material.

Precipitation, electrostatic

Separation of particles or droplets suspended in a gas or air. A large potential difference (12 to 30 kV dc) is required between the spaced electrodes in the precipitator. The charged panicles are attracted to an electrode of opposite charge and collected.

Precipitation, in chemistry

The sedimentation of a solid material from a liquid solution in which the material is present in amounts greater than its solubility in the liquid.

Precision (reproducibility)

The closeness of agreement between the results obtained by applying a given experimental procedure several times under prescribed conditions. The smaller the random part of the experimental errors which affect the results, the more precise is the method. A term not to be confused with accuracy which is a measure of the agreement between the true value and the measured value.

Precursor

A chemical compound which is released into the atmosphere, undergoes chemical change, and leads to a new (secondary) pollutant, is called a precursor of that species.

Pre-exponential factor

The term A which appears in the Arrhenius form of the rate coefficient expression, $k = Ae^{-Ea/RT}$.

Pressure

Force per unit area.

Pressure, gauge

The difference in pressure existing within a system and that of the atmosphere. Zero gauge pressure is equal to the atmospheric pressure.

Pressure, static

The pressure of a fluid at rest, or in motion exerted perpendicularly to the direction of flow.

Primary fines

Fines derived from structures present in wood and released after kraft pulping, before refining.

Primary mixture

A mixture obtained directly from two or more components intended for the preparation of more dilute calibration mixtures (called secondary or tertiary mixtures).

Primary pollutant

A pollutant emitted directly into the air from identifiable sources (e.g., SO_2, NO, hydrocarbons, etc.). Secondary pollutants, such as ozone, are generated within the atmosphere through chemical changes which occur in primary pollutants.

Primary wall

The lignin-rich outer wall of a papermaking fiber that is mostly removed by kraft pulping.

Primitive change

One of the conceptually simpler molecular changes into which an elementary reaction can be notionally dissected. Such changes include bond rupture, bond formation, internal rotation, change of bond length or bond angle, bond migration, redistribution of charge, etc. The concept of primitive changes is helpful in the detailed verbal description of elementary reactions, but a primitive change does not represent a process that is by itself necessarily observable as a component of an elementary reaction.

Principal quantum number

The number related to the amount of energy an electron has and therefore describing which shell the electron is in.

Prismatic habit

A shape of a large group of crystals that is very geometric and orderly. Sometimes the crystals line up in one direction.

Privileged structure

Substructural feature which confers desirable (often drug-like) properties on compounds containing that feature. Often consists of a semi-rigid scaffold which is able to present multiple hydrophobic residues without undergoing hydrophobic collapse.

Probe (in stack gas sampling)

A device, commonly in the form of a tube, used for sampling or measurement inside a duct, stack, volcano, vent, etc.

Prodrug

A prodrug is any compound that undergoes biotransformation before exhibiting its pharmacological effects. Prodrugs can thus be viewed as drugs containing specialized non-toxic protective groups used in a transient manner to alter or to eliminate undesirable properties in the parent molecule.

Product

The substance or substances that are produced in a chemical reaction.

Product development control

The term is used for reactions under kinetic control where the selectivity parallels the relative (thermodynamic) stabilities of the products. Product development control is usually associated with a transition state occurring late on the reaction coordinate.

Product-determining step

The step of a stepwise reaction, in which the product distribution is determined. The product-determining step may be identical to, or occur later than, the rate-controlling step on the reaction coordinate.

Promethium

Symbol: "Pm" Atomic Number: "61" Atomic Mass: (145)amu. This is one of the elements in the lanthanide series of inner transition elements. It may also be classified as a rare earth element. This element is not found in nature and has only been created in a lab. You will not find many uses for it in real life.

Property

Anything about matter which helps identify it.

Property space

Multidimensional representation of a set of compounds in which the axes represent quantifiable properties, such as molecular weight, log P, molar refractivity, etc., and individual compounds are represented by a vector or set of coordinates.

Proportion

An equality between two ratios.

Protactinium

Symbol: "Pa" Atomic Number: "91" Atomic Mass: 231.04amu. Protactinium is one of the elements in the actinide series of inner transition elements. It may also be classified as a rare earth element. It is a radioactive and unstable element and you will not find it in use anywhere.

Protease

An enzyme that hydrolyzes (breaks down a bond and adds water) proteins, especially to peptides.

Protecting group

A ground used in preventing undesired reactions.

Protection

A hypothetical mechanism to explain wet-strength effects as due to the chemical blocking of access to inter-fiber hydrogen bonds.

Protein

A molecule composed of a long chain of amino acids. Proteins are the principal constituents of cellular material and serve as enzymes, hormones, structural elements, and antibodies. The molar mass is usually above 100,000.

Protein kinases

Enzymes that phosphorylate certain amino acid residues (most often Ser, Thr, or Tyr) in specific proteins.

Protogenic (solvent)

Capable of acting as a proton (hydron) donor strongly or weakly acidic (as a Brønsted acid). The term is preferred to the synonym "protic" or the more ambiguous expression "acidic" by itself.

Proton

A proton is a particle found in the nucleus of every atom. It holds a positive charge (+). The mass of a proton is almost equal to the mass of a neutron. Electrons are much smaller than protons.

Proton affinity

The negative of the enthalpy change in the gas phase reaction (real or hypothetical) between a proton (more appropriately hydron) and the chemical species concerned, usually an electrically neutral species to give the conjugate acid of that species.

Protophilic (solvent)

Capable of acting as proton acceptor, strongly or weakly basic (as a Brønsted base). Also called HBA (hydrogen bond acceptor) solvent.

Pseudo-catalysis

If an acid or base is present in nearly constant concentration throughout a reaction in solution (owing to buffering or the use of a large excess), it may be found to increase the rate of that reaction and also to be consumed during the process. The acid or base is then not a catalyst and the phenomenon cannot be called catalysis according to the well-established meaning of these terms in chemical kinetics, although the mechanism of such a process is often intimately related to that of a catalysed reaction. It is recommended that the term pseudo-catalysis be used in these and analogous cases (not necessarily involving acids or bases).

Pseudopericyclic

A *concerted transformation* is pseudopericyclic if the primary changes in bonding occur within a cyclic array of atoms at one (or more) of which nonbonding and bonding atomic orbitals interchange roles. A formal example is the enol.

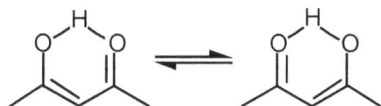

Because the pi and sigma atomic orbitals that interchange roles are orthogonal, such a reaction does not proceed through a fully conjugated transition state and is thus not a pericyclic reaction and therefore not governed by the rules that express orbital symmetry restrictions applicable to pericyclic reactions.

Psychrometry

The use of a wet-and-dry-bulb thermometer for measurement of atmospheric humidity.

Pure substance

A substance consisting of only one type of particle. It cannot be separated into simpler substances by physical means. E.g. filtration. Its properties are unique for that particular substance and are constant. ie. do not change. eg. melting and boiling point of water.

PVSK

The potassium salt of polyvinyl chloride, a highly charged, negative linear polymer often used in charge titrations.

Q

Qualitative

Qualitative descriptions are those that describe qualities and characteristics. For example, it could be a colour, a smell, or a feeling.

Quality assurance

The guarantee that the quality of a product (analytical data set, etc.) is actually what is claimed on the basis of the quality control applied in creating that product. Quality assurance is not synonymous with quality control. Quality assurance is meant to protect against failures of quality control.

Quality control

The maintenance and statement of the quality of a product (data set, etc.) specifically that it meets or exceeds some minimum standard based on known, testable criteria.

Quantitative

Quantitative descriptions are those that are based on numbers and exact figures, such as a weight or a temperature.

Quantitative structure-activity relationships (qsar)

Quantitative structure-activity relationships are mathematical relationships linking chemical structure and pharmacological activity in a quantitative manner for a series of compounds. Methods which can be used in QSAR include various regression and pattern recognition techniques.

Quantum

Something which comes in discrete units, for example, money is quantized (divided into units); it comes in quanta (divisions) of one cent.

R

Radiant energy

Energy which is transmitted away from its source, for example, energy that is emitted when electrons transition down from one level to another.

Radiation

Energy in the form of photons.

Radical

A radical is a group of atoms that appear in a compound and act as a group. Functional groups are classified as radicals. Two examples are NaCl and NaOH. In these examples, the chlorine ion and hydroxide functional group bond in similar ways with the sodium atom.

Radical centre(s)

The atom (or group of atoms) in a polyatomic radical on which an unpaired electron is largely localized. Attachment of a monovalent atom to a radical centre gives a molecule for which it is possible to write a Lewis formula in which the normal stable valencies are assigned to all atoms.

Radical ion

A radical that carries an electric charge. A positively charged radical is called a "radical cation" (e.g., the benzene radical cation $C_6H_6^+$); a negatively charged radical is called a "radical anion" (e.g., the benzene radical anion $C_6H_6^-$ or the benzophenone radical anion $Ph_2C\text{-}O^-$). Commonly, but not necessarily, the odd electron and the charge are associated with the same atom. Unless the positions of unpaired spin and charge can be associated with specific atoms, superscript dot and charge designations should be placed in the order $^{\cdot+}$ or $^{\cdot-}$ suggested by the name "radical ion", (e.g $C_3H_6^+$).

Radical pair (or geminate pair)

The term is used to identify two radicals in close proximity in solution, within a solvent cage. They may be formed simultaneously by some unimolecular process, e.g., peroxide decomposition, or they may have come together by diffusion.

Radioactive

Describes a substance with an unstable nucleus.

Radioactive decay

The 'fission' or splitting of a nucleus into smaller nuclei releasing energy as radiation.

Radioactivity

Radioactivity occurs when the nucleus of an atom breaks up into two or more pieces. A neutron is often released during radioactive decay.

Radiofrequency encoding

Strategy for identifying library members by physically associating them with a set of electronic devices which emit characteristic radio frequency signals upon stimulation with a radiofrequency energy source. These signals can be used to track the reaction history of each sample in a synthesis.

Radio-isotope
An isotope of a particular element that undergoes radioactive decay.

Radiolysis
The cleavage of one or several bonds resulting from exposure to high-energy radiation. The term is also often used loosely to specify the method of irradiation ("pulse radiolysis") used in any radiochemical reaction, not necessarily one involving bond cleavage.

Radiometry
The measurement of quantities associated with radiant energy. The quantities may also describe the variation of the energy with respect to other variables such as wavelength, time, position, direction (solid angle), area normal to the light, or projected area of emitting or receiving surfaces.

Radiosonde
A miniature radio transmitter with instruments in a package that is carried aloft (e.g., by an unmanned balloon) for broadcasting every few seconds by means of precise tone signals or other suitable method, the humidity, temperature, pressure, or other parameter.

Radium
Symbol: "Ra" Atomic Number: "88" Atomic Mass: 226.03amu. Radium is a member of the alkaline metals group. It was discovered by the Curies in 1898 and is a radioactive, white metal that is often luminescent

(glowing). You will find it in use for medicine, glowing paints, and the creation of radon gas.

Radon
Symbol: "Rn" Atomic Number: "86" Atomic Mass: (222)amu. It is one of the noble or inert gases. This element has not been found in nature and is a product of some nuclear reactions and the combustion of heavier elements. It is very dangerous and toxic to living organisms.

Rain out
The mechanism by which small particles in the clouds are removed by the formation of rain-drops; this is a different mechanism from wash out which is a process which occurs below cloud level. Both the terms rain out and wash out have not always been used in accordance with these definitions. For clarity they should be replaced by the term, in-cloud scavenging and below-cloud scavenging, respectively.

Raoult's law
This chemistry law shows that the vapour pressure above a mixture of two liquids is directly related to the amounts of the solute and solvents in the solution.

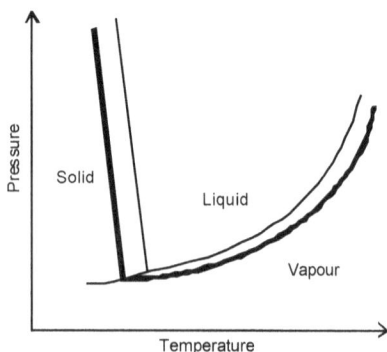

Rate law (or empirical differential rate equation)

An expression for the rate of reaction of a particular reaction in terms of concentrations of chemical species and constant parameters (normally rate coefficients and partial orders of reaction) only. For examples of rate laws see equations (1) to (3) under kinetic equivalence, and (1) under steady state.

Rate of Diffusion

This rate measurement is the speed at which molecules or atoms diffuse through a substance.

Rate-controlling step

A rate-controlling (rate-determining or rate-limiting) step in a reaction occurring by a composite reaction sequence is an elementary reaction the rate constant for which exerts a strong effect - stronger than that of any other rate constant - on the overall rate. It is recommended that the expressions rate-controlling, rate-determining and rate-limiting be regarded as synonymous, but some special meanings sometimes given to the last two expressions are considered under a separate heading. A rate-controlling step can be formally defined on the basis of a control function (or control factor) CF, identified for an elementary reaction having a rate constant k_i by $CF = (\partial \ln v / \partial \ln k_i)_{K_j,k_j}$ where v is the overall rate of reaction. In performing the partial differentiation all equilibrium constants K_j and all rate constants except k_i are held constant. The elementary reaction having the largest control factor exerts the strongest influence on the rate v, and a step having a CF much larger than any other step may be said to be rate-controlling.

Rate-determining step, rate-limiting step

These terms are best regarded as synonymous with rate-controlling step. However, other meanings that have been given to them should be mentioned, as it is necessary to be aware of them in order to avoid confusion. Sometimes the term rate-determining is used as a special case of rate-controlling, being assigned only to an initial slow step which is followed by rapid steps. Such a step imposes an upper limit on the rate, and has also been called rate-limiting.

Ratio

The relative size of two quantities expressed as the quotient of one divided by the other; the ratio of a to b is written as a:b or a/b.

Ratio coding

Encoding strategy in which the relative quantities of tags convey information about compound identity. In comparison to binary coding, more information may be obtained from a given tag set, but tag interpretation is more complex.

Ray cells

Cellulosic structures within a tree that conduct water and nutrients in a radial direction.

Reactant

The starting substance in a chemical reaction.

Reacting bond rules

(1) For an internal motion of a molecular entity corresponding to progress over a transition state (energy maximum), any change that makes the motion more difficult will lead to a new

molecular geometry at the energy maximum, in which the motion has proceeded further. Changes that make the motion less difficult will have the opposite effect. (This rule corresponds to the Hammond principle.

(2) For an internal motion of a molecular entity that corresponds to a vibration, any change that tends to modify the equilibrium point of the vibration in a particular direction will actually shift the equilibrium in that direction.

(3) Effects on reacting bonds (bonds made or broken in the reaction) are the most significant. The bonds nearest the site of structural change are those most strongly affected.

Reaction coordinate

A geometric parameter that changes during the conversion of one (or more) reactant molecular entities into one (or more) product molecular entities and whose value can be taken for a measure of the progress of an elementary reaction (for example, a bond length or bond angle or a combination of bond lengths and/or bond angles; it is sometimes approximated by a non-geometric parameter, such as the bond order of some specified bond). In the formalism of "transition-state theory", the reaction coordinate is that coordinate in a set of curvilinear coordinates obtained from the conventional ones for the reactants which, for each reaction step, leads smoothly from the configuration of the reactants through that of the transition state to the configuration of the products. The reaction coordinate is typically chosen to follow the path along the gradient (path of shallowest ascent/deepest descent) of potential energy from reactants to products.

Reaction mechanism

the series of individual reactions that occur in an entire sequence of reactions.

Reaction path

(1) A synonym for *mechanism*.
(2) A trajectory on the potential-energy surface.
(3) A sequence of synthetic steps.

Reaction rate

the speed at which a reaction occurs; typically measured as the change in concentration of either reactants or products over time.

Reaction stage

A set of one or more (possibly experimentally inseparable) reaction steps leading to and/or from a detectable or presumed reaction intermediate.

Reaction step

An elementary reaction, constituting one of the stages of a stepwise reaction in which a reaction intermediate (or, for the first step, the reactants) is converted into the next reaction intermediate (or, for the last step, the products) in the sequence of intermediates between reactants and products. Reaction with phosphorus pentachloride (PCl_5) is a characteristic of organic compounds containing a hydroxyl group and this reaction is used to identify these compounds in an organic analysis.

Reaction, elementary

A chemical reaction which describes a single step in a chemical reacting system. The formation of final products from initial reactants always takes place by one or more relatively simple steps (elementary reactions) in each of which the extent of transfer of atoms and molecular decomposition or rearrangement is very limited (a simple bond cleavage, etc.).

Reactive element

When an element is reactive, it is easily excited. It can combine with other elements very quickly and get involved in many chemical reactions.

Reactive size

A sizing agent such as ASA or AKD that undergoes a covalent reaction when heated in the presence of fibers.

Reactive, reactivity

As applied to a chemical species, the term expresses a kinetic property. A species is said to be more reactive or to have a higher reactivity in some given context than some other (reference) species if it has a larger rate constant for a specified elementary reaction. The term has meaning only by reference to some explicitly stated or implicitly assumed set of conditions. It is not to be used for reactions or reaction patterns of compounds in general.

Reactivity index

Any numerical index derived from quantum mechanical model calculations that permits the prediction of relative reactivities of different molecular sites. Many indices are in use, based on a variety of theories and relating to various types of reaction. The more successful applications have been to the substitution reactions of conjugated systems where relative reactivities are determined largely by changes of pi-electron energy.

Reactivity-selectivity principle (RSP)

This idea may be expressed loosely as: the more reactive a reagent is, the less selective it is. Consider two substrates S^1 and S^2 undergoing the same type of reaction with two reagents R^1 and R^2, S^2 being more reactive than S^1, and R^2 more reactive than R^1 in the given type of reaction. The relative reactivities (in log units, see selectivity) for the four possible reactions may notionally be represented as follows:

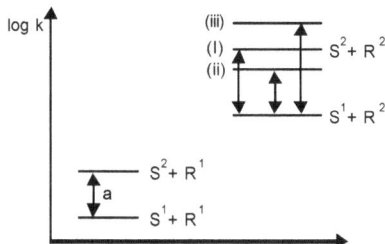

log k
(iii)
(I) $S^2 + R^2$
(ii)
                $S^1 + R^2$
          $S^2 + R^1$
    a
          $S^1 + R^1$

With the positions of $(S^1 + R^1)$, $(S^2 + R^1)$, and $(S^1 + R^2)$ fixed, there are three types of positions for $(S^2 + R^2)$: In position (i) the selectivity of R^2 for the two substrates, measured by a is the same as the selectivity of R^1 for the two substrates, also a. In position (ii) the selectivity of R^2 for the two substrates, measured by b, is less than the selectivity of R^1 for the two substrates, i.e. b < a. It is this situation which is in accord with the RSP. In position (iii) the selectivity of R^2 for the two substrates, measured by c, is greater than the selectivity of R^1 for the two substrates, i.e. c > a. This situation may be described as anti-RSP.

Reagent efficiency

The ratio of the number of library members prepared compared to the number which would have been prepared in a fully combinatorial library using the same building blocks. Lower reagent efficiency may be desirable in order to reduce the number of compounds to be synthesized or tested, for example by maximizing the number of members expected to have high activity in a library prepared by parallel synthesis.

Reagent partitioning

Phenomenon whereby the concentration of a compound within, for instance, a particle of solid support is higher or lower than of the bulk solution due to the physicochemical properties of the solid support.

Real gas

A real gas is one that you find in the real world. They have unique properties depending on the temperature and pressure. A perfect gas would be called an ideal gas.

Rearrangement stage

The elementary reaction or reaction stage (of a molecular rearrangement) in which there is both making and breaking of bonds between atoms common to a reactant and a reaction product or a reaction intermediate. If the rearrangement stage consists of a single elementary reaction, this is a "rearrangement step".

Receptor

A receptor is a molecule or a polymeric structure in or on a cell that specifically recognizes and binds a compound acting as a molecular messenger (neurotransmitter, hormone, lymphokine, lectin, drug, etc.).

Receptor mapping

Receptor mapping is the technique used to describe the geometric and/or electronic features of a binding site when insufficient structural data for this receptor or enzyme are available. Generally the active site cavity is defined by comparing the superposition of active to that of inactive molecules.

Recovery

The percentage yield of added analyte after it has passed a sequence of operations constituting a particular analytical scheme.

Recursive partitioning

Process for identifying complex structure-activity relationships in large sets by dividing compounds into a hierarchy of smaller and more homogeneous sub-groups on the basis of the statistically most significant descriptors.

Redox reaction

A reaction consisting of both reduction and oxidation.

Reduced species

In chemistry, a term used to characterize the degree of reduction (or oxidation) in atoms, molecules, and ions. An atom in a molecule or an ion which has a low oxidation state. An element or atom in a compound can be reduced by the reaction of an element or compound with hydrogen, while it can be oxidized by reaction with oxygen. A reduced species can be formed also through the gain of electrons (either at the negative electrode in a ceil or through transfer from another atom, ion, or group of atoms in a chemical reaction).

Reducing agent

a substance that loses electrons and undergoes oxidation. It "allows" the other substance to undergo reduction.

Reduction

The complete transfer of one or more electrons to a molecular entity (also called "electronation"), and, more generally, the reverse of the processes described under oxidation (2), (3).

Reduction reaction

A reaction in which a substance gains at least one electron.

Reductive elimination

The reverse of oxidative addition.

Reference material

A substance or mixture of substances, the composition of which is known within specified limits, and one or more of the properties of which is sufficiently well established to be used for the calibration of an apparatus, the assessment of a measuring method, or for assigning values to materials.

Reference procedure

Agreed method for determining one or more air quality characteristics where it is not practical to produce a reference material; the result obtained is defined as the measure of the air quality characteristic. For example, a gas such as NO_2 may be somewhat unstable when stored in a tank at low mixing ratios, so that the use of a more stable NO standard mixture in N_2 may be oxidized to NO_2 by O_3 in a specified manner referred to as the NO_2 reference procedure.

Refining

Passing pulp through a device that applies compression and shear forces onto the wetted fibers, causing fibrillation and increased flexibility.

Reflectance, spectral, directional

For a surface receiving radiation, ratio of the reflected radiant exitance to the incident irradiance. It may depend on wavelength and on direction of incidence, as indicated by the prefixes.

Regional metamorphism

Metamorphic rocks that have been formed in areas where heat and pressure combined to create the rock. Mountain areas are locations of regional metamorphism.

Regioselectivity, regioselective

A regioselective reaction is one in which one direction of bond making or breaking occurs preferentially over all other possible directions. Reactions are termed completely (100%) regioselective if the discrimination is complete, or partially (x%), if the product of reaction at one site predominates over the product of reaction at other sites. The discrimination may also semi-quantitatively be referred to as high or low regioselectivity.

Reinforcement

A hypothetical mechanism to explain wet-strength effects as due to formation of covalent bonds, adding to the effects of hydrogen bonds.

Relative density

The ratio of the density of a given substance to the density of a reference material at specified conditions of temperature and pressure; in the older literature this is called specific gravity.

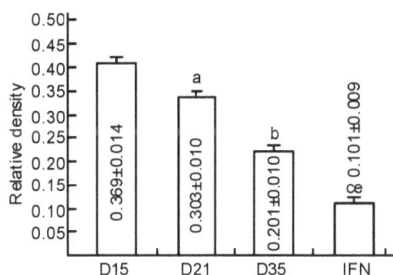

Relative humidity

The ratio, often expressed as a percentage, of the partial pressure of water in the atmosphere at some observed temperature, to the saturation vapour pressure of pure water at this temperature.

Relaxation

Passage of an excited or otherwise perturbed system towards or into thermal equilibrium with its environment.

Remote sensing (in atmospheric sciences)

The determination of substances in the atmosphere, or in emissions, or of meteorological parameters in the atmosphere, by means of instruments not in immediate physical contact with the sample being examined.

Reniform habit

A shape of a large crystal which has the arrangement of several small rounded balls stuck together. Think about some of those computer generated structures of molecules for this example.

Repeatability

Qualitatively, the closeness of agreement between successive results obtained with the same method on identical test material, under the same conditions (same operator, same apparatus, same laboratory and short intervals of time).

Reproducibility

Qualitatively, the closeness of agreement between individual results obtained with the same method on identical test material but under different conditions (different operators, different apparatus, different laboratories and/or different times). Quantitatively, the value below which the absolute difference between two single test results on identical material obtained by operators in different laboratories.

Repulping

Transforming waste paper back into fibers by immersion in water and strong mixing.

Residual fuel/oil

The liquid or semiliquid, high-boiling fraction of residue from the distillation of petroleum which is used as a fuel. After removal of the lower boiling fraction of crude oil, sold as petroleum gas, the somewhat higher boiling fraction becomes gasoline and diesel oil. A portion of the higher boiling fraction is "cracked" to yield additional gasoline.

Residual spectrum/background spectrum in mass spectrometry

Set of peaks recorded in the absence of a sample and due either to small air leaks or to the presence of molecules desorbed from the walls of the introduction device or the source, or from the pump fluid.

Residue

a) Portion of a chemical structure which can be identified as being derived from a particular building block; b) portion of a building block which is incorporated into the final product but is not part of the scaffold.

Resin

Insoluble polymeric material which allows ready separation from liquid phase materials by filtration; can be used to carry library members (i.e. solid support) or reagents, or to trap excess reagents or reaction by-products.

Resin acids

Component of softwood pitch having a ring structure; also used to make rosin size.

Resonance

In the context of chemistry, the term refers to the representation of the electronic structure of a molecular entity in terms of contributing structures. Resonance among contributing structures means that the wavefunction is represented by "mixing" the wavefunctions of the contributing structures. The concept is the basis of the quantum mechanical valence bond methods. The resulting stabilization is linked to the quantum mechanical concept of "resonance energy". The term resonance is also used to refer to the delocalization phenomenon itself.

Resonance effect

This is the term most commonly used to describe the influence (on reactivity, spectra, etc.) of a substituent through electron delocalization into or from the substituent. The use of the term obviates the need to attempt to distinguish between the operation of the mesomeric effect and the electromeric effect. (An alternative term with essentially the same meaning is "conjugative effect". At one time "tautomeric effect" was also used, but was abandoned because tautomerism implies reorganization of the atomic nuclei.) The effect is symbolized by R.

Resonance energy

The difference in potential energy between the actual molecular entity and the contributing structure of lowest potential energy. The resonance energy cannot be measured, but only estimated, since contributing structures are not observable molecular entities.

Response time

Time taken for an instrument to respond to a rapid change in value of the air quality characteristic. It consists of two major parts a) Lag time, the time taken to reach 10% of the final change in instrument reading; b) rise time (fall time), the time taken to pass from 10% to 90% of the final change in instrument reading. For instruments where transient oscillations occur in the approach to the final instrument reading, the rise time is considered to be the time taken for the oscillations to fall to less than 10% of the final change in instrument reading.

Restabilization

The result of adding too much low-mass cationic additive to furnish, such that all the surfaces become positive and repel each other.

Re-synthesis

Preparation of individual members or pools of a combinatorial library, normally to follow up on some property of interest identified in initial screening, and often in larger scale and/or greater purity than the original preparation.

Retention

The efficiency with which small particles (or additives) remain in the paper during its formation rather than staying with the white water.

Retention aids

Chemical additives, especially high-mass copolymers of acrylamide, designed to increase the retention efficiency of fine materials during paper formation.

Retention efficiency (in particle separation)

The ratio of the quantity of particles retained by a separator to the quantity entering it (generally expressed as a percentage).

Retention time in gas chromatography

The time between the beginning of the injection of a sample and the moment where there is emergence of the peak maximum of a stated component. This time is quite reproducible with a given pure component when the flows, temperature, etc., are carefully controlled.

Reversible reaction

a reaction that can proceed in both the forward and reverse direction; products can react to re-form the initial reactants.

Rhenium

Symbol: "Re" Atomic Number: "75" Atomic Mass: 186.21amu. This is one of the transition elements. Rhenium is never found free in nature, always bonded to other elements. This silvery-white metal is used in many alloys, flash photography, and even experiments with super-conductivity.

Rhodium

Symbol: "Rh" Atomic Number:"45" Atomic Mass: 102.91amu. Rhodium is one of the transition elements and in the platinum family. Rhodium is often used to harden platinum and found in spark plugs and highly reflective materials.

Rhombohedral

A form of precipitated calcium carbonate in which the particles are relatively "blocky".

Ringelmann chart

A chart which has been used in air pollution evaluation for assigning the degree of blackness of smoke emanating from a source. The observer compares the shades of grey (white to black) with a series of shade diagrams formed by horizontal and vertical black grid lines on a white background. A corresponding number, the Ringelmann number, is then assigned to the describe the best match; numbers range from O (white) to 5 (black).

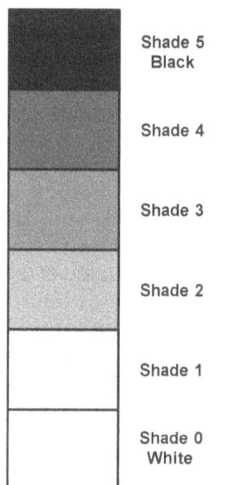

Shade 5
Black

Shade 4

Shade 3

Shade 2

Shade 1

Shade 0
White

Ritchie equation

The linear free energy relation:

$$\log k_N = \log k_0 + N_+$$

applied to the reactions between nucleophiles and certain large and relatively stable organic cations, e.g. arenediazonium, triarylmethyl, and aryltropylium cations in various solvents. k_N is the rate constant for reaction of a given cation with a given nucleophilic system (i.e. given nucleophile in a given solvent). k_0 is the rate constant for the same cation with water in water, and N_+ is a parameter which is characteristic of the nucleophilic system and independent of the cation. A surprising feature of the equation is the absence of a coefficient of N_+, characteristic of the substrate (cf. the s in the Swain-

Scott equation), even though values of N_+ vary over 13 log units. The equation thus involves a gigantic breakdown of the reactivity-selectivity principle. The equation has been extended both in form and in range of application.

Robotic system

Automated device where materials are transferred by the physical movement of a delivery device relative to the ultimate receptacle, or vice versa.

Rock

A rock is a group of minerals in a mixture. Volcanic rocks are excellent examples of rocks created by the super-heated mixing of many minerals.

Rosin acid

A mixture of water-insoluble carboxylic acids from conifers, mostly in the form of multi-ring compounds, in their protonated form.

Rosin size

Various products, derived from certain wood extractives, that can be added at the wet end in the presence of aluminium species to make paper resist water penetration after it has been dried.

Rotometer

A device, based on Stokes law, for measuring rate of fluid flow. it is a tapered vertical tube having a circular cross section in which a float moves in a vertical path to a height dependent upon the rate of fluid flow upward through the tube.

Rubidium

Symbol: "Rb" Atomic Number: "37" Atomic Mass: 85.47amu. One of the alkali metal group. This silvery-white, metallic element can be found in many alloys and amalgams.

Rules of Five: Lipinski's rules

Set of criteria for predicting the oral bioavailability of a compound on the basis of simple molecular features (molecular weight, c Log P, numbers of hydrogen-bond donors and acceptors). Often used to profile a library or virtual library with respect to the proportion of drug-like members which it contains.

Ruthenium

Symbol: "Ru" Atomic Number: "44" Atomic Mass: 101.07amu. Ruthenium is one of the transition elements. One of the members of the platinum group, this white metal can be found in alloys and corrosion resistant metals.

Rutherfordium

Symbol: "Rf" Atomic Number: "104" Atomic Mass: (261)amu One of the postactinide elements. Scientists have created these in labs and may have found only a few atoms of the element.

Rutile

A form of titanium dioxide having the highest refractive index of commonly used fillers.

S

S2 sublayer

Most massive part of a woody fiber, having cellulose molecules almost aligned with the fiber.

Safety-catch linker

A linker which is cleaved by performing two different reactions instead of the normal single step, thus providing greater control over the timing of compound release.

Salt

When you mix an acid and a base, the ionic compounds dissociate. In solution, the H and OH ions combine to form water. The other two ions combine to create a salt. A good example of a salt is NaCl when it is formed by solutions of NaOH (base) and HCl (acid).

Samarium

Symbol: "Sm" Atomic Number: "62" Atomic Mass: 150.40amu. This is one of the elements in the lanthanide series of inner transition elements. It may also be classified as a rare earth element. This silvery metal has many uses in metallic alloys. You may find it in nuclear reactors and even audio equipment.

Sample line

Line provided to remove a representative sample of the gas to be analysed and to conduct it to the sample point. It may include devices such as filters, dryers, or condensers (primary and secondary treatments of gas) which are necessary to prepare the sample for analysis.

Sample point

Point in the gas analysis installation beyond which it is assumed that no alteration of the sample occurs and the sample can be considered representative.

Sample probe

Device inserted into the gas to be sampled and to which is connected a sample line or a container for collecting the sample.

Sample, air

A quantity of air (sometimes of known volume), which is assumed to be representative of the air mass under investigation, and which is examined for air quality characteristics.

Sampler, dichotomous

Device for dividing a polydispersed aerosol particle population into two size fractions during sampling. The fractionation is based on the momentum differences of the particles which allow the larger particles to pass through a zone of stagnant gas.

Sampling train

The complete assemblage of equipment necessary to sample atmospheres.

Sampling, continuous
Sampling, without interruptions, throughout an operation or for a predetermined time.

Sampling, cryogenic
The collection of trace compounds from gaseous media by co-condensation with a major constituent (e.g., water vapour, CO_2, N_2, Ar) of the matrix.

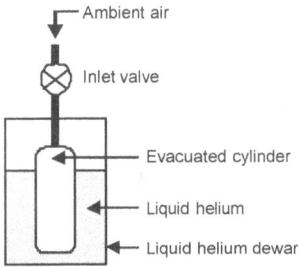

Cryogenic Sampling Method

Sampling, discontinuous
Sampling in which the sample flow is periodically interrupted but not necessarily at equal time intervals.

Sampling, grab
The taking of a sample (often in an evacuated bulb) in a very short time; preferred terms are instantaneous sampling or spot sampling.

Sampling, sequential
Repetitive sampling from the same gas to be analysed or from several gases to be analysed successively.

Sanitary land fill
An engineered burial of refuse. The refuse is dumped into trenches and compacted by bulldozer, where, it is hoped, aerobic metabolism by microorganisms decomposes the organic matter to stable compounds (H_2O, CO_2, etc.).

Saponification
The hydrolysis of an ester under basic conditions to form an alcohol and the salt of a carboxylic acid.

Saponifyable
Capable of being formed into a carboxylic acid soap upon addition of base (e.g. esters, and the protonated form of carboxylic acids).

Saturated
A solution in which the maximum amount of solute has been dissolved in the solvent. As you dissolve sugar in a glass of water there will come a point when you can dissolve no more sugar. The solution has become saturated. Steam from a boiling pot of water can also saturate the surrounding air.

Saturated solution
A solution that contains as much dissolved solute as it can under existing conditions.

Saturation transfer
A term used in nuclear magnetic resonance. When a nucleus is strongly irradiated, its spin population may partly be transferred to another nucleus by an exchange process.

Saturation vapour pressure
The pressure exerted by a pure substance (at a given temperature) in a system containing only the vapour and condensed phase (liquid or solid) of the substance.

Save-all
A device, usually based on disc screens, a screen cylinder, or floatation, that collects fine materials from white water so that they can be returned to the papermaking process.

Saytzeff rule

Dehydrohalogenation of secondary- and tertiary-alkyl halides proceeds by the preferential removal of the -hydrogen from the carbon that has the smallest number of hydrogens. Originally formulated by A. Saytzeff (Zaitsev) to generalize the orientation in b-elimination reactions of alkyl halides, this rule has been extended and modified, as follows: When two or more olefins can be produced in an elimination reaction, the thermodynamically most stable alkene will predominate. Exceptions to the Saytzeff rule are exemplified by the Hofmann rule. SAYTZEFF.

Sbr

Styrene-butadiene resin, a very common latex binder used in aqueous coating formulations.

Scaffold

Core portion of a molecule common to all members of a combinatorial library.

Scale

In meteorology, the size of the system. Microscale processes are the subject of micrometeorology, synoptic scale processes are studied in synoptic meteorology, etc.

Scale height

Distance given by kT/mg where k is the Boltzmann constant, T the temperature (K), m is the molecular mass, and g is the acceleration due to gravity. The scale height is equal to twice the distance through which a particle having kinetic energy kT/2 in the vertical direction can rise against the force of gravity.

Scalenohedral

A rosette shape of certain precipitated calcium carbonate particles that confer bulk and opacity to the paper.

Scandium

Symbol: "Sc" Atomic Number: "21" Atomic Mass: 44.96amu. Scandium is one of the transition elements from the fourth period. Scandium can be found in stars, crystals of aquamarine, in other minerals, and has possible uses in spacecrafts of the future.

Scanning in mass spectrometry

Variation of one or more operating parameters (electric, magnetic, etc.) of a spectrometer which makes it possible to cause the appearance, in the ion collector, of a succession of ions with increasing or decreasing mass to charge ratio.

Scattering (light)

An interaction of light with an object that causes the light to be redirected in its path.

Scattering angle

The angle between the direction of propagation of the scattered and incident (or transmitted) light.

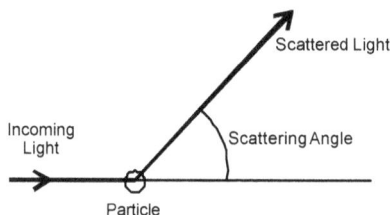

Scavenger

A substance that reacts with (or otherwise removes) a trace component (as in the scavenging of trace metal ions) or traps a reactive reaction *intermediate*.

Scavenger resin

Solid-supported reagent which will react with undesired materials (such as excess reagents) and remove them from solution.

Scavenging

The removal of pollutants from the atmosphere by natural processes, including scavenging by cloud water, rainout, and washout. This type of removal process is termed precipitation scavenging. Scavenging of airborne pollutants at surfaces of plant, soil, etc., is termed dry deposition.

Screen(s)

Device(s) to remove large solids such as fiber bundles and flakes from thin stock just before the headbox of a paper machine.

Scrubbing

A process used in gas sampling or gas cleaning in which components in the gas stream are removed by contact with a liquid surface or a wetted packing, on spray drops, droplets, or in a bubbler, etc.

Seaborgium

Symbol: "Sg" Atomic Number: "106" Atomic Mass: (263)amu. This is one of the postactinide elements. Scientists have created these in labs and may have only found a vew atoms of the element. You will not find these in use anywhere.

Seawater

Seawater is a complex mixture of 96.5 % water, 3.5 % salts, and smaller amounts of other substances, including dissolved inorganic and organic materials, particulates, and a few atmospheric gases. The world's oceans cover nearly 71 % (361 840 000 km^2) of the Earth's surface (510 100 000 km^2), with an average depth of 3 682.2 m. The density of seawater is higher than that of fresh water because of its higher salinity. Seawater's freezing point is lower than that of pure water and its boiling

point is higher. The average salinity of the ocean is 35 ‰, which means that for every kilograms of water, there are 35 g of salt. The relative abundance of the major salts in seawater are constant regardless of the ocean. Only six elements and compounds comprise about 99 % of sea salts: chlorine (Cl^-), sodium (Na^+), sulphur (SO_4^{2-}), magnesium (Mg^{2+}), calcium (Ca^{2+}), and potassium (K^+).

Chemical composition of 1kg seawater with a salinity of 35 %

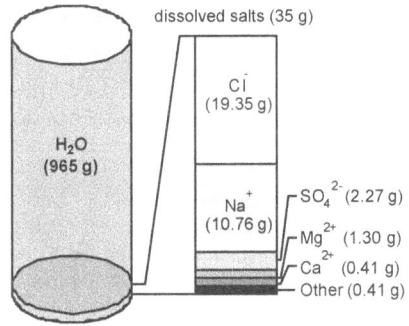

dissolved salts (35 g)

H_2O (965 g)

Cl (19.35 g)

Na^+ (10.76 g)

SO_4^{2-} (2.27 g)

Mg^{2+} (1.30 g)

Ca^{2+} (0.41 g)

Other (0.41 g)

Second messenger

A second messenger is an intracellular metabolite or ion increasing or decreasing as a response to the stimulation of receptors by agonists, considered as the "first messenger". This generic term usually does not prejudge the rank order of intracellular biochemical events.

Second order reaction

A reaction whose rate is dependent on the concentration of two reactants, leading to a reaction rate of Rate = k [X] [Y]

Secondary fines

Fines torn from fiber surfaces or resulting from fiber breakage during refining.

Secondary pollution (emissions)

The products of the primary pollutants which form through photochemical and thermal reactions in the atmosphere (O_3, peroxyacetyl nitrate, etc.).

Sedimentary rock
A rock type that has been created by the deposit and compression of sediment. This type of rock is created over millions of years while igneous rock can be created overnight. Sandstone is a good example of a sedimentary rock. The three main types of rock are igneous, sedimentary, and metamorphic.

Sedimentation
In the atmospheric sciences, the process of removal of an air borne particle from the atmosphere due to the effect of gravity.

Selectivity
The discrimination shown by a reagent in competitive attack on two or more substrates or on two or more positions in the same substrate. It is quantitatively expressed by ratios of rate constants of the competing reactions, or by the decadic logarithms of such ratios.

Selectivity factor
A quantitative representation of selectivity in aromatic substitution reactions (usually electrophilic, for monosubstituted benzene derivatives). If the partial rate factor, f, expresses the reactivity of a specified position in the aromatic compound PhX relative to that of a single position in benzene, then the selectivity factor S_f (expressing discrimination between p- and m-positions in PhX) is defined as $S_f = \lg (f_p^X/f_m^X)$.

Selenium
Symbol: "Se" Atomic Number: "34" Atomic Mass: 78.96amu. It is classified as a non-metal. Selenium is found in many forms. It may have red crystals or a grayish metal colour.

The element is used in solar cells, photocopiers, and it is a trace element in your diet. Too much selenium is poisonous.

Selex
"Systematic Evolution of Ligands by Exponential Enrichment". Process for identifying aptamers by iterative enrichment of oligonucleotide mixtures with respect to their ability to bind a target.

Semi-metal or metalloid
An element that has some of the properties of a metal and some of the properties of a non-metal. eg. silicon is a semi electrical conductor (metallic property) and is brittle (a non-metallic property).

Sensitivity
The rate of change of instrument reading with respect to the change of the value of the air quality characteristic.

Sequestration-enabling reagent
Reagent which converts undesired by-products or residual starting materials into a form which may more easily be removed from the reaction mixture by, for example, solid phase extraction or other phase switch.

Serine protease
A family of proteases, characterized by a serine amino acid at its active site.

Settling chamber
Chamber designed to reduce the velocity of gases in order to permit the settling out of fly ash. It may be either part of, adjacent to, or external to an incinerator.

Settling velocity
The terminal rate of fall of a particle through a fluid as induced by gravity or other external force.

Shear

A change in velocity with respect to distance perpendicular to the direction of flow.

Shells

A shell is the area around the center of an atom. The atom holds its electrons in these shells. There can be up to seven shells that hold 110 electrons.

Shielding

In the context of NMR spectroscopy shielding is the effect of the electron shells of the observed and the neighbouring nuclei on the external magnetic field. The external field induces circulations in the electron cloud. The resulting magnetic moment is oriented in the opposite direction to the external field, so that the local field at the central nucleus is weakened, although it may be strengthened at other nuclei (deshielding).

Si system

International System of Units. A system of measurement used in science. It includes the metric system and other measures. Standard units include the kilogram, liter, metre, and seconds.

SI unit

Stands for Systeme International d'Unites, a international system which established a uniform set of measurement units.

Sigma bonds

A type of covalent bond in which most of the electrons are located in between the nuclei.

Sigma, pi (σ, π)

The terms are symmetry designations, pi molecular orbitals being antisymmetric with respect to a defining plane containing at least one atom (e.g. the molecular plane of ethene), and sigma molecular orbitals symmetric with respect to the same plane. In practice the terms are used both in this rigorous sense (for orbitals encompassing the entire molecule) and also for localized two-centre orbitals or bonds, and it is necessary to make a clear distinction between the two usages. In the case of two-centre bonds, a pi bond has a nodal plane that includes the internuclear bond axis, whereas a sigma bond has no such nodal plane. (A delta bond in organometallic or inorganic molecular species has two nodes.) Radicals are classified by analogy into sigma and pi radicals. Such two-centre orbitals may take part in molecular orbitals of sigma or pi symmetry. For example, the methyl group in propene contains three C-H bonds, each of which is of local sigma symmetry (i.e. without a nodal plane including the internuclear axis), but these three "sigma bonds" can in turn be combined to form a set of group orbitals one of which has pi symmetry with respect to the principal molecular plane and can accordingly interact with the two-centre orbital of pi symmetry (pi bond) of the double-bonded carbon atoms, to form a molecular orbital of pi symmetry.

Sigmatropic rearrangement

A molecular rearrangement that involves both the creation of a new sigma bond between atoms previously not directly linked and the breaking of an existing sigma bond. There is normally a concurrent relocation of pi bonds in the molecule concerned, but the total number of pi and sigma bonds does not change. The term was originally restricted to intramolecular pericyclic reactions, and many authors use it with this connotation. It is, however, also applied in a more general, purely structural, sense. If such reactions are intramolecular, their transition state may be visualized as an association of two fragments connected at their termini by two partial sigma bonds, one being broken and the other being formed as, for example, the two allyl fragments in (a'). Considering only atoms within the (real or hypothetical) cyclic array undergoing reorganization, if the numbers of these in the two fragments are designated i and j, then the rearrangement is said to be a sigmatropic change of order [i,j] (conventionally [i] <= [j]). Thus the rearrangement (a) is of order [3,3], whilst reaction (b) is a [1,5]sigmatropic shift of hydrogen.

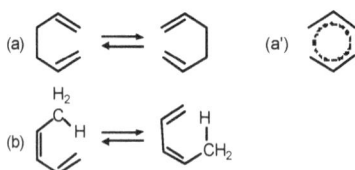

The descriptors a and s (antarafacial and suprafacial) may also be annexed to the numbers i and j; (b) is then described as a [1s,5s] sigmatropic rearrangement, since it is suprafacial with respect both to the hydrogen atom and to the pentadienyl system:

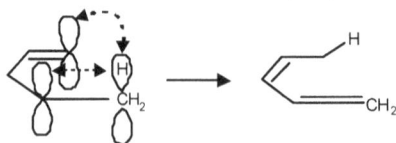

The prefix "homo" (meaning one extra atom, interrupting conjugation - cf. "homoaromaticity") has frequently been applied to sigmatropic rearrangements, but is misleading.

Significant figures
All certain digits in a measurement plus one uncertain digit.

Silicate mineral
A mineral that is made up of compounds with a silicon oxide group or silicon atom bonded to a metal. Topaz is a good example of a silicate mineral.

Silicon
Symbol: "Si" Atomic Number: "14" Atomic Mass: 28.09amu. Silicon is a delicate, non-metallic element. It is delicate because it is brittle. There is more silicon in the Earth's crust than any other element except oxygen. You will also find silicon in glass, pottery, computer chips, and bricks.

Silver
Symbol: "Ag" Atomic Number: "47" Atomic Mass: 107.87amu. It is one of the transition elements. Silver is one of man's precious metals and has been used for thousands of years. It has the highest thermal and electrical conductivity of any metal. You will find it used in photography, dentistry, electronics, mirrors, and explosives.

Silylene
(1) Generic name for H_2Si: and substitution derivatives thereof, containing an electrically neutral bivalent silicon atom with two non-bonding electrons.
(2) The silanediyl group (H_2Si), analogous to the methylene group (H_2C).

Simple elements
These are elements in the periodic table that have only one shell that is missing electrons. These simple elements include many of the first 18 elements. Carbon, oxygen, nitrogen are examples of simple elements.

Single bonds

When two atoms participate in a Covalent Bond and only share a single (one) electron the Covalent Bond formed is referred to as a Single Covalent Bond or just a Single Bond.

Single Bond

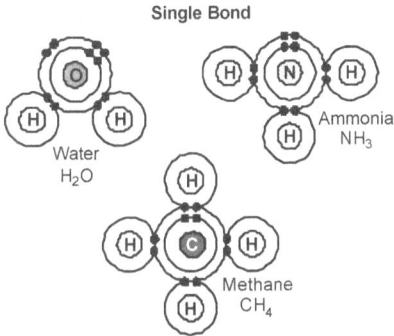

Water
H_2O

Ammonia
NH_3

Methane
CH_4

Single-electron transfer mechanism (SET)

A reaction mechanism characterized by the transfer of a single electron between the species occurring on the reaction coordinate of one of the elementary steps.

Single-step reaction

A reaction that proceeds through a single transition state.

Sink

In atmospheric chemistry, the sink is the receptor for material which is removed from the atmosphere. Because of long range transport of many pollutants such as SO_2, sulphuric acid and its salts, the sink region can be many hundreds of kilometres from the source region of the pollutants.

Sintering

The process by which fly ash produced in combustion of fuels such as coal, is baked (sintered) at a very high temperature. The sintered material is used in the manufacture of cinder blocks and other ceramic products. This term is also relevant to the enrichment of low grade ores and preparation of the charge for, e.g., a blast furnace. The sinter plant may be a significant source of pollution while serving to aid in the abatement of pollution for the blast furnace.

Site isolation

Property of solid supports, whereby functional groups are separated from each other by the polymeric framework, and thus, while they may be physically in close proximity, reduced levels of reaction between sites may be observed.

Site-specific delivery

Site-specific delivery is an approach to target a drug to a specific tissue, using prodrugs or antibody recognition systems.

Size press

Equipment for applying a polymeric solution to the surface of paper just after it has been dried for the first time, usually by means of a puddle and nip between rolls or by metering the solution onto a rubber roll.

Size reversion

A tendency for certain types of sized paper to gradually loose their water-resistant nature.

Sizing

1. "Internal" sizing is treatment of the fiber slurry so that the paper will resist fluids.
2. "Surface sizing" is addition of a film of starch solution or other material at the paper surface.

Skeleton equation

A chemical equation that is not balanced, with an unequal number of atoms on each side of the reaction. You may start with a hydrogen molecule on one side of the equation (two atoms) and create a compound that has eight hydrogen atoms. Although the formulas are correct, the equation is not balanced.

Slater-type orbital
An approximate atomic orbital that attempts to allow for electron-electron repulsion by scaling the nuclear charge for each orbital.

Slime
A slippery deposit composed of bacteria or fungal cells.

Slip
A condition of low friction coefficient - either sheet-to-sheet or sheet-to-equipment, often attributable to waxy materials or high AKD size addition level.

Slip plane
The hydrodynamic slip plane is an imaginary plane about 2-10 nm from a charged surface where ions closer to the surface act as if they are part of the surface and those outside act as if they are part of the surrounding aqueous solution.

Smog
The term originated in Great Britain as a popular derivation of "smoke-fog" and appears to have been in common use before World War I. It originally referred to the heavy pollution derived largely from coal burning (largely smoke filled air, rich in sulphur dioxide), and it probably was largely a reducing atmosphere. More common today in cities is an oxidising atmosphere which contains ozone and other oxidants.

Smog alert
Conditions indicated by meteorological forecasts, air sampiing, etc., where authorities responsible for air pollution control in a given area recommend or impose reduction of pollutant output by industry and other sources which contribute to the smog development. Alert levels of gaseous pollutants (carbon monoxide, nitrogen oxides, sulphur oxides, ozone) ate considered indicative of an approach to danger to public health. Usually several levels of alert with increasing hazard are used.

Smog chamber
A large confined volume in which sunlight or simulated sunlight is allowed to irradiate air mixtures of atmospheric trace gases (hydrocarbons, nitrogen oxides, sulphur dioxide, etc.) which undergo oxidation. In theory these chambers allow the controlled study of complex reactions which occur in the atmosphere.

Smog index
A mathematical correlation between smog and meteorological and/or pollutant concentrations associated with it. These are qualitative indices which are sometimes used in some urban communities to predict the degree of the air pollution which is expected for the coming day.

Smoke
Smoke is a fine suspension of solid particles in a gas. In general smoke particles range downward from about 50nm in diameter to less than 0.5nm in diameter. Smoke generally refers to a visible mixture of products given off by the incomplete combustion of an organic substance such as wood, coal, fuel oil etc. This airborne mixture general contains small particles (dusts) of carbon, hydrocarbons, ash etc. as well as vapours such as carbon monoxide, carbon dioxide, and water vapour.

Smoke abatement

Legal measures which a control agency of a community may take to enforce laws and regulations concerning smoke emission.

Smoke alarm

An instrument which can provide an objective method of continuous measurement of the smoke density. Such devices are often depend upon the attenuation of light, and they can actuate an alarm when the attenuation exceeds some predetermined amount.

Smokestack

A chimney which carries the products of combustion away from a combustion chamber.

Smuts

Agglomerates of soot that become detached from the wall of a chimney and are swept out by the flue gas and then fall in the vicinity of the stack.

Soap sizing

Achieving resistance to water penetration by adding the sodium salt of rosin at the wet end.

Sodium

Sodium was discovered by Sir Humphry Davy (England) in 1807. The origin of the name comes from the Latin word natrium meaning sodium carbonate. It is soft silvery-white metal. Fresh surfaces oxidize rapidly. Reacts vigorously, even violently with water. Reacts with water to give off flammable gas. Burns in air with a brilliant white flame. Sodium is obtained by electrolysis of melted sodium chloride (salt), borax and cryolite. Metallic sodium is vital in the manufacture of organic compounds. Sodium chloride (NaCl) is table salt. Liquid sodium is used to cool nuclear reactors.

Soft drug

A soft drug is a compound that is degraded in vivo to predictable non-toxic and inactive metabolites, after having achieved its therapeutic role.

Soiling

Visible damage to materials by deposition of air pollutants.

Sol

A fluid colloidal system of two or more components, e.g. a protein sol, a gold sol, an emulsion, a surfactant solution above the critical micelle concentration.

Solar radiation

The electromagnetic radiation emitted by the sun. The total range of wavelengths of light emitted by the sun (99.9% in the range from 150 to 4000 nm) is filtered on entering the earth's atmosphere, largely through the absorption by oxygen, ozone, water vapour, and carbon dioxide. Near sea level only light of wavelengths longer than about 290 nm is present.

Solid

One characteristic of a solid is that it might be hard. In the same way that a solid holds its shape, the atoms inside of a solid are not allowed to move around. The solid atoms and molecules are trapped in their places.

Solid phase extraction

Method for sample purification, whereby either the desired or undesired components of a mixture have preferential affinity for a solid material. Adding the mixture to the solid material then allows facile separation of the desired material by filtration.

Solid support

Insoluble, functionalized, polymeric

material to which library members or reagents may be attached (often via a linker) allowing them to be readily separated (by filtration, centrifugation, etc.) from excess reagents, soluble reaction by-products or solvents.

Solidification

A change in state from liquid to a solid. The particles slow down sufficiently for the attractive forces between them to be strong enough to hold the particles in fixed positions.

Solubility

The maximum amount of material, pure solid, liquid, or gaseous compound (grams, mol, etc.) which will dissolve at equilibrium in a given amount of solvent (100 g, 1 kg, 1 litre of solution etc.) at a given temperature. The system is at equilibrium (at a fixed temperature) when the solution phase as well as the solid, liquid, or gas phase remain in contact indefinitely without further net change in amount of either phase. The solubility of gases in water is often considered in terms of Henry's law.

Solubility curve

A graph showing the relationship between solubility and temperature.

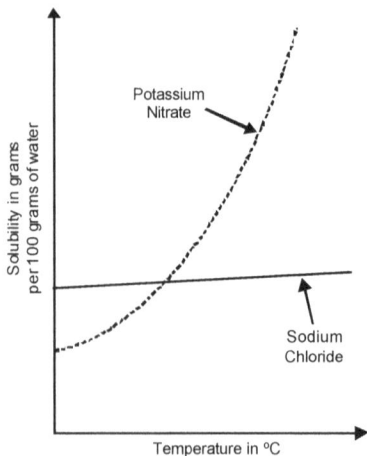

Solubility product constant

The equilibrium constant for the solution of a slightly soluble ionic compound. Symbol K_{sp}. K_{sp} is equal to the product of the concentrations of ions raised to powers equatl to the subscripts in their chemical formulas.

Soluble

Soluble is the ability of a substance to dissolve in another substance. Not all solutes are soluble in all solvents. Sugar and salt are compounds that are soluble in water.

Soluble support

An attachment, common to all library members, which renders the library components soluble under conditions for library synthesis, but which can be readily separated from most other soluble components when desired by some simple physical process. This process has been termed liquid phase chemistry. Examples of soluble supports include linear polymers such as polyethylene glycol, dendrimers or fuorinated compounds which selectively partition into fluorine-rich solvents.

Solute

A solute is the substance to be dissolved. Sugar would be the solute when you are dissolving sugar in water.

Solution

A homogeneous mixture of two or more elements or compounds. The term may be applied to mixtures of solids as well as liquids, but unless stated otherwise, solution normally refers to a liquid medium (e.g., H_2SO_4 in water).

Solvation

Any stabilizing interaction of a solute (or solute moiety) and the solvent or a similar interaction of solvent with groups of an insoluble material (i.e., the ionic groups of an ion-exchange resin). Such interactions generally involve electrostatic forces and van der Waals forces, as well as chemically more specific effects such as hydrogen bond formation.

Solvatochromic relationship

A linear free-energy relationship based on solvatochromism.

Solvatochromism

The (pronounced) change in position and sometimes intensity of an electronic absorption or emission band, accompanying a change in the polarity of the medium. Negative (positive) solvatochromism corresponds to a hypsochromic (bathochromic) shift with increasing solvent polarity.

Solvent

The part of the solution that the solute is dissolved in; typically the substance present in larger amounts. In aqueous solutions the solvent is water.

Solvent parameter

Quantitative measures of the capability of solvents for interaction with solutes. Such parameters have been based on numerous different physico-chemical quantities, e.g. rate constants, solvatochromic shifts in ultraviolet/visible spectra, solvent-induced shifts in infrared frequencies, etc. Some solvent parameters are purely empirical in nature, i.e. they are based directly on some experimental measurement. It may be possible to interpret such a parameter as measuring some particular aspect of solvent-solute interaction or it may be regarded simply as a measure of solvent *polarity*. Other solvent parameters are based on analysing experimental results. Such a parameter is considered to quantify some particular aspect of solvent capability for interaction with solutes.

Solvolysis

Generally, reaction with a solvent, or with a *lyonium ion* or *lyate ion*, involving the rupture of one or more bonds in the reacting solute. More specifically the term is used for *substitution, elimination* and *fragmentation* reactions in which a solvent species is the *nucleophile*.

Somo

A Singly Occupied Molecular Orbital (such as the half-filled *HOMO* of a radical).

Sonication

Irradiation with (often ultra)sound waves, e.g. to increase the rate of a reaction or to prepare vesicles in mixtures of surfactants and water.

Soot

Aggregations of black carbonaceous particles formed during incomplete combustion and which are deposited before being emitted from a chimney.

Sort and Combine

Use of directed sorting to facilitate library assembly. Related to pool/split protocol, but more commonly applied to macroscopic solid supports (such as pins and related carriers) where each library member is found on only one, or a small number of carriers.

Source

In atmospheric chemistry, the place, places, or group of sites or areas where a pollutant is released into the atmosphere. Point sources, elevated sources, area sources, multiple sources are often identified.

Span

Difference between the instrument readings for a stated value of air quality characteristic and a zero sample. By convention, this value of air quality characteristic is selected to be 95% of the upper limit of measurement.

Spatially addressable
Having the ability to identify at least part of the structure of a library component or pool by noting its physical location in an array.

Special salt effect
The initial steep rate increase observed in the kinetic electrolyte effect on certain solvolysis reactions, upon addition of some non-common ion salts, especially $LiClO_4$.

Species
In chemistry, a given kind of atom, molecule or radical which has a characteristic chemical structure and composition. A chemical species is a set of chemically identical atomic or molecular structural units in a solid array or of chemically identical molecular entities that can explore the same set of molecular energy levels on the time scale of the experiment.

Specific catalysis
The acceleration of a reaction by a unique catalyst, rather than by a family of related substances. The term is most commonly used in connection with specific hydrogen-ion or hydroxide-ion (lyonium ion or lyate ion) catalysis.

Specific gravity
The specific gravity is a comparison of the mass of a substance to the mass of water with the same volume. If you fill a cup with mercury, it has a greater mass than the same cup filled with water. Specific gravity is usually used to measure and compare the masses of liquids. Density is usually used to measure and compare the masses of solids.

Specific heat
The amount of heat energy required to raise the temperature of one gram of a substance by one degree Celsius. The specific heat of water is 4.184 J/ (g·°C)

Specific heat capacity
The heat needed to raise a gram of a substance temperature by a degree.

Specific surface area
The surface area of a sample of solid material, divided by its mass.

Spectator ion
an ion that is present during a reaction but does not undergo change; it appears on both sides of the reaction.

Spectrometry, optical (in trace component analysis of air)
Methods of identification of substances and determination of their concentration based upon the measurement of light transmittance at selected wavelengths or bands of wavelengths; see also mass spectrometry.

Spectrophotometer
Tool that measures the absorption or emission of electromagnetic radiation.

Spectrophotometry
Methods using a photometer to measure light intensity as a function of wavelength.

Spectroscopy
Is the analysis of the lines of light emitted from excited atoms as the electrons drop back through their orbitals. These lines give the energy and distances of the electronic orbitals.

Spheradiance, spectral

Alternate term suggested for Actinic flux.

Spin density

The unpaired electron density at a position of interest, usually at carbon, in a radical. It is often measured experimentally by electron paramagnetic resonance (EPR, ESR (electron spin resonance)) spectroscopy through hyperfine coupling constants of the atom or an attached hydrogen.

Spin label

A stable paramagnetic group (typically a nitryl radical) that is attached to a part of a molecular entity whose microscopic environment is of interest and may be revealed by the electron spin resonance (ESR) spectrum of the spin label. When a simple paramagnetic molecular entity is used in this way without covalent attachment to the molecular entity of interest it is frequently referred to as a "spin probe".

Spin trapping

In certain reactions in solution a transient radical will interact with a diamagnetic reagent to form a more *persistent* radical. The product radical accumulates to a concentration where detection and, frequently, identification are possible by EPR/ESR spectroscopy. The key reaction is usually one of attachment; the diamagnetic reagent is said to be a "spin trap", and the persistent product radical is then the "spin adduct". The procedure is referred to as spin trapping, and is used for monitoring reactions involving the intermediacy of *reactive* radicals at concentrations too low for direct observation.

Spontaneous change

Changes that occur on their own.

Spontaneous reaction

A reaction that will proceed without any outside energy.

Spreading

A time-dependent increase in wetted area when liquid is placed on a solid such as paper.

Spreading coefficient

A thermodynamic parameter that can be used to predict the best composition for a defoamer.

Stable

As applied to chemical species, the term expresses a thermodynamic property, which is quantitatively measured by relative molar standard Gibbs energies. A chemical species A is more stable than its isomer B if $D_rG^\circ > 0$ for the (real or hypothetical) reaction A   B, under standard conditions. If for the two reactions P   X + Y (DrG1°) Q   X + Z (DrG2°) $D_rG_1^\circ > D_rG_2^\circ$, P is more stable relative to the product Y than is Q relative to Z. Both in qualitative and quantitative usage the term stable is therefore always used in reference to some explicitly stated or implicitly assumed standard. The term should not be used as a synonym for unreactive or "less reactive" since this confuses thermodynamics and kinetics. A relatively more stable chemical species may be more reactive than some reference species towards a given reaction partner.

Stable suspension

A mixture of finely divided particles in a liquid in which the repulsive forces, due to like charges and/or adsorbed molecules having long fluid-loving tails extending into the fluid, prevent sticking collisions.

Stack gas

Gaseous waste products discharged to the atmosphere through a stack.

Stack height selection

The degree of dispersion of the stack effluent increases with the height of the stack. The maximum ground level concentration of pollutants and the point from the stack at which this occurs are complex functions of the wind turbulence and other meteorological factors as well as stack height. There are physical and practical limitations which control the choice of stack height: cost, air traffic hazards, aesthetic considerations, aerodynamic factors, vibration, materials, etc.

Stack sampling

Collection of representative gaseous and particulate samples of matter flowing through a duct or stack. Acceptable performance should indicate a collection efficiency of 95 ± 5 percent. Samples should be taken under isokinetic conditions to obtain an accurate representation of the particle size distribution in the effluent.

Standard

An exact value, or a concept, that has been established by authority or agreement, to serve as a model or rule in the measurement of a quantity or in the establishment of a practice or procedure, in air pollutant analysis, standard reference gases, liquids, or solids are used to calibrate equipment. The concentrations of standards specified by a government agency or private laboratory must be based upon accurate measurement techniques which are verifiable through cross checks and the use of unambiguous methods.

Standard conditions

Conditions used to complete formulas in chemistry. Standard conditions include atmosphere at sea level (760 torr) and the Kelvin value for the freezing point of water (273K).

Standard conditions for gases

Sometimes indicated with the abbreviation, STP. Temperature, 273.15 K (0 °C) and pressure of 10^5 pascals. IUPAC recommends that the former use of the pressure of 1 atm as standard pressure (equivalent to 1.01325×10^5 Pa) should be discontinued.

Standard electrode potential

The voltage obtained when a given half-cell is combined with a standard hydrogen half-cell, as measured under standard conditions (25°C, 1 M ion concentrations, 101.3 kPa pressure). Symbol E°.

Standard hydrogen half-cell

The reference electrode that is used to determine the electrode potential of other half-cells. The hydrogen half-cell, assigned a voltage of 0.00 V under standard conditions (25°C, 1 M ion concentrations, 101.3 kPa pressure). The hydrogen half-cell reaction is: $2 H^+_{(aq)} + 2e^{-}$"! $H_{2(g)}$

Standard pressure

The pressure measured at sea level on the Earth. Pressure can change if weather changes but standard pressure is measured as 760 millimetres of mercury on a barometer (torr).

Standard solution

This is a solution for which the scientist knows the concentration of solute and solvent.

Standard temperature and pressure (STP)

The temperature and pressure at which many scientific measurements are made. Typically refers to a temperature of 0 °C (273 K) and 101.3 kPa (or 1 atm pressure).

Starch

A long chain of carbohydrates formed in plants. It is often used as a food supply because it is a polysaccharide made of glucose units. You will see starches from wheat plants used everyday in pasta. Starch is originally created in plant cells.

State property

A state property is a quantity that is independent of how the substance was prepared. Examples of state properties are altitude, pressure, volume, temperature and internal energy.

States of Matter

Matter comes in many forms, shapes, and sizes. The big ones you should remember are solids, liquids, gases, and plasmas. Nearly all matter can be found in these four basic forms.

Stationary phase in gas chromatography

Solid or liquid which has reversible sorption properties, for the components to be analysed. The non-mobile phase in the chromatographic bed, on which the separation depends. For example, in gas-solid chromatography and liquid-solid chromatography the active solid, and in gas-liquid and liquid-liquid chromatography the liquid, but not the solid support.

Stepwise reaction

A chemical reaction with at least one reaction intermediate and involving at least two consecutive elementary reactions.

Stereoelectronic

Pertaining to the dependence of the properties (especially the energy) of a molecular entity in a particular electronic state (or of a transition state) on relative nuclear geometry. The electronic ground state is usually considered, but the term can apply to excited states as well. Stereoelectronic effects are ascribed to the different alignment of electronic orbitals in different arrangements of nuclear geometry.

Stereoelectronic control

Control of the nature of the products of a chemical reaction (or of its rate) by stereoelectronic factors. The term is usually applied in the framework of an orbital approximation. The variations of molecular orbital energies with relative nuclear geometry (along a reaction coordinate) are then seen as consequences of variations in basis-orbital overlaps.

Stereoselectivity

Stereoselectivity is the preferential formation in a chemical reaction of one stereoisomer over another. When the stereoisomers are enantiomers, the phenomenon is called enantioselectivity and is quantitatively expressed by the enantiomer excess; when they are diastereoisomers, it is called diastereoselectivity and is quantitatively expressed by the diastereomer excess. Reactions are termed (100%) stereoselective if the discrimination is complete or partially (x%) stereoselective if one product predominates. The discrimination may also be referred to semiquantitatively as high or low stereoselectivity.

Stereospecificity

(1) A reaction is termed stereospecific if starting materials differing only in their configuration

are converted into stereoisomeric products. According to this definition, a stereospecific process is necessarily *stereoselective* but not all stereoselective processes are stereospecific. Stereospecificity may be total (100%) or partial. The term is also applied to situations where reaction can be performed with only one stereoisomer. For example the exclusive formation of trans-1,2-dibromocyclohexane upon bromination of cyclohexene is a stereospecific process, although the analogous reaction with (E)-cyclohexene has not been performed.

(2) The term has also been applied to describe a reaction of very high stereoselectivity, but this usage is unnecessary and is discouraged.

Steric effect

The effect on a chemical or physical property (structure, rate or equilibrium constant) upon introduction of substituents having different steric requirements. The steric effect in a reaction is ascribed to the difference in steric energy between, on the one hand, reactants and, on the other hand, a transition state, (or products). A steric effect on a rate process may result in a rate increase ("steric acceleration") or a decrease ("steric retardation"). Steric effects arise from contributions ascribed to strain as the sum of (1) non-bonded repulsions, (2) bond angle strain, and (3) bond stretches or compressions.

Steric factor

Term (p) used in the older literature to describe the make up of the preexponential factor (A) in the Arrhenius equation for the rate coefficient:

$$A = pz,$$

where z is the collision number and p represents the probability of correct orientation for reaction upon collision between two reactants.

Steric hindrance

The original term for a steric effect arising from crowding of substituents.

Steric-approach control

Control of stereoselectivity of a reaction by steric hindrance towards attack of the reagent, which is directed to the less hindered face of the molecule. Partial bond making is strong enough at the transition state for steric control to take place. This suggests that the transition state should not be close to products.

Steroid

Steroids are lipids that are based on the cholesterol molecule. Steroids have three six-carbon rings, one five-carbon ring, and a side chain of some type. They are often used as hormones in organisms. Some steroids you may know are cholesterol, progesterone, or testosterone.

Stickies

Sticky materials in recycled papermaking pulp, often involving pressure-sensitive labels.

Stoichiometric

Involving chemical combination in simple integral ratios. Characterized by having no excess of reactants or products over that required to satisfy the balanced chemical equation representing the given chemical reaction.

Stoichiometry

The area of mathematics that is concerned with numerical relationships of chemical formulas and chemical equations.

Stoker

A machine for feeding coal into a furnace, and supporting it there during combustion.

Stopped flow

A technique for following the kinetics of reactions in solution (usually in the millisecond time range) in which two reactant solutions are rapidly mixed by being forced through a mixing chamber. The flow of the mixed solution along a uniform tube is then suddenly arrested. At a fixed position along the tube the solution is monitored (as a function of time following the stoppage of the flow) by some method with a rapid response (e.g. photometry).

Storage temperature, maximum

The temperature above which the indicated uncertainty of the composition of a standard substance or mixture may be altered because of physical, chemical, or physico-chemical reactions of the components of the mixture with each other or decompositions or reactions catalyzed at the wall of the gas cylinder.

STP

Abbreviation for standard temperature (273.15 K or 0 °C) and pressure (16 Pa); usually employed in reporting gas volumes. Note that flow metres calibrated in standard gas volumes per unit time often refer to volumes at 25 °C, not 0 °C.

Strain

Strain is present in a molecular entity or transition structure if the energy is enhanced because of unfavourable bond lengths, bond angles, or dihedral angles ("torsional strain") relative to a standard. It is quantitatively defined as the standard enthalpy of a structure relative to a strainless structure (real or hypothetical) made up from the same atoms with the same types of bonding. (The enthalpy of formation of cyclopropane is 53.6 kJ mol^{-1}, whereas the enthalpy of formation based on three "normal" methylene groups, from acyclic models, is -62 kJ mol^{-1}.

Stratopause

The stratopause (formerly Mesopeak) is the level of the atmosphere which is the boundary between two layers, stratosphere and the mesosphere. In the stratosphere the temperature increases with altitude, and the stratopause is the section where a maximum in the temperature occurs.

Stratosphere

The atmospheric shell lying just above the troposphere which is characterized by an increasing temperature with altitude. The stratosphere begins at the tropopause (about 10-15 km height) and extends to a height of about 50 km, where the lapse rate changes sign at the stratopause and the beginning of the mesosphere.

Streaming current

A method for estimating the charge demand of an aqueous sample by adding titrant to a device with a loose-fitting plastic piston reciprocating in a plastic cylinder fitted with two electrodes and a detection system.

Streaming potential

A method for estimating the relative magnitude of zeta potential at fiber surfaces by forcing aqueous solution through a mat or plug of fibers and noting how the electrical potential measured across the mat changes with applied pressure.

Strong acid

A strong acid is an acid that ionizes completely in an aqueous solution by losing one proton, according to the equation

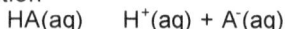

$$HA(aq) \quad H^+(aq) + A^-(aq)$$

For sulphuric acid which is diprotic, the "strong acid" designation refers only to dissociation of the first proton

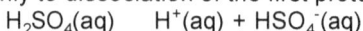

$$H_2SO_4(aq) \quad H^+(aq) + HSO_4^-(aq)$$

More precisely, the acid must be stronger in aqueous solution than hydronium ion, so strong acids are acids with a $pK_a < -1.74$. An example is HCl for which $pK_a = -6.3$. This generally means that in aqueous solution at standard temperature and pressure, the concentration of hydronium ions is equal to the concentration of strong acid introduced to the solution. While strong acids are generally assumed to be the most corrosive, this is not always true. The carborane superacid $H(CHB_{11}Cl_{11})$, which is one million times stronger than sulphuric acid, is entirely non-corrosive, whereas the weak acid hydrofluoric acid (HF) is corrosive and can dissolve, among other things, glass and all metals except iridium.

Strong base

A base that dissociates completely into a metal ion and hydroxide ion (or nearly so) in aqueous solution.

Strong electrolyte

A strong electrolyte is compound that ionizes one hundred percent in solution. Strong acids, bases, and salts are all strong electrolytes.

Strontium

Symbol: "Sr" Atomic Number: "38" Atomic Mass: 87.62amu. This element is a member of the alkaline metals family. Strontium is grouped with other barium-like minerals. It is reactive and oxidizes quickly, becoming a yellowish colour. You may find it in magnets, TV tubes, and nuclear reactors.

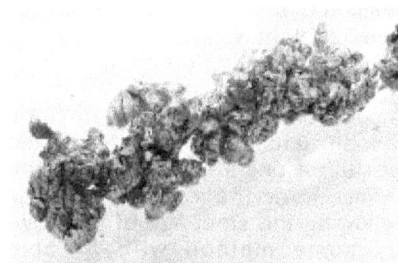

Structural formula

A chemical formula that shows how atoms are arranged within a moleucle or polyatomic ion. Each dash represents a single covalent bond.

Structure-activity relationship (SAR)

Structure-activity relationship is the relationship between chemical structure and pharmacological activity for a series of compounds.

Structure-based design

Structure-based design is a drug design strategy based on the 3D structure of the target obtained by X-ray or NMR.

SPC

Structure-property correlations refers to all statistical mathematical methods used to correlate any structural property to any other property (intrinsic, chemical or biological), using statistical regression and pattern recognition techniques.

Stuff box

An overflow chamber that provides a constant hydrostatic head before the stock pump that metres thick stock to a paper machine.

Sub-atomic

Small particles which make up the atom. ie. the proton, the neutron and the electron.

Subgroup

These are columns of transition and inner transition elements. They have electron similarities for the outer two or three electron orbitals.

Sub-library

A subset of a combinatorial library physically separated from the rest of the library, generally with one or more fixed building blocks.

Sublimation

A change in state from solid to gas without the formation of a liquid. eg. dry ice (solid carbon dioxide)

Sub-monomer synthesis

Process resulting in an oligomer in which each monomer residue is formed from two or more building blocks. This approach has been used for peptoid synthesis.

Subshell

One part of a level, each of which can hold different numbers of electrons.

Substituent

An atom or group of bonded atoms that can be considered to have replaced a hydrogen atom (or two hydrogen atoms in the special case of bivalent groups) in a parent molecular entity (real or hypothetical).

Substitution reaction

A reaction, elementary or stepwise, in which one atom or group in a molecular entity is replaced by another atom or group. For example,
$$CH_3Cl + OH^- \quad CH_3OH + Cl^-$$

Substrate

A chemical species, the reaction of which with some other chemical reagent is under observation (e.g., a compound that is transformed under the influence of a catalyst). The term should be used with care. Either the context or a specific statement should always make it clear which chemical species in a reaction is regarded as the substrate.

Successor complex

The radical ion pair which forms by the transfer of an electron from the donor D to the acceptor A after these species have diffused together to form the *precursor* or *encounter complex*:
$$A + D \quad (A\ D) \quad (A^-\ D^+)$$

Sulfate mineral

A mineral that is made up of compounds with a sulfate group bonded to a metal. Copper sulfate is a good example of a sulfate mineral. It is also known as chalcanthite.

Sulfate reducing bacteria

A type of bacteria that thrives in oxygen-free (anaerobic) environments, causing odors and corrosion of stainless steel.

Sulphide mineral

A mineral that is made of compounds with a sulphur atom bonded to a metal. Iron pyrite is a good example of a sulfide mineral with one iron atom bonded to two sulphur atoms.

Sulphur

Symbol: "S" Atomic Number: "16" Atomic Mass: 32.06amu. Sulphur is a non-reactive element and is classified as a non-metal. It is found in large amounts all over the Earth and is usually yellow. You'll also find sulphur in fertilizers, medicine, fireworks, and matches. There are also many minerals called sulfides and sulfates in which sulphur appears.

Sulphur dioxide (SO$_2$)

A major oxidation product of sulphur-containing compounds in fuels and the major sulphur species emitted from power plants, furnaces, and other combustion sources. It is oxidized eventually to sulphuric acid and its salts in the atmosphere by reaction with HO-radicals in the gas phase, and more rapidly in cloud-water, rain, and in ground water, where it exists largely as HSO$_3^-$ ion, by reaction with dissolved H$_2$O$_2$, O$_3$, and other oxidizing agents.

Superacid

A medium having a high acidity, generally greater than that of 100 wt.-% sulphuric acid. The common superacids are made by dissolving a powerful Lewis acid (e.g. SbF$_5$) in a suitable Brønsted acid, such as HF or HSO$_3$F. In a biochemical context "superacid catalysis" is sometimes used to denote catalysis by metal ions analogous to catalysis by hydrogen ions.

Supercritical carbon dioxide

Supercritical carbon dioxide (scCO$_2$) is a powerful, cheap, non-toxic and environmental friendly solvent. When used at a supercritical state (over 74 bar and 31 °C), it achieves similar solvating power as its organic competitors, such as hydrocarbons and chlorinated solvents. Supercritical carbon dioxide is one of few solvents that can be unrestrictedly used for food processing.

Supercritical fluid extraction

Supercritical fluid extractions (SFE) have solvating powers similar to liquid organic solvents, but with higher diffusivities, lower viscosity, and lower surface tension. The main advantages of using supercritical fluids for extractions is that they are inexpensive, contaminant free, and less costly to dispose safely than organic solvents. For non-destructive isolation choose SFE, which is simply the best technology for sensitive raw materials. For these reasons supercritical carbon dioxide (scCO$_2$) is the reagent used to extract caffeine from coffee and tea. Its gaslike behaviour allows it to penetrate deep into the green coffee beans, and it dissolves from 97 % to 99 % of the caffeine present.

Supersaturated

A solution that has more solute dissolved than is possible under normal circumstances. If you heat a glass of water that is saturated you can add more sugar to the solution. When that solution cools to the original temperature, it is considered supersaturated.

Supersaturated solution

A solution that is holding more dissolved solute than it normally can under a given set of conditions.

Supersaturation

a) In chemistry, an unstable system which has a greater concentration of a material in solution than would exist at equilibrium is said to be supersaturated.
b) In meteorology, supersaturation of an air mass with respect to H$_2$O vapour is of special interest. It is the saturation ratio minus one, or the percent supersaturation is the percent relative humidity minus 100.

Supramolecule

A system of two or more molecular

entities held together and organized by means of intermolecular (noncovalent) binding interactions.

Surface sizing

Application of a solution, often containing starch, to the surface of paper, usually in order to increase surface strength, and sometimes with addition of hydrophobic polymers.

Surface tension

The strength of the tendency of a liquid to adopt a shape having the minimum surface area (often forming a droplet).

Surfactant

A surface active agent, usually comprised of molecules with water-loving and water-hating groups, used for wetting, emulsifying, etc.

Suspended matter

All particulate material which persists in the atmosphere or in a flue gas stream for lengthy periods because the particles are too small in size to have an appreciable falling velocity.

Suspension

A mixture consisting of small particles of solid dispersed throughout a liquid. The appearance is cloudy(opaque) as light is scattered.

Swain-Lupton equation

A dual parameter approach to the correlation analysis of substituent effects, which involves a field constant (F) and a resonance constant (R). The original treatment was modified later.

Swain-Scott equation

The linear free-energy relation of the form $lg(k/k_0) = sn$ applied to the variation of reactivity of a given electrophilic substrate towards a series

of nucleophilic reagents. n is characteristic of the reagent (i.e. a measure of its nucleophilicity) and s is characteristic of the substrate (i.e. a measure of its sensitivity to the nucleophilicity of the reagent). A scale of n values is based on the rate coefficients k for the reaction of methyl bromide with nucleophiles in water at 25 °C, s being defined as 1.00 for these reactions and n being defined as 0.00 for the hydrolysis of methyl bromide.

Swamp gas

Swamp gas is a gas which develops by rottening of organic matter with no presence of air at all, e.g. at bottom of the swamp.

Symbiosis

The term was originally applied to describe the maximum flocking of either hard or soft *ligands* in the same complexes. For hydrocarbon molecules, symbiosis implies that those containing a maximum number of C-H bonds (e.g. CH_4) or C-C bonds (e.g. Me_4C) are the most stable.

Synchronization (principle of nonperfect synchronization)

This principle applies to reactions in which there is a lack of synchronization between bond formation or bond rupture and other primitive changes that affect the stability of products and reactants, such as resonance, solvation, electrostatic, hydrogen bonding and polarizability effects. The principle states that a product-stabilizing factor whose development lags behind bond changes at the transition state, or a reactant-stabilizing factor whose loss is ahead of bond changes at the transition state, increases the intrinsic barrier and decreases the "intrinsic rate constant" of a reaction.

Synchronous

A concerted process in which the primitive changes concerned (generally bond rupture and bond formation) have progressed to the same extent at the transition state is said to be synchronous. The term figuratively implies a more or less synchronized progress of the changes. However, the progress of the bonding change (or other primitive change) has not been defined quantitatively in terms of a single parameter applicable to different bonds or different bonding changes. The concept is therefore in general only qualitatively descriptive and does not admit an exact definition except in the case of concerted processes involving changes in two identical bonds.

Synoptic scale

The synoptic scale in meteorology (also known as large scale or cyclonic scale) is a horizontal length scale of the order of 1000 kilometres (about 620 miles) or more. This corresponds to a horizontal scale typical of mid-latitude depressions (e.g. extratropical cyclones). Most high and low-pressure areas seen on weather maps such as surface weather analyses are synoptic-scale systems, driven by the location of Rossby waves in their respective hemisphere. Low-pressure areas and their related frontal zones occur on the leading edge of a trough within the Rossby wave pattern, while surface highs form on the back edge of the trough.

Synthesis

When you take two elements or compounds and combine them to create a new compound.

Synthetic sizes

Alkenylsuccinic anhydride (ASA) and alkylketene dimer (AKD) hydrophobizing agents for wet-end addition.

Systemic

Systemic means relating to or affecting the whole body.

T

Tag

(a) One of a set of surrogate analytes which are used in a decoding process;

(b) Pendant function which allows a molecule to be selected from a mixture.

Talc

A very soft, platey, oil-loving mineral product used as a filler and also used (in finely divided form) for pitch control.

T-Amyl Methyl Ether (TAME)

Chemical formula of $C_2H_5C(CH_3)_2OCH_3$ and an atomic weight of 102.18 amu. It is listed as a volatile organic compound that can form explosive vapour or air mixtures under certain conditions. TAME is being researched to replace MTBE as a cleaner fuel additive, to reduce the harmful effects to ground water system from leaking MTBE storage facilities as well as the exhaust. TAME is one of the by-products of purifying crude oil to petrol and it can cause moderate skin irritation as well as dizziness if inhaled.

Tantalum

Symbol: "Ta" Atomic Number: "73" Atomic Mass: 180.95amu. Tantalum is one of the transition elements. This very hard, gray metal can be found in many alloys. It has also been used in surgical equipment, camera lenses, and even electronic capacitors.

Tar

Tar is a brown or black bituminous material, liquid or semi-solid in consistency, gained as a product of dry distillation of natural fuels like wood, or other organic materials.

T-Butylbenzene

Chemical formula is $C_{10}H_{14}$ molecular weight 134.21 grams. This chemical is highly flammable and easily ignited by heat, sparks or flames. It is also less dense than water and insoluble in water and is a colourless liquid. This chemical is an aromatic hydrocarbon used in hydrocarbon fuels. In combustion processes it contributes to the formation of mutagenic and carcinogenic compounds such as benzo(a)pyrene.

Tea-bag

A type of reaction vessel consisting of a porous mesh which encloses the resin but allows passage of reagents and solvents when immersed in an appropriate secondary container. Several tea-bags may be treated in a single vessel without mixing of the enclosed resins; manipulation of multiple tea-bags allows preparation of libraries by pool/split or directed sorting techniques.

Technetium

Symbol: "Tc" Atomic Number: "43" Atomic Mass: (98)amu. Technetium is one of the transition elements from period five. Technetium is an element that is not found in nature. Man has been able to create it in labs. It is a silvery-gray metal than has been used in steel and super conductors. It is radioactive.

Tele-substitution

A substitution reaction in which the entering group takes up a position more than one atom away from the atom to which the leaving group was attached.

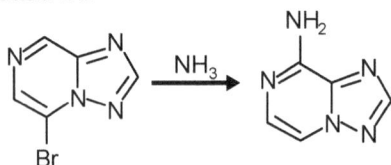

Tellurium

Symbol: "Te" Atomic Number: "52" Atomic Mass: 127.60amu. Tellurium is usually found with gold. It is used in many alloys and as a trace element in ceramics.

Temperature

A measure of the average speed or kinetic energy of the particles in a substance.

Temporary wet strength

Increased strength of treated paper, tested after initial, complete wetting, which decays within a few minutes or hours.

Tentagel

Trademark of Rapp Polymere GmbH, Tubingen, Germany. Beaded solid support with a crosslinked polystyrene core and grafted linear poly(ethylene glycol) (PEG) chains with terminal functional groups.

Teratogen

A teratogen is a substance that produces a malformation in a foetus.

Terbium

Symbol: "Tb" Atomic Number: "65" Atomic Mass: 158.93amu. Terbium is one of the elements in the lanthanide series of inner transition elements. It may also be classified as a rare earth element.

Term

Each compound or element in a chemical equation.

Termo-setting

Tending to become a permanently cross-linked, insoluble solid when heated.

Tetragonal crystal

A crystal that has a basic cube shape but is stretched out. It is almost rectangular when viewed from one side. Think about a candy bar for this one.

Tetrahedral intermediate

A reaction intermediate in which the bond arrangement around an initially double-bonded carbon atom (typically a carbonyl carbon atom) has been transformed from trigonal to tetrahedral. For example, aldol in the condensation reaction of acetaldehyde (but most tetrahedral intermediates have a more fleeting existence).

Thallium

Symbol: "Tl" Atomic Number: "81" Atomic Mass: 204.38amu. It is classified as a basic metal. Thallium is a very soft, silver-coloured metal. It is very toxic but still has uses in poisons and some photographic equipment.

Thematic libraries synthesis

Over the past several years, combinatorial chemistry has gradually realigned itself with changing business needs. In many organizations diversity-driven library production intended to broadly cover druglike chemical space has to a large extent been replaced by thematic as well as project-directed libraries.

Thermal conductivity

A measure of the amount of heat that can flow through a substance.

Thermal decomposition

Thermal decomposition is a chemical decomposition caused by heat. The decomposition temperature of a substance is the temperature at which the substance chemically decomposes. The reaction is usually endothermic as heat is required to break chemical bonds in the compound undergoing decomposition. If decomposition is sufficiently exothermic, a positive feedback loop is created producing thermal runaway and possibly an explosion.

Thermodynamic control (of product composition)

The term characterizes conditions that lead to reaction products in a proportion governed by the equilibrium constant for their interconversion and/or for the interconversion of reaction intermediates formed in or after the rate-limiting step.

Thermodynamics

The study of temperature, pressure, volume, and energy flow in chemical reactions.

Thermolysis

The uncatalysed cleavage of one or more covalent bonds resulting from exposure of a compound to a raised temperature, or a process in which such cleavage is an essential part.

Thermosphere

Atmospheric shell extending from the top of the mesosphere to outer space. It is a region of more or less steadily increasing temperature with height, starting at 70 or 80 km. It includes the exosphere and most or all of the ionosphere.

Thick stock

A mixture of papermaking pulp and other materials, after having been diluted with whitewater at a fan pump.

Thiol

A compound that contains the functional group composed of a sulphur atom and a hydrogen atom (-SH).

Thorium

Symbol: "Th" Atomic Number: "90" Atomic Mass: 231.04amu. This is one of the elements in the actinide series of inner transition elements. It may also be classified as a rare earth element. A very radioactive element that is used in reactors and in the process of making certain types of gas. One of the byproducts of the combustion of thorium is radium.

Three-dimensional Quantitative Structure-Activity Relationship (3D-QSAR)

A three-dimensional quantitative structure-activity relationship is the analysis of the quantitative relationship between the biological activity of a set of compounds and their spatial properties using statistical methods.

Thulium

Symbol: "Tm" Atomic Number: "69" Atomic Mass: 168.93amu. Thulium is one of the elements in the lanthanide series of inner transition elements. It may also be classified as a rare earth element.

Tin

Tin has been known since ancient times. The origin of the name comes from the Latin word stannum meaning tin. It is silvery-white, soft, malleable and ductile metal. Exposed surfaces form oxide film. Resists oxygen and water. Dissolves in acids and bases. Organic tin compounds may be highly toxic. Tin is principally found in the ore cassiterite (SnO_2) and stannine (Cu_2FeSnS_4). Used as a coating for steel cans since it is non-toxic and non-corrosive. Also in solder (33 %Sn:67 %Pb), bronze (20 %Sn:80 %Cu) and pewter. Stannous fluoride (SnF_2), a compound of tin and fluorine is used in some toothpaste.

Tincture

A solution in which the solvent is an alcohol.

Titanium

Symbol: "Ti" Atomic Number: "22" Atomic Mass: 47.90amu. This is one of the transition elements from period three. Titanium can be found in meteorites and many minerals from the Earth's crust.

Titanium dioxide

A white mineral filler having a high refractive index, making it effective for increasing the opacity of paper.

Titration

a procedure used to determine the concentration of a solution, involving reacting a solution with a known concentration with the solution with an unknown concentration. Often used with acids and bases.

Titrimetric methods

A class of volumetric analytical methods employing titration as the basis of quantitative measurement.

Tmp

Thermomechanical pulp, a high-yield pulp produced in a refiner.

Topliss tree

A Topliss tree is an operational scheme for analog design.

Torquoselectivity

The term refers to the preference for "inward" or "outward" rotation of substituents in conrotatory or disrotatory electrocyclic ring opening reactions.

Torr

Torr is a measurement of pressure. One millimetre of mercury on a barometer is equal to one torr. Standard pressure is equal to 760 torr.

Toxicity

The quality of being poisonous. It may be expressed as a fraction indicating the ratio of the smallest mass of the material which has some specified probability (often 50%) of causing death of some specific animal to the mass of the animal.

Toxin

Toxins are effective and specific poisons produced by living organisms. They usually consist of an amino acid chain which can vary in molecular weight between a couple of hundred (peptides) and one hundred thousand (proteins). They may also be low-molecular organic compounds. Toxins are produced by numerous organisms, e.g., bacteria, fungi, algae and plants. Many of them are extremely poisonous, with a toxicity that is several orders of magnitude greater than the nerve agents. Botulinum toxin, produced by the bacteria Clostridium botulinum, is the most poisonous substance known.

Trace element

This is an element of the periodic table that living organisms need to survive. These are not the major ones we need to survive (like oxygen); these elements are only needed in very small amounts.

Traceless linker

Type of linker which leaves no residue on the compound after cleavage.

Tracheid

The "fiber" of a softwood or conifer tree.

Transfer line

Line provided to carry the sample to be analysed from the sample point to the analytical unit without altering the composition of the sample.

Transferability

Transferability assumes invariance of properties, associated conceptually with an atom or a fragment present in a variety of molecules. The property, such as electronegativity, nucleophilicity, NMR *chemical shift*, etc. is held as retaining a similar value in all these occurrences.

Transformation

The conversion of a substrate into a particular product, irrespective of reagents or mechanisms involved. For example, the transformation of aniline ($C_6H_5NH_2$) into N-phenylacetamide ($C_6H_5NHCOCH_3$) may be effected by use of acetyl chloride or acetic anhydride or ketene. A transformation is distinct from a reaction, the full

description of which would state or imply all the reactants and all the products.

Transient (chemical) species

Relating to a short-lived reaction intermediate. It can be defined only in relation to a time scale fixed by the experimental conditions and the limitations of the technique employed in the detection of the intermediate. The term is a relative one. Transient species are sometimes also said to be "metastable". However, this latter term should be avoided, because it relates a thermodynamic term to a kinetic property, although most transients are also thermodynamically unstable with respect to reactants and products.

Transition coordinate

The reaction coordinate at the transition state corresponding to a vibration with an imaginary frequency. Motion along it in the two opposite senses leads towards the reactants or towards the products.

Transition element

Transition elements (also known as transition metals) are found in the middle section of the periodic table. They have two electron shells that are not filled. The shells are usually the outer two shells and are good conductors of electricity. Copper, silver and, and gold are examples of transition elements.

Transition state

In theories describing elementary reactions it is usually assumed that there is a transition state of more positive molar Gibbs energy between the reactants and the products through which an assembly of atoms (initially composing the molecular entities of the reactants) must pass on going from reactants to products in either direction. In the formalism of "transition state theory" the transition state of an elementary reaction is that set of states (each characterized by its own geometry and energy) which an assembly of atoms, when randomly placed there, would have an equal probability of forming the reactants or of forming the products of that elementary reaction. The transition state is characterized by one and only one imaginary frequency. The assembly of atoms at the transition state has been called an activated complex.

Transition state analogue

A substrate designed to mimic the properties or the geometry of the transition state of reaction.

Transition structure

A saddle point on a potential-energy surface. It has one negative force constant in the harmonic force constant matrix.

Transition-state analog

A transition-state analog is a compound that mimics the transition state of a substrate bound to an enzyme.

Transparent

The ability of light to clearly pass through a substance without being scattered.

Trapping

The interception of a reactive molecule or reaction intermediate so that it is removed from the system or converted into a more stable form for study or identification.

Tray water

Process water, containing fine materials, that drains from paper during its formation (a synonym for "cloudy white water").

Triclinic crystal

A triclinic crystal has a shape in which the arrangement of facets is random.

Triglycerides

Components of wood pitch consisting of three fatty acid moieties attached to glycerine by ester bonds.

Trigonal crystal

A trigonal crystal has a shape that has three sides and no specific length. It looks like an elongated triangle.

Trim addition

Addition of a portion of a certain papermaking additive to thin stock, after base-loading some to thick stock, to enable more rapid process control.

Triple bonds

When two atoms participate in a Covalent Bond and share three electrons with each other, the Covalent Bond formed is referred to as a Triple Covalent Bond or just Triple Bond. A common example of an organic compound containing a triple bond is acetylene ($HC=CH$).

Triple point

The single combination of pressure and temperature at which liquid water, solid ice, and water vapour can coexist in a stable equilibrium occurs at exactly 273.16 K (0.01 °C) and a partial vapour pressure of 611.73 pascals (ca. 6.1173 millibars, 0.0060373 atm). At that point, it is possible to change all of the substance to ice, water, or vapour by making arbitrarily small changes in pressure and temperature. Even if the total pressure of a system is well above triple point of water, provided the partial pressure of the water vapour is 611.73 pascals then the system can still be brought to the triple point of water.

0.0098 ºC   100 ºC
Triple Point   Boiling Point
Temperature

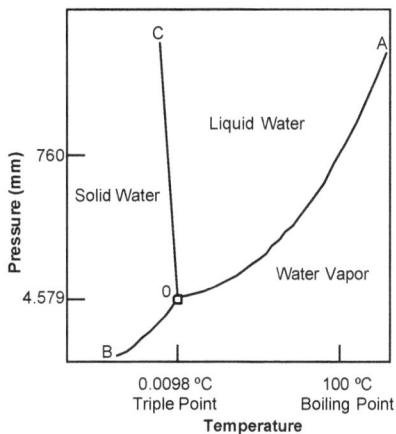

Troe expression

A semi-empirical description of the rate coefficient for a specific three body reaction [e.g.,
   $HO + NO_2 (+ M) \quad HONO_2 (+ M)$]
which represents well its pressure and temperature dependence in the region of transition between second and third order kinetics.

Tropopause

The region of the atmosphere which joins the troposphere and stratosphere, and where the decreasing temperature with altitude, characteristic of the troposphere ceases, and the temperature increase with height which is characteristic of the stratosphere begins.

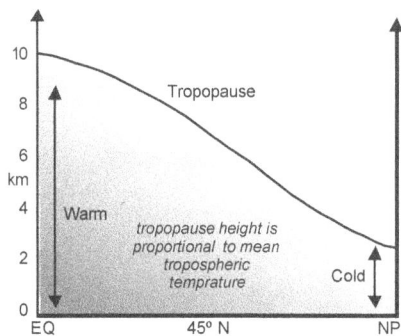

Troposphere

The lowest layer of the atmosphere, ranging from the ground to the base of the stratosphere (tropopause) at 10-15 km of altitude depending on the latitude and meteorological conditions. About 70% of the mass of the atmosphere is in the troposphere. This is where most of the weather features occur and where the chemistry of the reactive anthropogenic species released into the atmosphere takes place.

True formula

This formula tells you the number of atoms in a molecule for each element. Water has two hydrogen atoms and one oxygen atom when you look at the true formula.

Tungsten

Symbol: "W" Atomic Number: "74" Atomic Mass: 183.85amu. This is one of the transition elements from period six. Tungsten used to be called wolfram (thus the W). It is a light-gray metal found in many minerals. You many find it in electric components, power tools, paints, and even fluorescent lights.

Tunnelling

The process by which a particle or a set of particles crosses a barrier on its potential energy surface without having the energy required to surmount this barrier. Since the rate of tunnelling decreases with increasing reduced mass, it is significant in the context of isotope effects of hydrogen isotopes.

Turbidity

Turbidity is the cloudiness or haziness of a fluid caused by individual particles (suspended solids) that are generally invisible to the naked eye, similar to smoke in air. The measurement of turbidity is a key test of water quality.

Turbulence

Atmospheric eddies, mechanical or thermal, which are produced primarily by shearing stress or by convection. Atmospheric turbulence is primarily responsible for the dilution and mixing of atmospheric pollutants.

Turbulent fluctuation in stable air are mainly of high frequency with typical periods of seconds (mechanical turbulence).

Two-sidedness

The existence of differences in appearance or other properties of the two sides of paper.

U

Umpolung

Any process by which the normal alternating donor and acceptor reactivity pattern of a chain, which is due to the presence of O or N heteroatoms, is interchanged. Reactivity umpolung is most often achieved by temporary exchange of heteroatoms (N, O) by others, such as P, S, and Se.

Unbiased library

Library prepared from building blocks and scaffold chosen without bias towards a particular target.

Undetermined components

Components of the sample, the concentrations of which are not measured during the analysis.

Unit cell

The crystal structure of a material or the arrangement of atoms within a given type of crystal structure can be described in terms of its unit cell. The unit cell is a small box containing one or more atoms, a spatial arrangement of atoms. The unit cells stacked in three-dimensional space describe the bulk arrangement of atoms of the crystal. The crystal structure has a three-dimensional shape. The unit cell is given by its lattice parameters, which are the length of the cell edges and the angles between them, while the positions of the atoms inside the unit cell are described by the set of atomic positions (x_i, y_i, z_i) measured from a lattice point.

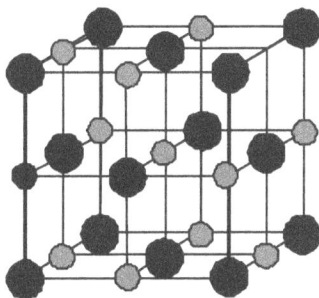

Universal library

A hypothetical compound collection which will show activity in all assays; a library with useful activity in many assays.

Unreactive

Failing to react with a specified chemical species under specified conditions. The term should not be used in place of *stable*, since a relatively more stable species may nevertheless be more *reactive* than some reference species towards a given reaction partner.

Unsaponifiable

Not capable of being formed into a carboxylic acid soap upon addition of base (e.g. not esters, not carboxylic acids).

Unsaturated

An unsaturated solution has not reached the maximum amount of solute. You can easily dissolve a tablespoon of sugar in a glass of water. Since you can still dissolve more the solution, it is considered to be unsaturated.

Unstable

The opposite of stable, i.e. the chemical species concerned has a higher molar Gibbs energy than some assumed standard. The term should not be used in place of reactive or transient, although more reactive or transient species are frequently also more unstable.

Upfield

A term used to describe the right direction on NMR charts. A peak to the right of another peak is described as being upfield from the peak.

Uranium

Symbol: "U" Atomic Number: "92" Atomic Mass: 238.03amu. Uranium is one of the elements in the actinide series of inner transition elements. It may also be classified as a rare earth element. A very radioactive metal that can be found in nuclear facilities, weapons, and submarines.

V

Vacuum
A vacuum is a space that has no pressure and no molecules inside. It is truly and empty space. Although space has a very low pressure (almost a vacuum), there are still particles out there.

Vacuum line
Gas-tight system of tubing equipped with accessories such as valves, manometers, pumps, etc., which enable a gas to be transported from one point to another.

Valence
The maximum number of univalent atoms (originally hydrogen or chlorine atoms) that may combine with an atom of the element under consideration, or with a fragment, or for which an atom of this element can be substituted.

Valence electrons
Electrons in the outermost energy level of an atom. Valence electrons are the electrons that participate in chemical bonding.

Valence isomer
A constitutional isomer interrelated with another by pericyclic reactions. For example, Dewar benzene, prismane and benzvalene are valence isomers of benzene.

Valence mechanism
This mechanism is the way an atom bonds to other atoms to create stable (full) electron orbitals.

Valence number
The valence is the number of electrons that can form compounds with other atoms. The valence number for the same element can be different. Sulphur has the valence numbers 2, 4, and 6 depending on the type of compound it forms.

Valence tautomerization
The term describes simple reversible and generally rapid isomerizations or degenerate re-arrangements involving the formation and rupture of single and/or double bonds, without migration of atoms or groups.

Van der Waals equation
An equation for non-ideal gasses that accounts for intermolecular attraction and the volumes occupied by the gas molecules.

Van der Waals forces
A weak attraction between molecules.

Vanadate mineral
A mineral that is made up of compounds with a vanadium oxide group or vanadium atom bonded to a metal. Vanadinite is a good example of a vanadate mineral.

Vanadium

Symbol: "V" Atomic Number: "23" Atomic Mass: 50.94amu. Vanadium is one of the transition elements. Vanadium can be found in some meteorites, crude oil, and many minerals.

Vapour

A vapour is closely related to a gas. Scientists define a vapour as "a compound in a gaseous state when its temperature is below the critical temperature." Steam is considered to be a vapour because it is in a gas state but the temperature is still below the critical temperature. Steam is liquid water suspended in a gas state. Helium gas is a true gas at room temperature. You may also see the spelling "vapour."

Vapour pressure

A property that is unique to each liquid. When the surrounding pressure of a system is below the vapour pressure, the liquid is able to evaporate.

Velocity

Speed of an object; the change in position over time.

Venturi

A device that entrains material into a fluid stream by taking advantage of the vacuum created by an expansion in the flow pattern.

Vessels

Structures within hardwood (deciduous) trees that conduct water from the roots up the tree.

Vinyl

An organic compound that contains a vinyl group (also called ethenyl), CH=CH2.

Virtual library

A library which has no physical existence, being constructed solely in electronic form or on paper. The building blocks required for such a library may not exist, and the chemical steps for such a library may not have been tested. These libraries are used in the design and evaluation of possible libraries.

Virtual screening

Selection of compounds by evaluating their desirability in a computational model. Also termed in silico screening.

Viscosity

The tendency of a liquid to resist flow; e.g. syrup has a higher viscosity than water.

Visibility

Defined as the greatest distance at which a black object of suitable dimensions can be seen and recognized against the horizon sky, or, in the case of night observations, could be seen and recognized if the general illumination were raised to the normal daylight level.

Vitreous solid

A vitreous solid has no specific organization of molecules. Steel is an example of a vitreous solid. Because of its combination of atoms, it does not have a specific melting point. It may become a liquid over a range of temperatures.

Volatile

A volatile compound has a lower boiling point than surrounding compounds. Volatility is a comparison. Alcohol is more volatile than water because it evaporates at a lower temperature.

Volt

A single volt is defined as the difference in electric potential across a wire when an electric current of one ampere dissipates one watt of power. It is also equal to the potential difference between two points 1 metre apart in an electric field of 1 newton per coulomb. Additionally, it is the potential difference between two points that will impart one joule of energy per coulomb of charge that passes through it.

Voltage
A measure of electric potential difference.

Volume
Measures the size of an object using length measurements in three dimensions.

W

Wall

The substance of a fiber between its outside and its lumen (interior space).

Wash out

The removal from the atmosphere of gases and sometimes particles by their solution in or attachment to raindrops as they fall.

Washing of pulp

Removal of pulping or bleaching liquors from cellulosic fibers either by
(a) dewatering, then diluting with "clean" white water, or
(b) displacement of the liquor by spraying wash water onto a mat of fibers.

Wave

A signal which propagates through space, much like a water wave moves through water.

Wavelength

On a periodic curve, the length between two consecutive troughs (low points) or peaks (high points).

Waxes

Water-hating natural substances in wood, rich in alkyl ($-CH_2-CH_2-$) groups.

Weak acid

A substance that only partly dissociates into hydrogen ions and a conjugate base upon addition to water.

Weak electrolyte

A weak electrolyte is a compound that does not ionize one hundred percent in solution. The lower the percentage, the weaker the electrolyte. Weak acids and bases are often weak electrolytes. Water is also considered a weak electrolyte.

Wet bulb temperature

In psychrometry, the temperature of the sensor or the bulb of a thermometer in which a constantly renewed film of water is evaporating. The temperature of the water used to renew the film must be at the temperature of the gas. See psychrometry.

Wet chemistry

An informal term, meaning the type of chemical test that can be performed by adding a solution to a sample to be analyzed and observing a colour change, etc.

Wet end of a paper machine

Roughly speaking, the parts of a papermaking process between pulping (or bleaching) and wet-pressing of the paper.

Wet web strength

The strength of a wet sheet of paper after its formation but before it has ever been dried.

Wet-strength

The strength of a sheet of paper after it has been exposed to a standard solution for a standard length of time, but often expressed as a ratio vs. the dry strength.

Wettability
The relative ease with which a certain solid surface accepts liquids, usually defined in terms of the angle of contact of a flat solid with an air-liquid interface.

White pitch
Deposits on papermaking equipment, a major component of which is latex binder from coated paper or broke.

White water
Process water within a paper machine system, especially referring to water that is drained from paper as the sheet is being formed.

Whiteness
A subjective impression of white appearance, usually favoring a bluish tint.

Wind rose
A wind rose is a graphic tool used by meteorologists to give a succinct view of how wind speed and direction are typically distributed at a particular location. Historically, wind roses were predecessors of the compass rose (found on maps), as there was no differentiation between a cardinal direction and the wind which blew from such a direction. Using a polar coordinate system of gridding, the frequency of winds over a long time period are plotted by wind direction, with colour bands showing wind ranges.

Wire
Informal synonym for forming fabric, the continuous screen on which paper is formed.

Work
Expression of the movement of an object against some force.

X

Xenobiotic

A xenobiotic is a compound foreign to an organism (xenos [greek] = foreign).

Xenon

Symbol: "Xe" Atomic Number: "54" Atomic Mass: 131.29amu. It is one of the noble or inert gases. This non-reactive element has been made into several compounds in the lab. The pure gas is used in lasers, headlights, and in medicine.

X-ray fluorescence

An analytical method for determination of the ratio of different metal ions in an ash sample.

X-ray photoelectron spectroscopy

Technique for determining the elemental composition at a solid surface by measuring the energy of elctrons emitted in response to X-rays of different frequency.

Y

Yield of paper pulp

The ratio of pulp solid mass to the solid mass of the original wood that it was derived from. High-yield pulps are produced by mechanical refining or grinding. Kraft pulps are relatively "low yield".

Ytterbium

Symbol: "Yb" Atomic Number: "70" Atomic Mass: 173.04amu. Ytterbium is one of the elements in the lanthanide series of inner transition elements. It may also be classified as a rare earth element. This silvery metal can be found in several minerals. It is never found as a pure element in nature, always in compounds.

Yttrium

Symbol:"Y" Atomic Number:"39" Atomic Mass: 88.91amu. This is one of the transition elements found in period five of the periodic table. One of the rare Earth metals, yttrium is used in TV tubes, alloys, and has even been found on the Moon.

Z

Z-direction

The direction perpendicular to the plane of a sheet of paper.

Zero gas or zero sample

Substance or mixture of substances resembling, as closely as possible, the matrix of the actual air sample to be measured, but characterized by a value of the air quality characteristic which is not detectable by the method used.

Zeta potential

The average electrical potential near to the surfaces of particles or fibers suspended in water, evaluated by a method involving relative motion of the solids versus the liquid.

Zinc

Symbol: "Zn" Atomic Number: "30" Atomic Mass: 65.38amu. Zinc is one of the transition elements found in period four. Zinc is another metal that has been used for thousands of years. This bluish-white metal can be found in many alloys, paint, fluorescent lights, and in the process of making plastics.

Zirconium

Symbol: "Zr" Atomic Number: "40" Atomic Mass: 91.22amu. This is one of the transition elements found in period five of the bale of elements. Zirconium is found in many minerals.

This grayish-white metal can be found in nuclear reactors, corrosion resistant alloys, magnets, and some gemstones.

Zucker-Hammett hypothesis

This hypothesis states that, if in an acid catalyzed reaction, $lg\,k_1$ (first-order rate constant of the reaction) is linear in H_o (Hammett acidity function), water is not involved in the transition state of the rate-controlling step. However, if $lg\,k_1$ is linear in $lg[H^+]$, then water is involved. This has been shown to be incorrect by Hammett himself.

Z-value

An index of the ionizing power of a solvent based on the frequency of the longest wavelength electronic absorption maximum of 1-ethyl-4-methoxycarbonylpyridinium iodide in the solvent. The Z-value is defined by $Z = 2.859 \times 10^4/l$ where Z is in kcal mol^{-1} and l is in nm.

Zwitterionic compound

A neutral compound having electrical charges of opposite sign, delocalized or not on adjacent or nonadjacent atoms. Zwitterionic compounds have no uncharged canonical representations. Sometimes referred to as inner salts, ampholytes, dipolar ions (a misnomer). For example: $H_3N^+CH_2C(=O)O^-$, glycine.

Appendix – I
The Greek Alphabet

Letters	Name	Letters	Name
A	alpha	N	nu
B	beta		xi
	gamma	O	omicron
	delta		Pi
E	epsilon	P	rho
Z	zeta		sigma
H	eta	T	tau
	theta	Y	upsilon
I	iota		phi
K	kappa	X	Chi
	lambda		psi
M	mu		omega

Fundamental Constants

Constant	Symbol	Value in SI units
acceleration of free fall	g	$9.806\ 65$ m s^{-2}
Avogadro constant	L, N_A	$6.022\ 141\ 79(30) \times 10^{23}$ mol^{-1}
Boltzmann constant	$k = R/N_A$	$1.380\ 6504(24) \times 10^{-23}$ J K^{-1}
electric constant	$_0$	$8.854\ 187\ 817 \times 10^{-12}$ F m^{-1}
electronic charge	e	$1.602\ 176\ 487(40) \times 10^{-19}$ C
electronic rest mass	m_e	$9.109\ 382\ 15(45) \times 10^{-31}$ kg
Faraday constant	F	$9.648\ 3399(24) \times 10^{4}$ C mol^{-1}
gas constant	R	$8.314\ 472(15)$ J K^{-1} mol^{-1}
gravitational constant	G	$6.674\ 28(67) \times 10^{-11}$ m^3 kg^{-1} s^{-2}
Loschmidt's constant	N_L	$2.686\ 7774(47) \times 10^{25}$ m^{-3}
magnetic constant	$_0$	$4\ \times 10^{-7}$ H m^{-1}
neutron rest mass	m_n	$1.674\ 927\ 211(84) \times 10^{-27}$ kg
Planck constant	h	$6.626\ 068\ 96(33) \times 10^{-34}$ J s
proton rest mass	m_p	$1.672\ 621\ 637(83) \times 10^{-27}$ kg
speed of light	c	$2.997\ 924\ 58 \times 10^{8}$ m s^{-1}
Stefan-Boltzmann constant		$5.670\ 400(40) \times 10^{-8}$ Wm^{-2} K^{-4}

SI Units

Base and dimensionless SI units

Physical quantity	Name	Symbol
Length	metre	m
mass	kilogram	kg
time	second	s
electric current	ampere	A
thermodynamic temperature	Kelvin	K
luminous intensity	candela	cd
amount of substance	mole	mol
*plane angle	radian	rad
*solid angle	steradian	sr

*dimensionless units

Derived SI units with special names

Physical quantity	Name of SI unit	Symbol of SI unit
frequency	hertz	Hz
energy	joule	J
force	newton	N
power	watt	W
pressure	pascal	Pa
electric charge	coulomb	C
electric potential difference	volt	V
electric resistance	ohm	
electric conductance	Siemens	S
electric capacitance	farad	F
magnetic flux	weber	Wb
inductance	henry	H
magnetic flux density (magnetic induction)	tesla	T
luminous flux	lumen	lm
illuminance	lux	lx
absorbed dose	gray	Gy
activity	becquercl	Bq
dose equivalent	sievert	Sv

Decimal multiples and submultiples to be used with SI units

Submultiple	Prefix	Symbol	Multiple	Prefix	Symbol
10^{-1}	deci	d	10	deca	da
10^{-2}	centi	c	10^2	heclo	ii
10^{-3}	milli	m	10^3	kilo	k
10^{-6}	micro		10^6	mega	M
10^{-9}	nano	n	10^9	giga	G
10^{-12}	pico	p	10^{12}	tera	T
10^{-15}	femto	f	10^{15}	peta	P
10^{-18}	atto	a	10^{18}	exa	E
10^{-21}	zepto	z	10^{21}	zetta	Z
10^{-24}	yocto	y	10^{24}	yotta	Y

Conversion of units to SI units

From	To	Multiply by
in	m	2.54×10^{-2}
ft	m	0.3048
sq.in	m^2	6.4516×10^{-4}
sq.ft	m^2	9.2903×10^{-2}
cu.in	m^3	1.63871×10^{-5}
cu.ft	m^3	2.83168×10^{-2}
l(itre)	m^3	10^{-3}
gal(lon)	l(itre)	4.546 09
miles/hr	$m\ s^{-1}$	0.477 04
km/hr	$m\ s^{-1}$	0.277 78
lb	kg	0.453 592
gcm^{-3}	$kg\ m^{-3}$	10^3
lb/in^3	$kg\ m^{-3}$	$2.767\ 99 \times 10^4$
dyne	N	10^5
poundal	N	0.138 255
lbf	N	4.448 22
mmHg	Pa	133.322
atmosphere	Pa	$1.013\ 25 \times 10^5$
hp	W	745.7
erg	J	10^{-7}
eV	J	$1.602\ 10 \times 10^{-19}$
kW h	J	3.6×10^6
cal	J	4.1868

Appendix – II
The Electromagnetic Spectrum

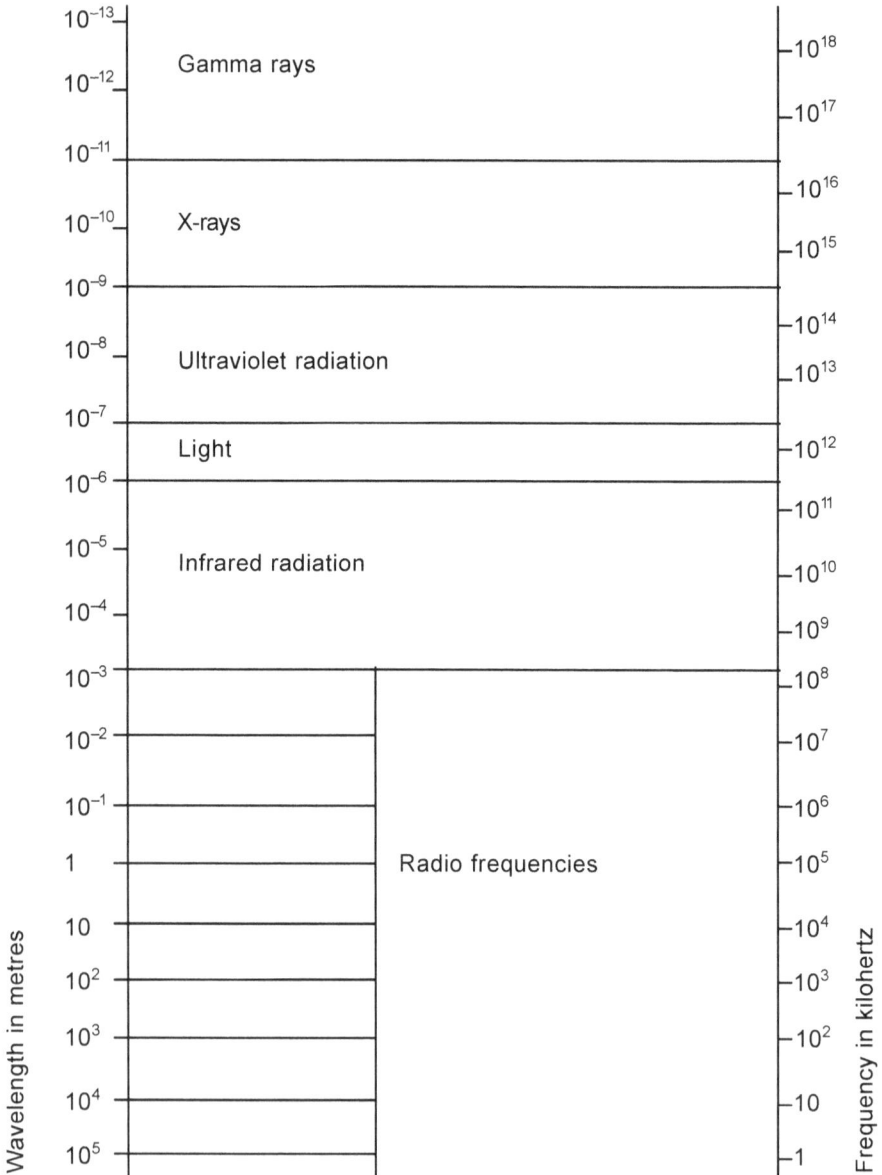

Wavelength in metres		Frequency in kilohertz
10^{-13}	Gamma rays	10^{18}
10^{-12}		10^{17}
10^{-11}		10^{16}
10^{-10}	X-rays	10^{15}
10^{-9}		10^{14}
10^{-8}	Ultraviolet radiation	10^{13}
10^{-7}		10^{12}
10^{-6}	Light	10^{11}
10^{-5}	Infrared radiation	10^{10}
10^{-4}		10^{9}
10^{-3}		10^{8}
10^{-2}		10^{7}
10^{-1}		10^{6}
1	Radio frequencies	10^{5}
10		10^{4}
10^{2}		10^{3}
10^{3}		10^{2}
10^{4}		10
10^{5}		1

Appendix – III
The Periodic Table

Appendix – IV
The Chemical Elements

Element	Symb	a.n.	r.a.m.	Element	Symb	a.n.	r.a.m.
actinium	Ac	89	227*	iold	Au	79	196.967
aluminium	A]	13	26.98	lafhium	Hf	72	178.49
americium	Am	95	243*	lassium	Hs	108	265*
antimony	Sb	51	121.75	lelium	He	2	4.0026
argon	Ar	18	39.948	holmium	Ho	67	164.93
arsenic	As	33	74.92	hydrogen	H	1	1.008
astatine	At	85	210*	indium	In	49	114.82
barium	Ba	56	137.34	iodine	I	53	126.9045
berkelium	Bk	97	247*	iridium	Ir	77	192.20
beryllium	Be	4	9.012	iron	Fe	26	55.847
bismuth	Bi	83	208.98	krypton	Kr	36	83.80
bohrium	Bh	107	262*	lanthanum	La	57	138.91
boron	B	5	10.81	lawrencium	Lr	103	256*
bromine	Br	35	79.909	lead	Ph	82	207.19
cadmium	Cd	48	112.41	lithium	Li	3	6.939
caesium	Cs	55	132.905	lutetium	Lu	71	174.97
calcium	Ca	20	40.08	magnesium	Mg	12	24.305
californium	Cf	98	251*	manganese	Mn	25	54.94
carbon	C	6	12.011	meitnerium	Mt	109	266*
cerium	Ce	58	140.12	mendelevium	Md	101	258*
chlorine	Cl	17	35.453	mercury	Hg	80	200.59
chromium	Cr	24	52.00	molybdenum	Mo	42	95.94
cobalt	Co	27	58.933	neodymium	Nd	60	144.24
copper	Cu	29	63.546	neon	Ne	10	20.179
curium	Cm	96	247*	neptunium	Np	93	237.0482
darmstadtium	Ds	110	271*	nickel	Ni	28	58.70
dubnium	Db	105	262*	niobium	Nb	41	92.91
dysprosium	Dy	66	162.50	nitrogen	N	7	14.0067
einsteinium	Hs	99	254'	nobelium	No	102	254*
erbium	Er	68	167.26	osmium	Os	76	190.2
europium	Eu	63	151.96	oxygen	O	8	15.9994
fermium	Fm	100	257*	palladium	Pd	46	106.4
iluorine	F	9	18.9984	phosphorus	P	15	30.9738
"rancium	Ft	87	223*	platinum	Pi	78	195.09
gadolinium	Gd	64	157.25	plutonium	Pu	94	244*
gallium	Ga	31	69.72	polonium	Po	84	210'
germanium	Ge	32	72.59	potassium	K	19	39.098

R.a.m values with asterisk denote mass number of the most stable known isotope

Element	Symb	a.n.	r.a.m.
praseodymium	Pr	59	140.91
promethium	Pm	61	145
protactinium	Pa	91	231.036
radium	Ra	88	226.0254
radon	Rn	86	222*
rhenium	Re	75	186.2
rhodium	Rh	45	102.9
roentgenium	R8	111	272*
rubidium	Rb	37	85.47
ruthenium	Rυ	44	101.07
rutherfordiiim	Rf	104	261*
samarium	Sm	62	150.35
scandium	Sc	21	44.956
seaborgium	Sg	106	263*
selenium	Se	34	78.96
silicon	Si	14	28.086
silver	Ag	47	107.87
sodium	Na	11	22.9898
strontium	Sr	38	87.62
sulphur	S	16	32.06
tantalum	Ta	73	180.948

Element	Symb	a.n.	r.a.m.
technetium	Tc	43	98*
tellurium	Te	52	127.60
terbium	Tb	65	158.92
thallium	Tl	81	204.39
thorium	Th	90	232.038
thulium	Tm	69	168.934
tin	Sn	50	118.69
titanium	Ti	22	47.9
tungsten	W	74	183.85
ununbium	Uub	112	285*
ununtrium	Uut	113	284*
ununquadium	Uuq	114	289^s
ununpentium	Uup	115	288"
ununhexium	Uuh	116	292'
uranium	U	92	238.03
vanadium	V	23	50.94
xenon	Xe	54	131.30
ytterbium	Vb	70	173.04
yttrium	V	39	88.905
zinc	Zn	30	65.38
zirconium	Zr	40	91.22

Appendix – V
Nobel Prizes in Chemistry

Year	Name of prizewinner (s)	Nature of work or discovery
1901	Jacobus Henricus Van't Hoff (1852-1911) Dutch	Discovery of the laws of chemical dynamics and osmotic pressure in solutions
1902	Hermann Emil Fischer (1852-1919) German	Work on sugar and purine syntheses
1903	Svante August Arrhenius (1859-1927) Swedish	The electrolytic theory of dissociation
1904	Sir William Ramsay (1852-1916) British	Discovery of the inert gaseous elements in air and the determination of their place in the periodic system
1905	Johann Friedrich Wilhelm Adolf Von Baeyer (1835-1917) German	Advancement of organic chemistry and the chemical industry through work on organic dyes and hydroaromatic compounds
1906	Henri Moissan (1852-1907) French	Investigation and isolation of the element fluorine, and for his electric furnace
1907	Eduard Buchner (1860-1917) German	Biochemical researches and the discovery of cell-free fermentation
1908	Lord Ernest Rutherford (1871 -1937) New Zealand-British	Investigations into the disintegration of the elements and the chemistry of radioactive substances
1909	Wilhelm Ostwald (1853-1932) Latvian-German	Work on catalysis and investigations into the fundamental principles governing chemical equilibria and rates of reaction
1910	Otto Wallacfi (1847-1931) German	Pioneering work in the field of alicyclic compounds
1911	Marie Curie (1867-1934) Polish-born French	Discovery of the elements radium and polonium, the isolation of radium, and the study of this element
1912	Victor Grignard (1871-1935) French Paul Sabatier (1854-1941) French	Discovery of the Grignard reagent Method of hydrogenating organic compounds in the presence of finely divided metals
1913	Alfred Werner (1866-1919) German-born Swiss	Work on the linkage of atoms in molecules, especially in inorganic chemistry

Year	Name of prizewinner (s)	Nature of work or discovery
1914	Theodore William Richards (1868-1928) US	Accurate determinations of the atomic weights of many chemical elements
1915	Richard Martin Willstatter (1872-1942) German	Work on plant pigments, especially chlorophyll
1918	Fritz Haber(1868-1934) German	The synthesis of ammonia from its elements
1920	Walther Hermann Nernst (1864-1941) German	Work in thermochemistry
1921	Frederick Soddy (1877-1956) British	Work on the chemistry of radioactive substances and investigations into the origin and nature of isotopes
1922	Francis William Aston (1877-1945) British	Discovery, by means of his mass spectrograph, of isotopes in a large number of nonradioactive elements
1923	Fritz Pregl (1869-1930) Austrian	Invention of the method of microanalysis of organic substances
1925	Richard Adolf Zsigmondy (1865-1929) Austrian-German	Demonstration of the heterogenous nature of colloid solutions and for the methods developed to study them
1926	Theodor Svedberg (1884-1971) Swedish	Work on disperse systems
1927	Heinrich Otto Wieland (1877-1957) German	Investigations of the constitution of the bile acids and related substances
1928	Adolf Otto Reinhold Windaus (1876-1959) German	Work on the constitution of the sterols and their connection with the vitamins
1929	Sir Arthur Harden (1865-1940) British Hans Karl August Simon Von Euler-Chelpin (1873-1964) German-Swedish	Investigations on the fermentation of sugar and fermentative enzymes
1930	Hans Fischer (1881-1945) German	Work on the constitution of haemin and chlorophyll, especially the synthesis of haemin
1931	Carl Bosch (1874-1940) German Friedrich Bergius (1884-1949) German	Contributions to the invention and development of chemical high pressure methods
1932	Irving Langmuir (1881-1957) US	Discoveries and investigations in surface chemistry

Year	Name of prizewinner (s)	Nature of work or discovery
1934	Harold Clayton Urey (1893-1981) US	Discovery of heavy hydrogen (deuterium)
1935	Frederic Joliot (1900-1958) French Irene Joliot-Curie (1897-1956) French	Synthesis of new radioactive elements
1936	Petrus (Peter) Josephus Wilhelmus Debye (1884-1966) Dutch	Contributions to our knowledge of molecular structure through investigations on dipole moments and on the diffraction of X-rays and electrons in gases
1937	Sir Walter Norman Haworth (1883-1950) British	Investigation of carbohydrates and vitamin C
	Paul Karrer (1889-1971) Russian-Swiss	Investigations on carotenoids, flavins, and vitamins A and B2
1938	Richard Kuhn (1900-1967) Austrian-born German	Work on carotenoids and vitamins (declined the award because of political pressure but later received the diploma and the medal)
1939	Adolf Friedrich Johann Butenandt (1903-1995) German	Work on sex hormones
1939	Leopold (Lavoslav) Stephen Ruzicka (1887-1976) Croatian-Swiss	Work on polymethylenes and higher terpenes
1943	George De Hevesy (1885-1966) Hungarian-born Swedish	Work on the use of isotopes as tracers in the study of chemical processes
1944	Otto Hahn (1879-1968) German	Discovery of the fission of heavy nuclei
1945	Artturi Ilmari Virtanen (1895-1973) Finnish	Research and inventions in agricultural and nutrition chemistry, especially for a fodder-preservation method
1946	James Batcheller Sumner 7-1955) US	Discovery that enzymes can be crystallized
	John Howard Northrop (1891-1987) US Wendell Meredith Stanley US (1904-1971)	Preparation of enzymes and virus proteins in a pure form
1947	Sir Robert Robinson (1886-1975) British	Investigations on plant products of biological importance, especially the alkaloids
1948	Arne Wilhelm Kaurin Tiselius (1902-1971) Swedish	Work on electrophoresis and adsorption analysis, especially discoveries concerning the complex nature of the serum proteins

Year	Name of prizewinner (s)	Nature of work or discovery
1949	William Francis Giauque (1895-1982) US	Contributions to the field of chemical thermodynamics, particularly the behaviour of substances at very low temperatures
1950	Otto Paul Hermann Diels (1876-1954) German Kurt Alder (1902-1958) German	Discovery and development of the diene synthesis (the Diels-Alder reaction)
1951	Edwin Mattison McMillan (1907-1991) US Glenn Theodore Seaborg (1912-1999) US	Work on the chemistry of the transuranium elements
1952	Archer John Porter Martin (1910-2002) British Richard Laurence Millinqton Synge (1914-1994) British	Invention of the technique of partition chromatography
1953	Hermann Staudinger (1881-1965) German	Discoveries in the field of macromolecular chemistry
1954	Linus Carl Pauling (1901-1994) US	Work on the nature of the chemical bond and its application to the elucidation of the structure of complex substances
1955	Vincent Du Vigneaud (1901-1978) US	Work on biochemically important sulphur compounds, especially for the first synthesis of a polypeptide hormone
1956	Sir Cyril Norman Hinsheiwood (1897-1967) British Nikolay Nikolaevich Semenov (1896-1986) Soviet	Studies of the mechanism of chemical reactions
1957	Lord Alexander R. Todd (1907-1997) British	Work on nucleotides and nucleotide coenzymes
1958	Frederick Sanger (1918-) British	Work on the structure of proteins, especially insulin
1959	Jaroslav Heyrovsky (1890-1967) Czech	Discovery and development of polarography
1960	Willard Frank Libby (1908-1980) US	Discovery and development of the technique of carbon-14 dating
1961	Melvrn Calvin (1911-) US	Work on carbon dioxide assimilation in plants
1962	Max Ferdinand Perutz (1914-2002) Austrian-British Sir John Cowdery Kendrew (1917-1997) British	Studies of the structures of globular proteins

Year	Name of prizewinner (s)	Nature of work or discovery
1963	Karl Ziegler (1898-1973) German Giulio Natta (1903-1979) Italian	Discoveries concerning the chemistry and technology of high polymers
1964	Dorothy Crowfoot Hodgkin (1910-1994) British	Determinations by X-ray techniques of the structures of important biochemical substances
1965	Robert Burns Woodward (1917-1979) US	Achievements in the art of organic synthesis
1966	Roberts. Mulliken (1896-1986) US	Work concerning chemical bonds and the electronic structure of molecules using molecular orbital theory
1967	Manfred Eigen (1927-) German Ronald George Wreyford Norrish (1897-1978) British Lord George Porter (1920-2002) British	Studies of extremely fast chemical reactions, effected by disturbing the equlibrium by means of very short pulses of energy
1968	Lars Onsager (1903-1976) Norwegian	Discovery of sugar nucleotides and their role in the biosynthesis of carbohydrates
1969	Sir Derek H. R. Barton (1918-1998) Odd Hassel (1897-1981) Norwegian	Development of the concept of conformation and its application in chemistry
1970	Luis F. Leioir(1906-1987) Argentinian	Discovery of sugar nucleotides and theri orla in the biosynthesis of carbohydrates
1971	Gerhard Herzberg (1904-1999) German-Canadian	Work on the electronic stucture and geometry of molecules and free radicals
1972	Christian B. Anfinsen (1916-1995) US	Work on ribonuclease, especially the connection between the amino acid sequence and the active conformation
	Stanford Moore (1913-1982) US William H. Stein (1911-1980) US	Contribution to the understanding of the connection between chemical structure and catalytic activity of the active centre of the ribonuclease molecule
1973	Ernst Otto Fischer (1918-2007) German Sir Geoffrey Wilkinson (1921-1996) British	Pioneering work, performed independently, on the chemistry of the sandwich compounds

Year	Name of prizewinner (s)	Nature of work or discovery
1974	Paul J. Fiory (1910-1985) US	Theoretical and experimental work on the physical chemistry of macromolecules
1975	Sir John Warcup Cornforth (1917-) Australian-British	Work on the stereochemistry of enzyme-catalysed reactions
1975	Vladimir Prelog (1906-1998) Bosnian-Swiss	Work on the stereochemistry of organic molecules and reactions
1976	William N. Lipscomb (1919- JUS	Studies on the structure of boranes, illuminating problems of chemical bonding
1977	Ilya Prigogine (1917-2003) Russian-Belgian	Contributions to non-equilibrium thermodynamics, particularly the theory of dissipative structures
1978	Peter D. Mitchell (1920-1992) British	Formulation of the chemiosmotic theory
1979	Herbert C. Brown (1912-2004) British-US GeorgWittig (1897-1987) German	Development of the use of boron- and phosphorus-containing compounds, respectively, into important reagents in organic synthesis
1980	Paul Berg (1926-) US	Fundamental studies of the biochemistry of nucleic acids, with particular regard to recombinant DNA
	Walter Gilbert (1932-) US Frederick Sanger (1918-) British	Contributions concerning the determination of base sequences in nucleic acids
1981	Kenichi Fukui (1918-1998) Japanese Roald Hoffmann (1937-) Polish-US	Theories, developed independently, concerning the course of chemical reactions (frontier-orbital theory and the Woodward-Hoffmann rules)
1982	Sir Aaron Klug (1926-) Lithuanian-British	Development of crystallographic electron microscopy and the structural elucidation of biologically important nucleic acid-protein complexes
1983	Henry Taube (1915-2005) Canadisn-US	Work on the mechanisms of electron-transfer reactions, especially in metal complexes
1984	Robert Bruce Merrifield (1921-2006) US	Development of methodology for chemical synthesis on a solid matrix

Year	Name of prizewinner (s)	Nature of work or discovery
1985	Herbert A. Hauptman (1917-) US Jerome Karle (1918-) US	Development of direct methods for the determination of crystal structures
1986	Dudley R. Herschbach (1932-) US Yuan T. Lee (1936-) Taiwanese John C. Polanyi (1929-) Canadian	Research on the dynamics of chemical elementary processes
1987	Donald J. Cram (1919-2001) US Jean-Marie Lehn (1939-) French Charles J. Pedersen (1904-1989) Norwegian	Development and use of molecules with structure-specific interactions of high selectivity (crown ethers and cryptands)
1988	Johann Deisenhofer(1943-) German Robert Huber (1937-) German Hartmut Michel (1948-) German	Determination of the three-dimensional structure of a photosynthetic reaction centre
1989	Sidney Altman (1939-) Canadian-US Thomas R. Cech (1947-) US	Discovery of the catalytic properties of RNA
1990	Elias James Corey (1928-) US	Development of the theory and methodology of organic synthesis (retrosynthetic analysis)
1991	Richard R. Ernst (1933-) Swiss	Development of high resolution nuclear magnetic resonance (NMR) spectroscopy
1992	Rudolph A. Marcus (1923-) Canadian-US	Work on electron-transfer reactions in chemical systems
1993	Kary B. Mullis (1944-) US	Discovery of the polymerase chain reaction
	Michael Smith (1932-2000) British-Canadian	Work on oiigonudeotide-based site-directed mutagenesis and its use for protein studies
1994	George A. Olah (1927-) Hungarian-US	Work on carbocation chemistry
1995	Paul Crutzen (1933-) Dutch Mario J.Molina (1943-) Mexican-US F. Sherwood Rowland (1927-) US	Work in atmospheric chemistry, particularly the formation and decomposition of ozone
1996	Robert F. Curl (1933-) US Sir Harold W. Kroto (1939-) British Richard Smalley (1943-2005) US	Discovery of fullerenes
1997	Paul D. Boyer (1918-) US John E.Walker (1941-) British JensC. Skou(1918-) Danish	Elucidation of the mechanism underlying the synthesis of ATP Discovery of an ion-transporting enzyme, Na+,K+-ATPase
1998	Walter Kohn (1923-) Austrian-US John A. Pople (1925-2004) British	Development of density-functional theory Development of computational methods in quantum chemistry

Year	Name of prizewinner (s)	Nature of work or discovery
1999	Ahmed H.Zewail (1946-) Egyptian	Studies of the transition states of chemical reactions using femtosecond spectroscopy
2000	Alan J. Heeger (1936-) US Alan G- MacDiarmid (1927-2007) New Zealand-US HidekiShirakawa (1936-) Japanese	Discovery and development of conductive polymers
2001	Williams. Knowles (1917-) US Ryoji Noyori (1938-) Japanese K. Barry Sharpless (1941-) US	Work on chirally catalysed hydrogenation reactions Work on chirally catalysed oxidation reactions
2002	John B. Fenn(1917-) US Koichi Tanaka (1959-) Japanese	Development of ionization methods for mass spectrornetric analyses of biological macromolecules
	Kurt Wuthrich (1938-) Swiss	Development of NMR spectroscopy for determining the structure of biological macromolecules in solution
2003	Peter Agre (1949- JUS	Discovery of water channels in cell membranes
	Roderick MacKinnon (1956-) US	Structural and mechanistic studies of ion channels in cell membranes
2004	Aaron Ciechanover (1947-) Israeli Avram Hershko(1937-) Hungarian-Israeli Irwin Rose (1926-) US	Discovery of ubiquitin-mediated protein degradation
2005	Yves Chauvin (1930-) French Robert H. Grubbs (1942-) US Richard R. Schrock (1945-) US	Development of the metathesis method in organic synthesis
2006	Roger D. Kornberg (1947-) US	Studies of the molecular basis of eukaryotic transcription
2007	Gerhard Ertl (1936-) German	Studies of chemical processes on solid surfaces
2008	Osamu Shimomura (1928 -) Japan Martin Chalfie (1947 -) US Roger Y. Tsien (1952 -) US	Green fluorescent protein, GFP
2009	Venkatraman Ramakrishnan (1952 -) India Thomas A. Steitz (1940 -) US Ada E. Yonath (1939 -) Israel	Structure and function of the ribosome
2010	Richard F. Heck (1931 -) US Ei-ichi Negishi (1935 - China Akira Suzuki (1930 -) Japan	Palladium-catalyzed couplings in organic synthesis
2011	Dan Shechtman (1941 -) Israel	Discovery of quasi crystals

Popular Science

Author: Vikas Khatri
Format: Paperback
Language: English
Pages: 160
Price: ` 110

Experiments are an inseparable part of any scientific study or Research. In this book, the author has tried to simplify science to the readers, particularly the school-going students through easy and interesting experiments. All the experiments given in the book are based on some scientific phenomena, such as atmospheric pressure, high and low temperatures, boiling, freezing and melting points of solids, liquids and gases, gravitational force, magnetism, electricity, solubility of substances, etc. Thus, read and carry out each of these fun-filled experiment in your homes or schools under the supervision and guidance of your teachers, parents or elders.

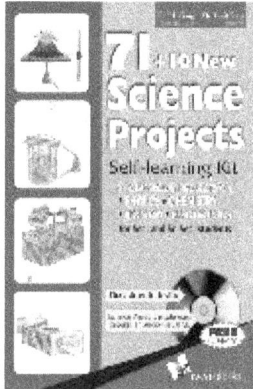

Author: Dr. C.L. Garg & Dr. Amit Garg
Format: Paperback
Language: English
Pages: 120
Price: ` 140

81 Classroom projects on: Physics, Chemistry, Biology& Electronics for Sec. & Sr. Sec. Students. Science projects and models play a pivotal role in inculcating scientific temper in young minds and in harnessing their skills. Students of classes 10 th, 11th & 12 th have to work on such projects and these carry much weight in the overall performance.
All these aspects have been considered during the compilation of the projects and models. This book will also be an ideal choice for parents interested in enhancing scientific temper of their children and for hobbyists.

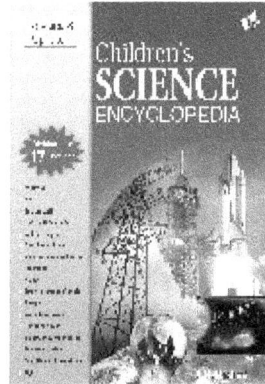

Author: A.H. Hashmi
Format: Paperback
Language: English
Pages: 206
Price: ` 495

Complete science homework compen-dium for children aged 8 to 16. Through Short paragraphs and great pictures the book explains all about, Environment, Transport, Energy, Communi-cation, Electricity & Magnetism, Light & Sound, Chemistry, Universe, Earth, Animal & Plants, Human Body and others in 17 sections! Guaranteed to build scientific temper in children to excel in studies! Equally useful for parents and guardians to understand and explain to the youngsters the different areas of scientific world in which we live. Competitive exam candidates will also be greatly benefitted in getting a short and crisp answer to their inquisitiveness.
A must have book for every home!

www.ingramcontent.com/pod-product-compliance
Lightning Source LLC
Chambersburg PA
CBHW070358270326

41926CB00014B/2609